Songs of the Finnish Migration

A BILINGUAL ANTHOLOGY

EDITED BY
THOMAS A. DUBOIS
B. MARCUS CEDERSTRÖM

A volume in the series Languages and Folklore of the Upper Midwest published in collaboration with the Center for the Study of Upper Midwestern Culture at the University of Wisconsin-Madison.

Joseph Salmons and James P. Leary, Series Editors

Songs of the Finnish Migration:
A Bilingual Anthology

Based on the Anthology
Reisaavaisen Laulu Amerikkaan,
edited by Simo Westerholm

Translated into English and with additional notes by
Thomas A. DuBois
B. Marcus Cederström
Hilary-Joy Virtanen

Kansanmusiikki-instituutti
KIJ 109

The University of Wisconsin Press
2019

Kansanmusiikki-instituutti
Jyväskyläntie 3
69600 Kaustinen, Finland
www.kansanmusiikki-instituutti.fi

The University of Wisconsin Press
728 State Street, Suite 443
Madison, Wisconsin 53706-1428
uwpress.wisc.edu

Sheet music by **Thomas A. DuBois** & **B. Marcus Cederström**
Layout by **Jimmy Träskelin**

Printed in the United States of America
ISBN 978-0-299-32714-9
ISSN 0355-9876

Esipuhe
Foreword

Simo Westerholm's 1983 *Reisaavaisen laulu Amerikkaan: Siirtolaislauluja* [The Traveler's Song to America: Songs of Migrants] was a joint publication of the Kaustinen Folk Music Institute and the Central Organization of Folk Music. Bringing together a wide range of songs related to the migration of Finnish-speaking Finns to North America, the work aimed at making these songs available to modern singers as well as historians and others interested in the movement of Finnish people to the United States and Canada during the nineteenth and early twentieth centuries. Culled from archival sources, manuscripts, sound recordings, and a wide array of published song books, the collection aimed to present the variety of different musical responses to the migration experience that arose among Finnish emigrants, their friends and family back home in Finland and their immediate descendants.

Songs were selected with particular attention to their lyrics: Westerholm looked in particular for songs that describe the migration experience, present attitudes toward the homeland or the host country, and depict the emotions associated with immigration to North America. The resulting collection was arranged thematically, and we have kept the songs' order as in Westerholm's original. The anthology begins with Section I, Jäähyväiset/Farewells **(Songs 1–14)**, which provides examples of the kinds of songs composed prior, during, or immediately after the migration experience. Songs express the confidence and optimism of emigrants, their adventures en route to America, and their immediate experiences upon arrival. A number of the songs describe the emotional turmoil of departure, either for the emigrant or for the loved ones left behind. Next comes Section II, Perillä/Arrived **(Songs 14–31)**: here we find the immigrant confronting the realities of life in the new country, including homesickness, labor injustice, and frustration. After these songs, Westerholm included a set of "piirileikkilauluja" songs sung in ring dances in Finland. These songs reflect the ways in which people, including children, in Finland imagined their friends, family members and loved ones far off in America. Many of the songs Westerholm selected were originally performed in Ostrobothnia, the area from which the bulk of emigrants came. We have labeled this Section III, Kotona/At Home **(Songs 32–54)**. The final section of Westerholm's anthology, Section IV Levyllä/On the Turntable **(Songs 55–81)** presents a small sampling of the some 800 different Finnish American songs recorded on American record labels prior to 1950. They reflect the vibrant musical culture that grew up in Finnish communities, particularly through performances staged in Finn Halls across the continent. Here the songs of Hiski Salomaa and Arthur Kylander in particular are of note.

Many of the songs in Westerholm's anthology were originally published without melodies and so, Westerholm had to find or create melodic transcriptions to accompany the words of the songs. Finding suitable melodies was sometimes challenging and involved careful archival work, not only in the collections of the Folk Music Institute but also the archives of the Finnish Literature Society. Also important as a source were broadsides catalogued by Arvid Hultin in 1931 and collected in the broadside collections of the University of Helsinki Library as well as sound recordings produced in North America by immigrant musicians. Collections by Kerttu Talvitie and Aatos Rinta-Koski were also incorporated, as were songs drawn from the repertoire of Arthur Kylander, transcribed through the efforts of Erik Lindström.

As the headnotes to the various songs indicate, Westerholm often sought out suitable melodies from archival sources and fitted the published words to the tunes. Sometimes, as the headnotes indicate, the same song was performed to different melodies in different regions or eras. We have faithfully copied Westerholm's original transcriptions and note that it is sometimes a little challenging to know exactly how the words of a given stanza are supposed to fit with the melody. On the English-translation side, we have labored to make texts that fit well with the melodies Westerholm provided, although the different stress system of English and its shorter word length means that we often faced a challenge in figuring out how to fill out a given line with both the original's meaning and the song's metrical and melodic demands. If our translations seem clunky or unwieldy at times, feel free to alter them in ways you see fit!

In his collection, Westerholm tended to preserve Finnish texts as they appeared in previous publications, but he adjusted melodies where necessary to better mesh songs and musical scores, or to provide musical settings where these had not been provided, e.g., as in the case of broadsides. Harmonies and chords provided by Timo Valo aimed at adapting the songs for standard *pelimanni* performance; some of the harmonies provided by Willie Larsen and Julia Kylander in late 1930s recordings were also incorporated into the transcriptions. The ultimate aim of Westerholm's collection was to make the songs available to readers of the text in a useable and informative manner.

Given the collection's original aim of making the songs available to a modern readership, both as objects of historical interest and as materials to possibly learn and perform, the task of translating the songs into English for a North American audience required not simply careful attention to the meanings of the lyrics but also a commitment to producing idiomatic "singable" translations into English that could be performed on stage or at home. With Simo Westerholm's blessing, and the strong encouragement of Jim Leary, the leading North American scholar in Finnish American folk song, this work of translation began in Madison at the University of Wisconsin, where a team of translators made up primarily of Sara Tikkanen, Hilary Virtanen, and Tom DuBois worked to produce first a close translation and transcription of the songs and then an idiomatic translation that could be sung to the melodies provided. The work of producing singable versions proceeded slowly over a number of years and was finally brought to completion by Marcus Cederström and Tom DuBois in 2015. By that time, regrettably, Simo Westerholm had passed away. Nonetheless, the translation team felt it important to bring the collection to publication, particularly to help fulfill Westerholm's dream of reacquainting Finns and Finnish Americans with the rich musical portrait of the migration that was produced by musicians and enjoyed by their audiences during the era of greatest Finnish immigration to North America. This collection can prove a useful supplement to the magnificent text, translation, and sound recording compilation of Finnish songs included in Leary's seminal *Folk Songs of Another America: Field Recordings of the Upper Midwest, 1937–1946,* a work that places Finnish songs from Upper Midwest singers alongside counterparts in a wide array of other languages, indigenous and immigrant, collected in the region during the 1930s and '40s[1]. While **Folk Songs of Another America** provides insightful overviews of actual singers and the ways in which they performed and employed their songs in their lives, the present collection provides the reader with transla-

---

1   Leary 2015

tions that can help make these songs part of modern singers' repertoires, both in Finnish and in English.

Two further notes on the translations included in this anthology are in order. First, our goal was to produce *singable* translations, not *literal* ones. In many cases, as the reader knowledgeable in Finnish may note, we have been able to stay fairly close to the Finnish originals in our texts. But seldom will one find exact word-for-word or line-for-line translations here. Instead, we have aimed to ensure that each English stanza reproduces at least the *gist*—and as much as possible of the specific meaning—of the original stanza in Finnish, even if we have avoided translating unfamiliar idioms or reproducing the Finnish original's sometimes tricky syntax or wording. We hope that readers conversant in Finnish will enjoy comparing the Finnish and English texts to see where we've stayed close and where we've strayed. Within the context of Finnish language instruction, comparison of the Finnish and English texts may elicit useful discussions of idiomatic phrases, connotations, or interpretations.

Second, we wish to note that throughout our work, we have tried to match the tone of the originals, making the English translations imitate the stylistic features of the Finnish texts, be they steeped in highflown rhetoric, winking humor, or jocular slang. It is sometimes easy for the American ear to interpret the Finnish love of minor keys as melancholic or moody, and so we wanted to make sure that the translations indicated clearly what we took to be the main tone or emotional content of the originals. At times we may have introduced the wrong tone, however, conveying a seriousness where the original is lighthearted, or humor where the original is poignant and sad. Songs can mean different things to different people or be interpreted in different ways, and we hope that our translations do not do damage to the effects and essences of the songs we translate or the reader's/singer's experience of them. We welcome your feedback on our wording and translations!

I. Jäähyväiset. Farewells.
Songs 1–14.

It is important to recognize the diversity of Finnish migrant experiences. Speakers of Finnish and closely related languages immigrated to North America not only from Finland, but also from northern Sweden and northern Norway. So too, those coming from Finland sometimes spoke Swedish or Sámi as their native languages or came from families or communities that were decidedly multilingual[1]. They arrived in New York City, Boston, Montreal, Québec, and elsewhere. They came permanently or stayed for a time and then returned home. Some traveled between the USA and other countries, notably Canada and Australia. During their travels, and throughout their lives in the New World, they passed through different stages and emotions, dealing with the complex issues of love, work, cultural adjustment, aging, and life in general. Given the complexity and variety of these experiences, it is striking how comparatively uniform the musical accounts of migration can seem. Broadsides produced for popular consumption in Finland, like popular music more generally, sought to speak to the most readily recognizable emotional experiences of singers and audiences. In the case of songs about parting, they tend to narrate and therefore reinforce the most prevalent migration story—i.e., a departure from southern or western Finland, travel by a combination of train and ship through Scandinavia and England and then across the Atlantic to New York City, with an immediate continuation from there to the American Midwest, where the promise of homestead lands and economic independence proved a powerful, almost mythical, draw. Despite this relative uniformity, however, we can also see in the songs of this section some striking differences in perspective and emotions. While they give us a glimpse of what song publishers and perhaps their audiences imagined as the most typical emigrant experiences, they also provide nuance to these portrayals through diverging details, emphases, and evaluations. One can sense in these songs an articulation of the ways Finns of the time *imagined* migration, and perhaps some of the standards by which they took stock of their own experiences or those of friends or loved ones they knew among the hundreds of thousands of migrants who journeyed from Scandinavia to North America during the nineteenth and early twentieth centuries.

---

1   Lindström 2003, Österlund-Pötzsch 2003, Olin 2004

Songs of Confidence (Songs 3, 4, 10).

Nineteenth-century Finnish migrants to America were both male and female, high-born and low. In a country that was still overwhelmingly agricultural and that offered few industrial opportunities (at least in comparison to countries like England or the United States), landlessness and a mounting rural population were vexing issues for both men and women. Mark Knipping[1] presents statistics on Finnish landlessness at the turn of the twentieth century: in 1901, only 23% of the rural population of Finland lived on land they owned. Another 32% were *torpparit* (crofters)—individuals or families that rented their holdings from a landowner and paid an annual rent in cash payments, crops, and supplemental donated labor. A further 43% of the rural population was entirely landless: people in this category worked primarily as hired hands on the farms of others or as itinerant workers. The issues of landlessness and rural poverty would shape Finnish politics markedly both before and after Finnish independence in 1917, and greatly colored the experiences and outlooks of those people who chose to emigrate to North America during the latter decades of the nineteenth century and down into the early 1920s[2].

In the district of Ostrobothnia, particularly south Ostrobothnia—home to some 120,000 of the roughly 300,000 Finnish emigrants that left Finland prior to 1920—new ideas of citizenry and identity became established with an intensity unlike anywhere else in Finland[3]. By the 1880s, at the close of a century that had seen the tripling of the local population, youth in the district were organizing local club houses and producing newspapers aimed at self realization and advancement. Emigration became a tool for finding new ways of life, and in many villages upwards of ten percent of the local populace chose to leave Finland for a new life abroad[4]. If Ostrobothnians figured prominently in immigration to the USA, the situation was even more dramatic in Canada, where they represented some two-thirds of the immigrant population coming from Finland[5]. In **Song 20** "Kauhea tapaturma kaivannossa/Tragic Mine Accident" that focuses on a mining accident in the American Midwest, (included in Section II of this anthology) fully five of the six men killed in the accident came from South Ostrobothnia. The remaining victim is identified as having come from Merijärvi, in North Ostrobothnia.

Aspects of the emigration experience—particularly its physical demands and its economic cost—selected for a particular demographic profile, and published broadsides often suggest a migrant who is male, young, confident, and looking for advancement. The emigrant who is able to afford passage to America often comes from a reasonably well-off family, e.g., one that has some land of its own. Yet the emigrant is not usually described as the heir to the farm (i.e., usually an oldest son), but rather is described as a younger son, someone expected to live out a life as a farmhand on his father's and later, on his older brother's, farm or to strike out on an adventure like emigration to make his own way in the world. As a Finnish immigrant to Wisconsin wrote: "The son of a small landowner, I enjoyed bread and warmth at home until my eldest brother became master of the farm. From that time on home no longer felt like home, and the prospect of becoming a hired hand in my own community was not attractive. There was no way by which I could become a landowner, and I knew no vocation save that of a farmer. So to America!"[6]. **Song 10**, "Amerikaan siirtolaisen laulu /Song of the Immigrant to America," published in Rauma in 1893 by Frans Juho Järwinen of Eura, makes this economic situation of the inscribed emigrant clear:

---

1   Knipping 2008, 7
2   Kirby 1989, Sulkunen 1989, Lindström 2003
3   Kirby 1989, 75–77
4   Kirby 1989, 77
5   Lindström 2003, 9
6   Knipping 2008, 8

Ameriikka Suomen poikain
On nyt paras turva,
Kun ei saata veljellänsä
Oleskella orja.
—

America there's no other
For a Finnish man young and brave,
There you're not stuck with your brother
Having to work as his slave.

Emigration seemed to offer a ticket out of a life determined by family circumstances and birth order, and Järwinen's final stanza suggests that redressing the inequities and injustices of Finnish landlessness represents the only surefire way of curtailing the era's rampant emigration:

Eläköhön tasa-arvo,
Kuolkohon raha-valta,
Sitten eivät Suomen pojat
Lähde kotomaalta.
—

Let equality find a footing
Let the power of money die.
Then we Finns will not be needing
From our native land to fly.

The confidence, even bravado, of some of the published songs is striking, particularly given the stereotype of Finnish hesitance and humility. **Song 4**, "Amerikkaan Aikeet/Plans for America," a broadside printed in Vaasa, Ostrobothnia, in 1888, displays this sense of confidence from its very opening:

Amerikkaan aivon lähteä niin ois mulla mieli,
Suomen niemi on nuorelle poijalle kuljeskella pieni.
—

To America I'll go, yes, I would see that country!
For a guy who is spry such as I, this here Finland's just too tiny.

The song announces clearly the gender and economic situation of the singer, who describes himself as a "nuori poika," "a young guy." In nineteenth-century Finnish, *poika* was used for both younger and older men, provided they hadn't married or come into an inheritance that would make them a *mies* ("man"), *aviomies* ("husband") or *isäntä* ("farmer/head"). The singer uses the image of "Suomen niemi," ("the Finnish headland"), not so much as to suggest a particular region or place within the country but rather, to use the typical Finnish topography of lakesides, spits and islands as a metaphor for the constricting nature of Finnish society. Ostrobothnian villages were often sited alongside rivers or lakes, and farming there involved considerable expected co-operation between neighbors, whose fields were often closely intermingled in ways determined by medieval systems of taxation and inheritance[1]. A young man of energy and promise, a man wanting independence and autonomy, needed freer environs to explore.

The economics of the singer's situation is clearly set forth in the second stanza of the same song:

---

1   Virtanen and DuBois 2000, 69

Amerikkaan aijottu matka ei oo kovin kallis,
Senkään suhteen kuin on sieltä tuleva suuri saalis.

—

Tickets to America don't seem very costly,
When I think of the great rewards that my trip will net me.

The cost of a ticket is described in terms of cost/benefit analysis, as an economic investment. The Finnish text, translated here as "cash," actually describes the "suuri saalis"—the big "catch" or "plunder"—that the emigrant will gain from migration, employing the familiar vocabulary of fishing and hunting to describe the anticipated outcomes of migration to a foreign country. As the subsequent stanzas detail, America seemingly offers endless opportunity, described particularly in connection with cash earnings. Cash was a relatively new element of life for rural Finns in the nineteenth century, replacing older systems of barter and subsistence with a novel sense of freedom of action: one could work a job, earn an income, and then use the money in whatever way a person wanted[1]. This freedom of movement lent the "footloose" emigrant—like the turn-of-the-century logger—a sense of seeming empowerment that contrasted with the more scripted, staid life trajectories of those "lucky" eldest sons who could inherit the farm[2]. Thus, it is not entirely surprising that **Song 3**, Salomon Ruuskanen's 1888 broadside "Nuorten poikajien Ameriikaan menosta/Young Men off to America," depicts a main character who is in fact an eldest son, breaking the hearts of father, mother, and girlfriend by his insistence to leave Finland on an adventure to America. Taking leave of his love at the dock, he declares:

Älä sinä helluni ennen sure,
Ja sure sitten vasta,
Laiva se lähtee rannalta
Eikä näkymästä lakkaa.

—

"Don't shed a tear, my true love dear,
You can cry once the ship has parted.
Now while the ship is upon the wave, let its image your heart save,
Once my journey's started.

The singer's cavalier attitude about the ramifications of his departure for the girl left behind is a topic explored in later stanzas of the song, as we shall see below. The disadvantages of living in a cash economy, unmentioned in these songs, are taken up in other more critical songs, as we shall see in Section II of this anthology.

Songs of Humility (Songs 1, 5, 9).

Not all songs popular or popularized during this era show such exuberance, however. Often, they explore, or at least touch on, the anxieties and emotional strains that emigration could bring. Some songs, like **Song 1**, "Nuori poismuuttaja/The Young Emigrant," were in fact translations of existing songs from other languages, often Swedish or English. Creating Finnish versions of songs that had become popular abroad was a sure-fire means of generating income for broadside writers and printers. Such songs also helped Finnish audiences become acquainted with international trends and ideas. The conventional handling of the farewell scene in **Song 1**—the sentimental conversation between the young emigrant and his weeping true love—has little to indicate a specifically Finnish experience of departure, and the song's closing stanza, with its opening

---

1   Talve 1998, 94–95
2   DuBois 2005

line "Hyvästi vuoret, laakso lemuavainen"/Farewell you mountains and you fragrant valley" does not seem particularly descriptive of a Finnish landscape. Borrowing songs was not an exclusively Finnish endeavor: Audiences of the late nineteenth and early twentieth centuries were in no way adverse to sampling the music of other cultures: even within the English-language context, Americans readily sang of "taking the high road to Loch Lomond," or what a long way it was to Tipperary, without necessarily knowing (or caring) exactly where those places were. What is central in **Song 1**, and others like it, is the emotional core of a parting between lovers, in which the emigrant tries to balance his enthusiasm for his impending journey/adventure with a genuine (or feigned?) acknowledgement of the emotional damage his departure will visit upon his beloved.

In **Song 5**, "Suomalaisen lähtö Amerikkaan/The Finn's Departure to America," the self-confidence characteristic of other emigrant songs is augmented by a clearer enunciation of the migrant's earnest and hardworking ways:

> Kuin mää kuljen kunnialla,
> Voitan kaikki eteeni,
> Voitan vieraan kovan leivän
> Ahkeralla työlläni.
>
> —
>
> As I march forth with my honor
> Troubles all I'll pull through
> Humble bread I'll ably get
> Through the honest labor I'll do.

The song's description of "kova leipä" ("hard" i.e., humble, bread) and "ahkera työ" ("diligent work") suggest a singer not out to have a fun time but rather someone willing and able to devote himself to getting ahead abroad.

In **Song 9**, "Amerikkaan aikovan hyvästijättö/The Goodbye Song of the American Traveler," a broadside published in Tampere in 1891, the singer addresses his friends and family with a sense of remorse for his past misdeeds:

> Nyt surulla alotan lauluni tään,
> Teill' vanhat mun ystäväni.
> Ja tiedoksi annan mun rivini nää
> Ja suruisen sydämmeni.
> Mä ystävät teitä niin pettänyt oon,
> Ja itseni saattanut turmijoon.
> Vaan anteeks' mul' antakaa kuitenki ne,
> Ett'ei meit' luojamme rankaise.
>
> —
>
> Now sorrowfully will I this my song begin
> For all of my old friends back there;
> My feelings I've set down in these lines herein,
> For my heart does great sorrow bear.
> My friends, I deceived you, your trust I betrayed,
> And led myself verily into harm's way.
> But friends, please forgive me, I beg you indeed
> That in the hereafter from Judgment I'm freed.

The singer describes his words as "rivini" ("my lines"), implying that the song is a quotation of a letter or a song. The singer seems to have already emigrated, a detail which ties the song more to those discussed in Section II. The singer expresses sorrow at having left Finland, at having not facilitated the travel of his sister, and at having somehow experienced deception at the hands of his love, a topic to which we will return below. In any case, the song evinces little of the bravado and jollity that one can note in the songs discussed above. It depicts leave-taking as a painful affair, often filled with recriminations and regrets that would haunt the migrant ever after.

Musical Travelogues and Advice (Songs 6, 7, 8, 12)

Some songs reflect the informational purposes of broadsides and singing in a Finland that was increasingly sending emigrants abroad. Suomen Höyrylaiva Osakeyhtiö, the Finnish Steamship Company, founded in 1883, held a monopoly on the transporting of Finns to England, where they could join with passengers from other countries on one of the large steamships that regularly crossed the Atlantic[1]. The company's ships—the Urania, Sirius, Polaris, Arcturus and Titania—were massive, and could hold upwards of 500 third-class passengers at a time. The songs in this section also detail the passage of emigrants from Finland to Stockholm, however, and from there by train to the west coast city of Gothenburg (Göteborg). From Gothenburg, the passengers would join up with other emigrants from Sweden and Norway before boarding a boat headed for England, generally Hull, but sometimes London. And from there, the travelers would board another train to Liverpool, where they would embark on the longest leg of the journey, and the most perilous: the transatlantic crossing to New York. In **Song 8** "Uusi laulu Ameriikkaan matkustajista/A New Song About the Travelers to America," published by Otto Brander in Pori in 1892, the singer seems intent on chronicling every step of the journey, including the friendliness of the English captain, the din of London, the speed of British trains, the woes of ocean storms and seasickness, the joy of catching sight of New York harbor at last, the meeting with Finns in New York, and the anxiousness of the new immigrants to leave New York for the promised farmlands of the Upper Midwest. Illustrative of the song's tone is the stanza about London:

> Maailman suurimpaan kaupunkihin,
> Temsen suu'n, Londonin saavuttihin,
> Voi ihmisvirtaa, pyörivää, rannalla tuoll'
> En matkallani nähnyt viel' satamass' muoll'.
>
> —
>
> The Thames River greets our ship that's now come,
> to the great city that is known as London.
> Its shores are all crowded and with people do teem,
> For me it is something I never have seen.

One can imagine the song equipping a would-be emigrant with the knowledge and advice needed for an effective crossing.

Other songs, however, such as **Song 6** "Nuorukaisen hyvästijättö Amerikkaan lähteissä/A Youth's Farewell when Leaving for America," published by P. Myllykorpi in Tampere in 1890, takes its details rather loosely: here the traveler reaches Hull before Gothenburg. The song depicts the Atlantic crossing as far less perilous or uncomfortable, noting:

> Ja ne laivat oli raudasta
> Rakettu ja ne oli suuria
> Ettei trengännyt reisaavan
> Murheesta itkiä.

---

1   Knipping 2008, 10

—
Those ships there they were mighty,
built of iron and steel,
So that no one who was on them
any worry should feel.

Occasionally one finds the multiplicity of line meanings that folklorists associate with folksongs of greater age, suggesting that the broadsides as published reproduced songs that were circulating in one way or another in oral tradition. In **Song 7** "Reisaavaisen laulu Ameriikkaan/The Traveller's Song of Going to America," published by Kustaa Luhtala in Tampere in 1891, for instance, the singer tells of fears lessening after ten days at sea:

Kymmenen päivän reisattua
Meiltä huolet jo väheni
Kun tuo kuuluisa Ameriikka
Meitä jo läheni.

—
'Twas ten long days that we sailed this way
till at last the land drew near.
America came now in sight
and that shore calmed our many fears.

The rather innocuous line "Meiltä huolet jo väheni" ("our worries lessened") is closely related to the grimmer "Meistä puolet väheni" ("we were reduced by half") in the rendering of a similar passage in **Song 6**, P. Myllykorpi's 1890 "Nuorukaisen hyvästijättö Ameriikkaan lähteissä/A Youth's Farewell when Leaving for America," also published in Tampere:

Kaksi viikkoa reisattua
Meistä puolet väheni,
Kun tuo kuuluisa Ameriikka
Meitä jo läheni.

—
When two weeks on the water
had cut our ranks by two
Then we saw at last America
rise out of the blue.

Similarly, the description of the voyage's sturdy ships in **Song 6** quoted above, is echoed by a similar stanza in **Song 7**:

Laivat on raudasta rakettu
Ja ne on niin pitkiä
Niin ettei tartte reisaavaisen
Pelvosta itkeä.

—
Those sailing ships they are well-equipped;
they are built of iron strong.
No traveler needs to be afraid
on such ships big and sleek and long.

The traveler need not "pelvosta itkeä" ("cry for fear"), just as the traveler in **Song 6** need not "murheesta itkeä" ("cry for sorrow"). Broadside writers did not hesitate to reproduce each others' insights when these could lead to profit, and the songs often evince similarities of wording, tone, and style.

Often the travelogue songs point to the same high ideals and optimism of the emigrants discussed in the songs above: the emigrants are leaving behind the subservience and control as well as the material limitations that would have been their lot if they stayed in Finland. Songs 6 and 7 speak of no longer having to kowtow to the rich and the clergy, a point echoed, as noted above, by the assertion of **Song 10** that equality at home would stop young Finns from leaving their homeland. Occasionally, however, a song could present an opposing view. In **Song 12** "Ameriikkaan lähtö/Going to America," composed by Juho Marjakangas and published in Oulu in 1893, the exuberance of other departure songs is strongly countered. Marjakangas depicts the leave-taking as tragic and ill-informed and has little positive to say for the cash economy awaiting emigrants on their arrival in America. As the singer warns: "Ei ole onni kaikilla/Ameriikan raitilla" ("Joy is not everywhere/on the route to America"). (In the singable translation, in accordance with the overall tone and content of the song, we have rendered these lines as "The money does not grow on trees/And life for them is not a breeze".) The singer decries the misleading, avaricious acts of emigrants and bosses alike in America and suggests that life in Finland would be far more secure and pleasant. Questioning the American quest for wealth, symbolized most evocatively by the Gold Rush and other mining crazes, the singer asks:

> Mitäs sä teet nyt kullalla
> Kun peityt mustall' mullalla,
> Käyt' kohti kuolemaa
> Josta tulee kutsut tuonelaan.
> —
> What do you do with all that gold
> When at your death you're set in mold
> You'll walk with Death and wait your turn
> To leave this world, your fate to learn.

Clearly, one needs to have one's wits about one when leaving Finland for a life in a distant, unscrupulous, and potentially dangerous place. And the American quest for wealth can imperil not only one's earthly life but one's fate in the hereafter as well.

Affairs of the Heart (Songs 2, 3, 11, 13, 14)

Few topics are as popular in Western popular music as explorations of affairs of the heart. Such is the case with Finnish emigration songs as well. Often questions of love, rejection, or betrayal play large or subtle parts in the songs of departure. In **Song 3**, Salomon Ruuskanen's 1888 broadside "Nuorten poikajien Ameriikaan menosta/Young Men off to America," discussed above, the male singer's cavalier attitude toward the dilemma his leaving creates is met, rather exceptionally, with an equally strong female response and perspective. A female point of view is established already in the song's very first stanza:

> Pojat ne ottivat Amerikkaan
> Kymmenen vuoden pestin,
> Monesta nätistä likasta on tullut
> Ameriikan leski.
> —

Men went to work in America
and for ten long years they stayed.
Emigration changed their girlfriends' station,
as they're into "widows" made.

The prospect of becoming an "Amerikan leski," an "America widow" looms large for the women whose boyfriends or husbands departed, a topic discussed in detail in **Song 14**, as we shall see below. In **Song 3**, however, we hear the voice of one such woman left behind as her boyfriend experiences the realities of his new life in America. After some time, as the song details, the man becomes homesick and despondent, writing sentimental letters home and asking his true love to come join him. Interestingly, the female persona at the center of these stanzas of the song does not simply comply with the man's request. Rather, she considers her options in order to decide what she would like to do. In the end, her observation of pairing birds convinces her of the appropriateness of joining her boyfriend abroad:

Meinasin meinasin meinasin olla
Ja meinasin olla yksin
Vaan katselin taivahan lintuja
Kuin niitä oli aina kaksi.
—
Long and hard I thought it out,
and I looked up in the sky.
There in the heavens all the birds of the feather
they just ever in pairs did fly.

Presumably the woman will accept the offer of a ticket to America and will be united again with the man she loves, or chooses to love.

Men might be to leave Finland out of a sense of overweaning ambition and self-centeredness, as many of the songs above indicate. But in a number of emigrant songs, blame for the man's actions is shifted to the woman left behind, as the songs aver male emigration as the result of a broken heart. **Song 13** "Lähtölaulu/Departure Song," collected from the farmwife Kerttu Talvitie (born 1912) of Kauhajoki, makes this idea of emotional culpability clear:

Kättä sinä annoit mulle pilkalla
Sinä pidit minua vain illan hupina.
Sinä valloitit mun nuoren sydämen,
Ja ryöstit vielä ensirakkauden.
—
You paid attention but went and deceived me.
You played your wiles and captured me with your art.
My true devotion then you took from me,
Turning my head and stealing away my heart.

What is not exactly clear in the song is who jilted whom, or why. Nonetheless, it is certain that the separation of the two lovers through emigration has been caused not by economic conditions but by emotional turmoil. The singer asks the lover to return someday to honor the singer's grave but does not expect to meet again in this life.

Where most of the songs in this anthology narrate the experience of unnamed men and women, two songs in this section describe the romantic experiences of named characters. In **Song 2** "Akseli ja Hilda/Akseli and Hilda," published as a broadside in Helsinki in 1875, we meet with a very different sort of parting, in which the woman leaves for America with her father, while her male truelove remains behind in Finland. The song is a translation from the Swedish song "Aksel och Hilda," written by the Swedish songster Johan Henrik Chronwall (1851–1909)[1]. Its popularity in Finland is reflected by the fact that it was reprinted some thirty-five times between 1875 and 1914[2]. In the Finnish song, which closely matches the Swedish original, Hilda's father disapproves of Akseli's lowborn background. He brings his daughter to live with him in California, where she pines for her boyfriend. On his deathbed, the father regrets his harshness and blesses the union. The distraught Hilda, now bereft of father and boyfriend, sighs out Akseli's name into the wind. At this point, in Chronwall's Swedish original, a male water spirit (a *näcke*) intervenes to reunite the couple:

> Och näcken han spelte på böljan upp en sång
> Och framför jungfrun trädde en yngling smärt och lång.[3]
> —
> And the *näcke* played on the wave a song
> And before the maiden stood a young man slender and tall.

Although the näcke is familiar in Finnish tradition as the *näkki*, the translator of Chronwall's song chose to replace the normally mischievous or ill-willed supernatural figure with Vellamon neitonen, ("maiden of Vellamo"), a kind of mermaid that Elias Lönnrot transformed into the post-drowning embodiment of his character Aino in Poem 5 of the *Kalevala*. The equivalent lines in the Finnish song read:

> Kun aalloissa lauloi Vellamon neitonen
> Niin Hildan eteen astui sen oiva sulhonen.
> —
> An overhearing mermaid, did sing upon a wave
> Akseli her dear bridegroom stood there before her brave.

The couple, reunited through the kindness of a supernatural being, are able to marry and live happily ever after. The song's events appear to have little to do with any actual experiences of male and female emigrants, but reflect the ways in which distant America—specifically in this song, California—figured into the imaginative lives of a Finnish populace increasingly familiar with emigration.

Song 11 "Kaarlo ja Alma/Kaarlo and Alma," a ballad popular in turn-of-the-century Finland, tells a very different story of a pair of lovers. It was composed, like **Song 10**, by Frans Juho Järwinen (1857–1918) and first appeared in print in Rauma in 1893. Järwinen was an avid composer and publisher, producing some eighty songs during his career[4]. Kaarlo emigrates to America, asking his true love Alma to wait for him while he amasses wealth abroad. He intends to earn money in New York and then return to Finland so that the couple can marry and start their life together. A scheming associate, however—Petturi—writes to Alma in the guise of Kaarlo and asks her to come join him in New York. Alma dutifully does so, while simultaneously, the faithful Kaarlo returns to Finland to be reunited with his future bride. When Alma arrives in New York, Petturi finds her and pressures her to give her heart to him instead. A confused Kaarlo, unable to locate Alma in Finland, realizes what has happened and rushes back to New York to find and rescue her:

---

1   Chronwall 1893
2   Asplund 1994, 327
3   Chronwall 1893
4   Asplund 1994, 405

Tuumasi tuossa hetken
Niin seikat selveni,
Kuultua Alman retken
Näin Kaarlo takaisin.

—

He was in consternation
And then it all came clear.
He heard her destination
And rushed to find her there.

Kaarlo stabs Petturi to death, as the song declares:

Petturi maahan vaipuu
Virtaen verensä
Näin oli palkka saatu
Kavalustyöstänsä.

—

Petturi falls down bleeding
And writhes upon the ground.
His punishment proceeding,
his wage he now had found.

Aside from reinforcing the prevalent nineteenth-century image of Finnish men as knife-wielding menaces, the song seems to reflect, in a thoroughly fictionalized and improbable manner, the marked paucity of eligible Finnish women in America and the lengths a lonely man might go to try to find a Finnish wife. The song doesn't tell us whether or not Kaarlo and Alma are able to be united in marriage after Kaarlo's violent act; in any case, it is clear that Alma is innocent of any blame. Her honor contrasts with ballads in other immigrant communities of the day, e.g., the very popular Irish American ballad "Lily of the West." There, the song's main character stabs his rival, a nobleman, after discovering that his true love has been two-timing on him:

I rushed up to my rival, a dagger in my hand,
I tore her from his arms and boldly did him stab;
Being mad with desperation my dagger pierced his breast
And I was betrayed by Mary, the Lily of the West[1].

The song, broadly popular in Ireland, also had an American variant, in which the woman lived in Louisville and was named Flora.

If most departure songs in the Finnish tradition present a male perspective, **Song 14** "Amerikan leski/America Widow" provides a striking contrast. Published as a broadside in 1905, the song was credited to Elisa Valkama of Kauhajoki, herself an "America widow." The song opens mournfully but matter-of-factly:

Minä olin Amerikan leski ja sillä mina laulan niistä,
Usein mina olen silmäni kuivannut murhen kyynelistä.

—

Since he left me, that two-timing husband, I have so many pangs of sorrow.
It's a well-known thing in these here parts, an America widow.

---

1   Mhic Grianna 1953

The singer tells of the ostracism and loneliness of an abandoned woman and of the tendencies of others to blame her for her husband's disappearance. She describes gossiping neighbors, her long-suffering and supportive mother-in-law, her husband's sending of divorce papers, and a host of other details. The warning at the outset of her song is forceful:

Jos se on sitte vihitty vaimo taikka nuori likka,
Niin ei saa päästää ystäväänsä ikänä Amerikkaan.
—
If you are a good upstanding wife or a happily engaged young girl,
Never let your husband take to the road, or go traveling to the New World.

Real life and the world of popular song intersect in sometimes deceptive ways. In certain respects, the songs above reflect very concrete and cogent details of the Finnish emigrant experience: the prevalence of South Ostrobothnia as a place of origin, the typical route of emigrants traveling from Finland to New York, and the various economic and cultural factors motivating the decision to leave one's homeland. But the songs also portray an imagined world, a way of viewing emigration that grew up on both sides of the Atlantic and in a variety of different countries, including Finland. This imagined world was one in which actions were never neutral but rather heroic or villainous. The emigrant's choice to leave Finland was applauded as enterprising and brave, or deplored as foolhardy and unkind. The emotional intensity of the departure songs underscores the poignancy of emigration for many Finns, both those who traveled away and those who stayed behind. In Section II, we examine the musical accounts of emigrants-turned-immigrants, the songs composed about life as it unfolded in the New World. There again, we will see both factual elements and a broad emotional evaluation of the often traumatic decision to relocate to a distant shore. Songs gave voice to people's concerns, perceptions, and convictions, especially in face of the uncertainty of a life-changing migration. On many levels, the words of **Song 3** speak an unavoidable truth: "Ei sitä tiedä lähteissänsä/Kuka sieltä kotia palaa" ("They didn't know as they got ready to go/If they would somehow sometime return").

1. Nuoren poismuuttajan lähtö kotimaasta
The Young Emigrant's Departure from the Homeland

From the broadside collection "Neljä uutta ja suloista laulua" [four new and beloved songs] translated into Finnish by Sampo. Published in Turku in 1872. Melody taken from *Suomen kansan sävelmiä II. Laulusävelmiä*. Ed. Ilmari Krohn. Helsinki 1904–1933. Melody no. 469, collected in Rantasalmi 1890.

O, nei - to, mik - si mur - heel - lis - na nos - tat sun si - ni - sil - mäs
Oh mai - den, now you turn your eyes so tear - ful up towards the clouds that

koh - ti pil - vi - ä? Mun, ys - tä - vä - si, vie - lä ker - ran koh - taat, ett'
drift a - cross the sky? But love of mine, oh some-day you'll be cheer - ful, when

kyy - ne - lee - si saa - tan pyyh - ki - ä.
I come back to wipe your tears all dry.

O, neito! miksi murheellisna nostat
Sun sinisilmäs kohti pilviä?
Mun, ystäväsi, vielä kerran kohtaat,
Ett' kyyneleesi saatan pyyhkiä.

Minua olet sä onnellisempi,
Sill' satamahan jäät sa suotusaan,
Kuin meren myrskysäälle minun lempi
Jo kodistani laitti kulkemaan.

Jos sinusta ja pohjolan saloista
Lapsuuden kodista mä eroan,
Niin molemmille pohjantähti loistaa
Ja osoittaapi rauhan satamaan.

Kuin lähden minä siskoin leikkimaista,
Jäät sinä, armas, niiden suosioon;
Vaan muista aina silloin nuorukaista,
Kuin lähti synkän onnen huomioon.

Taas kerran, jos sen Luoja siten suopi
Mun eteläinen, kautta merien,
Sun helmoihisi, armahani, tuopi —
Ja kotimaahan lapsen kadonneen.

Hyvästi siis! Mä Jumalani huomaan
Ja Kaikkivallan suojaan antaun.
Sun näen taas; — vaan anon vielä suomaan
Minulle hyväst'jättö suutelun.

Hyvästi siis! on ehkä viime kerran,
Kuin hellää kättäsi nyt puistelen! —
Ken rakastaisi kuitenkin sen verran,
Kuin minä sinua, oi armanen!

Hyvästi vuoret, laakso lemuavainen,
Kuss' kulunut on aika lapsuuden!
On toivossamme koti taivahainen;
Jos täällä en, sun siellä kohdanneen.

O maiden now you turn your eyes so tearful
Up towards the clouds that drift across the sky
But, love of mine, oh someday you'll be cheerful,
When I come back to wipe your tears all dry.

As in the peaceful harbor you're remaining
I think that fortune smiles on you not me.
For I shall be upon the waves complaining
So far from home and tossed by storm and sea.

If from your side stern fortune now must take me
And from my backwoods home I must go forth,
Yet on us both the North Star will shine brightly,
And point a peaceful harbor from the north.

I leave you with all of my family's favor
Amid the meadows where my sisters play,
The mem'ry of my sorrow may you savor
As I, to test my fortune, sail away.

I hope that if the blessed Lord allows me
Then from the southern strands, 'cross sea and foam,
To your own arms my Savior will return me,
A waif returning to his childhood home.

Farewell my love into the Lord's protection
I humbly to His care my life bestow.
I ask of you a sign of your affection
A kiss to warm my heart as forth I go.

Farewell my love, this moment may be our last
That ever I may press your lovely hand,
But who in all the world both present and past
Could ever hold you with a love as grand?

Farewell you mountains and you fragrant valley,
Where peacefully I spent my childhood years.
Inside my heart I long for heaven holy
If not before, then there we'll cease our cares.

2. Akseli ja Hilda
Akseli and Hilda

From the broadside collection "Neljä uutta kaunista laulua" [Four new beautiful songs]. Published in Helsinki in 1875. The song has been published a number of times and the melody provided here has also been used for many other broadside ballads. Melody collected from Elli Virkkala of Kaustinen, 1947, conserved in the archives of the Finnish Literature Society.

Is - tu-en i - ha-nas - sa raik - kas-sa leh - dos - sa Ak - se-li se - kä HIl - da hä - nen
Deep in a love-ly for - est, there on a sum-mer's night, Aks - el - i and his Hil - da they are

mor - si-a - men - sa. kau - nii - na ke - sä yö - nä he⎯ rak - ka-uu - des-taan pu -
cloaked in wa-ning light. The young man and his bride, how they spoke of love ser - ene, re -

hui - vat, muis - tu - tel - len mui - nais-ta on - ne - aan.
mem - bering while to - ge - ther the - hap - pi - ness they'd seen.

Istuen ihanassa raikkaassa lehdossa
Akseli sekä Hilda hänen morsiamensa
Kauniina kesäyönä he rakkaudestaan
puhuivat, muistutellen muinaista onneaan.

Ikävä vaan myös hauska se yö oli Hildalle
Hän armastansa lempi nojais sen rinnalle
Hän suruissansa lauloi ja huolin huokaili:
»Hyvästi kauniit lehdot; hyvästi rakkaani».

Pois minun Pohjolasta isäni tahtoopi;
hän Kaliforniahan huomenna lähteepi,
Hän minun viepi muassaan ja meidät eroittaa,
Sä hänen mielestänsä oot halpa arvolta.

No hyvästi siis kulta hän sinun vieköön vaan,
Mä hänen arvoisensa en tosin olekkaan.
Siis jään nyt yksin tänne rannalle itkemään;
Vaan unohtaa en taida milloinkaan ystävään!

Kuitenkin täältä rientää mä aivon Pohjolaan
Sen tähtitaivahia kauniita katsomaan.
Se ikävässänikin on aina iloni
Jos vaan on onnellinen mun oma Hildani.

Nyt laiva lainehilla jo tuolla häilyypi,
Sen kanssa Hilda kauas kotoaan kulkeepi;
Vaan rannalle jäi Akseli yksin seisomaan,
Hän raukka kovin suree eroa kullastaan.

Vaan Hilda yksin istuu ja miettii suruisna
Uudessa kotimaassaan, raikkaissa lehdoissa;
Hän muistaa ystävätään min jätti Pohjolaan
Miksikäs jäi hän sinne niin yksin suremaan.

Vaan päivät vuodet vieri ja ajat muuttuipi,
Niin isä kerran Hildan tykönsä kutsuupi;
Nyt on jo myöskin hänen mielensä muuttunut,
Ei ole hän nyt enää Akseliin suuttunut.

Kuuleppas tyttäreni mun oma lapseni
mä väärin olen tehnyt sen sanoi tuntoni.
Sun suruus olen syypää kun sulhos hylkäsin
Jos Akseli ois täällä hän olis omasi.

Näin kuolinhetkellänsä nyt vanhus jutteli;
Hän suri sitä että Akselin hylkäsi.
Nyt oli Hilda yksin isänsä kuoltua
Hän suruissansa raukka taas istui lehdossa.

Se oli yksi ilta auringon laskussa
Kun Hilda sulhoansa muisteli surussa;
Hän muisti Akselin sen nimen lausuupi.
sen tuuli yli meren sulholle kuiskaapi.

Kun aalloissa lauloi Vellamon neitonen.
Niin Hildan eteen astui sen oiva sulhonen;
Ah tulee sylihini, kuin sulosti se soi
Se rakkaus kun minun luoksesi tänne toi.

Sun oma Akselisi viel' olen yhäti
Mä Pohjolasta riensin taas tänne luoksesi
En enää kotilaaksoissa voinut viihtyä
Kun kyhkyiseni sieltä pois täytyi lähteä.

Ah tulee Akselini; nojan rintaani
Se ompi satamasi ja olet iloni
Oi Suomi kotimaani! Oi sulo Pohjola!
Sun ylistystäs mahtaa pilvetkin kaikua.

Rakkain jumalatar lehtohon katsahti
kun Akseliosa syliin nyt Hilda istahti
Syleilyt suutelotkin ne arvaa jokainen
semmoinen Suomen neito joll' on vaan sulhanen.

Nyt tahdomme siis tähän vaan vielä lisätä
Ett' Akseli ja Hilda nyt elää yksissä
Pian vietettihin näiden rakastavaisten häät
He ovat onnelliset, elävät lemmessä.

Deep in a lovely forest there on a summer's night,
Akseli and his Hilda they are cloaked in waning light,
The young man and his bride, how they spoke of love serene,
Rememb'ring while together the happiness they'd seen.

Pretty but yet painful for Hilda was that night,
Sighing of her sorrow and the star-crossed lovers' plight.
With her head upon his shoulder, and her back upon his sleeve,
Of forest and of lover at once she must take leave.

"Far now away from Finland father is taking me,
for distant California we are leaving certainly.
He will take me oh so far off, and part me thus from thee,
For in his hard opinion, you're not of quality."

"Go with my love then sweetheart, father you must obey
I am not his equal, here in Finland I must stay.
But here alone I'll miss you and on this shore I'll cry,
Rememb'ring you my sweetheart until the day I die."

"Mournfully from this parting, far to the north I'll flee,
where the starry night sky, I'll look at gratefully.
Its beauty always gladdens my heart in its distress,
If only I am certain of my Hilda's happiness."

Watching the ship's departure, somberly sail away,
Taking lonely Hilda to Cal-i-for-ni-a.
But on the shore stands Aksel, he stands there all alone,
And watches as his sweetheart now sails far from her home.

Now there in California, lost in her woeful plight,
Hilda is so lonely in the woodlands of delight.
She ponders her dear true love "oh, why did he have to stay,
Remembering his sweetheart and pining all the day?"

As the years are passing, hearts they can change as well.
Father, he called Hilda, "I've got something you to tell.
My opinion now has altered, for that Akseli low-born
That suitor is no longer the object of my scorn."

"Listen my little daughter, my beloved child
Cruelly did I treat you, for my jealousy was wild.
I forced a lovers' parting and dealt your heart a blow,
If Akseli were here now, I'd accept him as your beau."

Finally with his last breath, Father he slowly said
Blessings upon their marriage he gave on his deathbed.
And poor Hilda abandoned on that dismal dying day,
She sat there weeping sadly, in a forest far away.

Early in the eve'ning as the sun went down,
Hilda she said "Aksel" as she sadly now did frown.
As she now pictured her Aksel, a wind it started near
And blew across the ocean to alight upon his ear.

An overhearing mermaid did sing upon a wave,
Akseli her dear bridegroom stood there before her brave.
"Oh come into my arms now, how sweet the words they sound,
for through the pow'r of love now, we have each other found!"

"It is I your Aksel who now here stands by
Far from the distant north lands your love has drawn me nigh.
There in our native valleys no longer could I stay,
When from that place my love bird was forced to fly away."

"Can it be my Aksel, guardian of my heart,
It is your safe harbor and you my joy's true art!
Oh Finland my dear homeland, oh north land that I love,
Now even in the heavens your praise sounds up above!"

"My beloved goddess," Akseli he did sigh,
Hilda so contented in her love's embrace did lie
How long they held each other anyone can surely guess
Who's seen a Finnish maiden with the man she loves the best.

Happily ever after, ends our lovers' tale,
Akseli and his Hilda, their love will never fail.
Now at last they are united with wedding vows so true
And all their hopes are realized as only love can do.

3. Nuorten poikajen Ameriikkaan menosta
Young Men off to America

From the broadside collection "Kaksi laulua," [Two songs] published by Salomon Ruuskanen. Published in Tampere in 1888. Melody notated by Aatos Rinta-Koski from farmwife Kerttu Talvitie (born 1912) of Kauhajoki. Collector's archives.

Poi - jat ne ot - ti - vat A - mer - ik - kaan— kym - me - nen vuo - den   pes - tin
Men went to work in A - mer - i - ca and for ten   long— years they   stayed—

Mo - ne - sta nä - tis - tä   li - kas - ta   on tul - lut - A   me - rii - kan les - ki
Em - i - gra-tion changed their girl friends'— sta-tion as they're in - to— "wi-dows" made

Pojat ne ottivat Amerikkaan
kymmenen vuoden pestin,
Monesta nätistä likasta on tullut
Ameriikan leski.

Pojat ne astuvat laivahan
Niin kapteeni tervehteli,
Siinäkös poikasten silmistä
Ne vedet pyörähteli.

Pojat ne menevät Ameriikasta
Hakemahan rahaa,
Ei sitä tiedä lähteissänsä
Kuka sieltä kotia palaa.

Älä sinä helluni ennen sure
Ja sure sitten vasta,
Laiva se lähtee rannalta
Eikä näkymästä lakkaa.

Eikä ne pojat talojansa asu
Ne menevät Amerikkaan,
Tänne jättävät suremaan
Niin monen mamman likkaa.

Pojat ne menevät Amerikkaan
Ja neidolle tulee suru,
Kuin pääsevät Atlannin toiselle puolet.
niin hotellista pelin ääni kuuluu

Minä olen mammani ainoa poika
Ja elelen tällä lailla,
Ja aikani meinaan kulutella
Vierahilla mailla.

Helluni kirjan lähetti
Sieltä New Yorkin kaupungista,
Eikä se ollut erokirja
Se oli rakkauden lista.

Helluni kirjan kirjoitti
Ja siinä oli i ja ässä,
Siitähän sen saa arvata
Että on surun ikävässä.

Helluni kirjan kirjoitti
Se on lukittu sinetillä,
Ja siinä oli päällen kirjoitus
Että tulisitko piletillä.

Meinasin meinasin meinasin olla
Ja meinasin olla yksin,
Vaan katselin taivahan lintuja
kuin niitä oli aina kaksi,

Kaksipa poikaa papalla
ja vanhinta mamma suree,
Eikä sitä tiedä mitä vielä
nuoremmastakin tulee.

Pojat ne seilaa Amerikkaan
Atlannin meren yli,
Ja voi kun me vielä saisimme istua
Suomen neitojen syliin.

Pojat ne menevät Amerikkaan
Ennen juhannusta,
Ja niin olen jäänyt hellustani
Kun kuivanu oksa puusta.

Ameriikan keskellä
on vesiharmaa taulu,
Ja siihen oli kirjoitettu
Suomen poikajen laulu.

Ameriikan laivan maston nenäs
on lippu liehuvainen,
Nuorella pojalla luonto
on kuin koski kiehuvainen.

Pojat ne menevät Suomesta
sinne Ameriikan maahan,
Sieltä ne sitten lähettelee
Hellullensa rahaa.

Pappa se sanoi pojalle
että taloni annan sulle,
Jäisitkö sitten kotiasi
huvitukseksi mulle.

Pappa se suree poikaansa
ja eikä se sure suotta,
Kun jäi hyvästi jättelemätä
kymmeneksi vuotta.

Hyvät on mun hyljännyt
ja huonosta en minä huoli,
Nyt on aika valitella
kun ikä on vielä nuori.

Mua on luotu tähän maailmaan
ristiksi ihmisille,
Ikuiseksi harmiksi
noille raharikkahille.

Wirren tämän lopetan
ja pitemältä en laula,
Jos Ameriikas tekee vääryyttä
niin pannan naru kaulaan.

Men went to work in America
and for ten long years they stayed.
Emigration changed their girlfriends' station
as they're into "widows" made.

Men climbed a-board the trans-Atlantic,
as "All a-board" they're calling.
Oh, the sorrows of those girls who are left behind,
their tears they just keep on falling.

Men hurried off to America,
for the fortune that they would earn.
They didn't know as they got ready to go
if they would somehow sometime return.

"Don't shed a tear, my- true love dear,
you can cry once the ship has parted.
Now while the ship's upon the wave let its image your heart save
once my journey's started."

Men left their boyhood homes behind
and their bold steps they did not falter.
Back in their homeland sat their sweethearts waiting
for their chance to reach the altar.

Men when they left for America,
to all hearts they were sorrow bringing.
Off on the Atlantic's other side they've forgotten their good brides,
for room service they're ringing.

"I am my mother's only son,
and I now want to live this way
I want to be footloose and free in a land so full of glee
That's so far away."

"My love he sent me a letter here,
it was mailed from New York City.
It was a letter that did promise me better,
it was chocked full of words so pretty."

"My love he wrote me from far away,
he did send me a loving line.
I could see between his I and his P
that 'twas for me that he did pine."

My love he sent me a lonesome note,
in an envelope he did stick it.
"Will you come across the sea and live out here with me
if I send you a ticket?"

Long and hard I thought it out,
and I looked up in the sky.
There in the heavens all the birds of the feather
they just ever in pairs did fly.

Mother she has two fine young sons,
but she frets for her oldest one
Nobody knows for him what fortune it holds,
or what the younger will become.

Off to a distant shore they go
as the sail of their ship unfurls.
Oh what a day, if we could only just stay
here in the arms of our Finnish girls.

They took their leave on a fine June day,
as they sailed off so bright and boldly.
I'm left behind to feel that I'm like a withered tree,
a pine branch he's snapped off coldly.

There is a sign in America
that out in the rain has grayed.
There on that plaque you can read front to back
all those Finlanders' song displayed.

Up on the deck of that sailing ship,
flew a flag in the breeze so mild.
It is true when I say this to you
that a boy's like a rapids wild.

From here in Finland forth they go,
to this distant land's far parts.
Money they earn now with a letter they yearn
now for to send to their dear sweethearts.

Father he said "My only home
I will give to you right today
If you endeavor here to stay then forever
you've a place free and clear to stay."

Father he had some good reason
to shed for his son some tears.
Off for adventure now his son he did venture,
he was gone for ten long years.

Some of the best they have passed me by,
with jilting I have been stung.
Most of the rest well they just don't pass my test,
I can complain while I'm still young.

I have been planted on this earth
so the back of the rich will sag.
I was created yes it's been so stated
as a drag on their money bag.

Now ends my song of America,
and I say to you what the heck
Do something wrong and then before very long
they will have noosed you around the neck.

4. Amerikkaan aikeet
Plans for America

From the broadside collection "Kolme kaunista laulua" [Three beautiful songs]. Publsihed in Vaasa in 1888. Melody *Suomen kansan sävelmiä II. Laulusävelmiä.* Ed. Ilmari Krohn. Helsinki 1904–1933. Melody no. 1837, collected in Isokyö, 1905.

Amerikkaan aivon lähteä niin ois mulla mieli,
Suomen niemi on nuorelle poijalle kuljeskella pieni.

Amerikkaan aijottu matka ei oo kovin kallis,
Senkään suhteen kuin on sieltä tuleva suuri saalis.

Palkka siellä on monin kerroin, kyllä se työstä riittää.
Nyt mä menen ensi kerran ja aivon Suomen heittää.

Toistamiseenkin menevät sinne, jotka on nauttia saanu
Hyvää palkkaa ja takaisin tultua heiltä ompi laannu.

Kyllähän tään Suomenkin maan mieleni voi muistaa,
Kuitenkin sinne päästyäni surun annan luistaa.

Mutta rakkaus Suomeheni tavaksi on tullu,
Maa on tuhatjärvinen ja omaksi tät' on luullu.

Iloisest' tätä mielessäni kuvailen mä aina,
En voi siellä ijäti olla kun rakkaus Suomeen painaa.

Kuitenkin siellä ruumiini työssä täydellisesti olkoon
Sille, joka työtä tekee, siitä kunnia tulkoon.

En mä tahdo työtöinnä olla enkä jouten viettää
Aikaa, sillä jos mitä kylvän sitä myös saan niittää.

Suru ei voi mitään saada aikaan onnen maassa,
Raha tekee moninkerroin täällä suomelassa.

To America I'll go, yes, I would see that country!
For a guy who is spry such as I, this here Finland's just too tiny.

Tickets to America, they aren't so very costly.
If one thinks of the wealth and the cash the adventure there will net me.

Wages there are mighty high, plentiful work to have there.
At this time when I'm still in my prime I can from this Finland get clear.

All the other men who've gone there, such good things they tell me.
Such a bountiful wage at my stage, I can say will not repel me!

Of my distant homeland Finland I will think tomorrow.
Once I get to the place I am set for that's when I'll feel some sorrow.

Finland though is dear to me, its thousand lakes I love so.
As I go to that land far away I'll still feel that love I do know.

Happily I see my homeland in my mind's eye ever.
Such a love it must come from above, so I just can't leave forever.

Even if it weighs on me I will just keep on working.
Honor comes to the one who'll not run once begun, labor not shirking.

Never will I loaf 'round idly, or spend my time a'drinking.
What you sow you should know you will mow, that is something well worth thinking!

Sorrow there or homesick care just has no use in that land.
Money there it just can't com-pare there's so much more than in Finland.

5. Suomalaisen lähtö Amerikaan
The Finn's Departure to America

Westerholm provided no notes about the origin of this song or tune.

Luo - jan suu - ren suo-si - os - ta Ai - von mä nyt rei - sa - ta. I - loi - sil - le
With the good Lord at my side I'll glad - ly head off on my way, To my friends who

ys - tä - vil - le läh - tö - vir - ren vei - sa - ta.
are so mer - ry I'll sing fare - well on this day.

Luojan suuren suosiosta
Aivon mä nyt reisata,
Iloisille ystäville
Lähtövirren veisata.

Toimeni mä kokoon laitan
Otan matkan eteeni;
Lähden ulos Atlantille,
Amerikaan kulkuni.

Jossa suuret linjalaivat
Kuljettavat aalloille,
Yli meren pauhaavaisen
Toisen kodin rannoille.

Mitä siellä mahtaa tulla
Esteet monen kaltaiset,
Hyvät, huonot seuraukset,
Onnelliset ottelut.

Kuin mää kuljen kunnialla
Voitan kaikki eteeni,
Voitan vieraan kovan leivän
Ahkeralla työlläni.

Kauvan olen täällä ollut
Kotoväen keskellä
Siunatkaat siis vielä mua
Viimeisellä hetkellä.

Isänmaani rakkahainen
Jääköön kanssa hyvästi
Sitä toivoo lähteväinen
Sydämmestään hyvästi.

With the good Lord at my side
I'll gladly head off on my way,
To my friends who are so merry
I'll sing farewell on this day.

With my trip to America
spreading forth in front of me,
I will pack all my belongings
for the trip out on the sea.

Where the sturdy ocean liners
ply the great waves and the foam,
O'er the ocean I will travel
to the shores of my new home.

Much will face me on this journey,
I shall be put to the test.
Some things will prove mighty challenges
while some happen for the best.

As I march forth with my honor
troubles all I'll pull through,
Humble bread I'll ably get
through the honest labor I'll do.

For a long while I have tarried
with the home folk around here.
So your blessing grant unto me
as my leaving it now draws near.

To my dearest native country
I will bid now farewell.
From a traveler now on his way
but whose heart it loves you well.

6. Nuorukaisen hyvästijättö Amerikaan lähteissä
A Youth's Farewell when Leaving for America

From the broadside collection "Kaksi aivan uutta ja kaunista laulua" [Two very new and beautiful songs] written and published by W. Myllykorpi, also known as Ritala. Published in Tampere in 1890. Melody *Suomen kansan sävelmiä II. Laulusävelmiä.* Ed. Ilmari Krohn. Helsinki 1904–1933. Melody no. 1733, collected in Uuraansalmi 1901.

Joka tä - tä Suo-men - maa - ta tar - kas - ti kat - se - lee, ei - pä tääl - lä ol - la
If you look at this Fin - land it is ea - sy to see, That the young men with am -

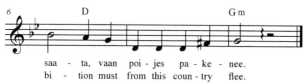

saa - ta, vaan poi - jes pa - ke - nee.
bi - tion must from this coun - try flee.

Joka tätä Suomenmaata
Tarkasti katselee,
Niin eipä täällä olla saata,
Vaan poijes pakenee.
Kun laivat ne rannasta erkani,
Niin itkivät neitoiset;
Hurraahuudot kuului
Isänmaalle rakkaalle.

Stockholmin sillalla meitä
Ensi kerran vastaan otettiin
Ja kun kuultiin minne reisattiin,
Niin roskat ne korjattiin.
Ja sitte me lähdimme reisaamaan
Aina Hullin kaupunkiin,
Siellä me flikkoja nähdä saimme,
Käsi kaulalla käveltiin.

Sitte me lähdimme reisaamaan
Läpi Engliskan maan
Ja kaksi päivää reisattua
Göteborgiin tulimma.
Ja sitte me lähdimme ajamaan
Noilla vaunuilla uljailla,
Ja kuuden tunnin kuluttua
Niin Liverpooliin tulimma.

Ja kun Liverpoolista lähdettiin,
Niin meri oli edessämme;

Ilo se muuttui murheeksi,
Vaikka malja oli kädessämme.
Ja ne laivat oli raudasta
Rakettu ja ne oli suuria,
Ettei trengännyt reisaavan
Murheesta itkiä.

Aallot ne käydä pärskätti,
Että Märskorit kastuivat
Ja silloinpa nuorukaiset
Ne murheesta astuivat.
Ja kun tuuli se rupeaa käymään,
Niin aallot ne yltyvät,
Ja silloinpa nuorukaisen
Sydän häilyypi.

Kaksi viikkoa reisattua
Meistä puolet väheni,
Kun tuo kuuluisa Ameriikka
Meitä jo läheni.
Ei trengännyt herroja palvella
Eikä myöskään kumartaa,
Vaan niinkuin omille armaillensa
Asian toimittaa.

Nyt astuimma me maalle
Täällä uudessa kotomaass'
Ja koska täältä palaamme,
Ei tiedä sanoa.

If you look at this Finland,
it is easy to see,
That the young men with ambition
must from this country flee.

The maidens they are crying
as the men head to sea,
From the ship decks they cry "Farewell"
as they leave their country.

When we got first to Stockholm
they met us with delight,
when we told them where we're headed
they fixed our boat up tight.

We headed on our travels
and we landed at Hull,
With a girl under each shoulder,
our time there was not dull!

We set off for more travel
across that great England.
And by morning of the third day
we reached Gothenburg strand.

By fancy railroad carriage
we did reach Liverpool.
It was barely six short hours
till we saw that fine jewel.

We took leave of that city,
the sea it lay ahead,
Though we drank deep from our tankards,
we felt sorrow instead.

Those ships there they were mighty,
built of iron and steel,
So that no one who was on them
any worry should feel.

The winds that blew across us
started ships' sails to fill,
The excitement of the moment
cheered the men's hearts as well.

When two weeks on the water
had cut our ranks by two
Then we saw at last America
 rise out of the blue.

You need not serve the wealthy
nor bow down as they pass,
But attend to your own business
and you'll earn your own cash.

We come ashore at last
to this homeland we like well.
Will we ever leave this country?
Well you can never tell.

7. Reisaavaisen laulu Ameriikkaan
The Traveler's Song of Going to America

Broadside published by Kustaa Luhtala. Published in Tampere in 1891. Melody *Suomen kansan sävelmiä II. Laulusävelmiä.* Ed. Ilmari Krohn. Helsinki 1904–1933. Melody no. 1357, collected in Suomussalmi 1902–05.

A - lo - tan mi - nä lau - lu - ni taas täl - lä - kin ta - val - la. Ja
I'll sing this day in my nor - mal way as it is my wont to do. I'll

ai - on läh - te - ä rei - saa - maan si - tä maa - il - maa la - ve - aa.
tell you how I am lea - ving now, for to tra - vel the whole world through.

Alotan minä lauluni
Taas tälläkin tavalla.
Ja aijon lähteä reisaamaan
Sitä mailmaa laveaa.

Ameriikkaan mennä meinaan
Ja sinne nämä pojat muuttaa
Me katselemme mailman avaruutta
Ja asuntoa uutta.

Kun Suomen rannasta lähdettiin
Niin maistettiin maljasta,
Hurraa huuto kuuluu,
Isänmaasta armaasta.

Tukholmin sillalla ensi kerta,
Meitä vastaan otettiin
Kun kuulivat mihin reisaamme
Niin värkkimme korjattiin.

Siitä me läksimme ajamaan
Niillä vaunuilla uljailla
Kahden päivän reisattua
Gööteporiin tulimme.

Englannin meri kaupunki
Jota Hulliksi sanottiin
Sepä nyt ensiksi
Meitä vastaan tuleepi.

Siitä me läksimme ajamaan
Englannin maata pitkin
Että se kuuluisa Liverpooli
Jo nähdä saataisiin.

Atlantin meri aukeni
Iso ja lavia
Vaan kyllä Herra laivamme
Vielä laittaa haminaan.

Irlannin järven saaret
Jotka ensiksi kierrettiin
Mitä niillä reisaavilla
Siinä liene mielessäkin.

Laivat on raudasta rakettu
Ja ne on niin pitkiä
Niin ettei tartte reisaavaisen
Pelvosta itkeä.

Atlantin aallot on korkeita
Ja välit on pitkiä.
Monen raukan reisaavan
Täytyy pelvosta itkeä.

Kymmenen päivän reisattua
Meiltä huolet jo väheni
Kun tuo kuuluisa Ameriikka
Meitä jo läheni.

Ei siellä helssata herroja
Ei pappia palvella
Vaan niinkuin vertaisellensa
Saa asiansa toimittaa.

I'll sing this day in my normal way,
as it is my wont to do
I'll tell you how I am leaving now,
for to travel the whole world through.

I'm headed off to America,
in the world I mean to roam,
The wide, wide world I will see unfurled
as I find me a fine new home.

On parting day we raised a cup
and we toasted our Finland.
We sailed away, with a "Hip-hurray!"
raised a shout for our dear homeland.

Before too long we had sailed along,
so that Stockholm we did see.
And when we said where we now did head,
then the ship it was made ready.

From there we road in carriages bold,
and it took us two days' time,
But then we'd see Gothenburg's beauty,
and our stay there it was prime.

We traveled next to a place called Hull,
it's a city of England.
And there we found many a sight and sound
on that great city's bustling strand.

Our next stop it was at Liverpool,
where we got a chance to rest.
A fine city it did seem to be,
it is known to be England's best.

Before us lay the great Atlantic,
with its waves and stretches wide.
The only way we could cross someday
was if God He would be our guide.

We sailed quite soon out past Ireland,
till we left its shores behind.
I wonder what all those folk aboard
they were harboring in their minds?

Those sailing ships they are well-equipped;
they are built of iron strong.
No traveler needs to be afraid
on such ships big and sleek and long.

The ocean waves tossed us down and up
and the distances are great.
And truth to tell in the mighty swell
 many feared that this was their fate.

'Twas ten long days that we sailed this way
till at last the land drew near.
America came now into sight a
nd that shore calmed our many fears.

There is no need the rich man to greet,
or to kow-tow to the priest.
But all can do what they mean to do,
from the greatest down to the least.

8. Uusi laulu Ameriikkaan matkustajista
A New Song about the Travelers to America

Broadside published by Otto Brander. Published in Pori in 1892. Melody "Juho ja Hilma," *Suomen kansan sävelmiä II. Laulusävelmiä.* Ed. Ilmari Krohn. Helsinki 1904–1933. Melody no. 1196, collected in Isokyrö 1905.

Hy - vä - sti su - loi - nen syn - ty - mä - maa nyt ai - von mi - nä mat - kus - taa
I'll say my fare - well oh land of my birth! I'm off to A - me - ri - ca

A - me - rik - kaan, kuin muut - to - lin - tu luo - tu o - len kul - ke - ma - han niin
for all I'm worth! I'll cross the man - y coun - tries and the waves of the sea; I'm

kau - vak___ si mai - den ja mer - ien taa.
just like a mi - gra - ting bird fly - ing free.

Hyvästi suloinen syntymämaa
Nyt aivon minä matkustaa Amerikkaan,
Kuin muuttolintu luotu olen kulkemahan
Niin kauvaksi maiden ja merien taa.

Pohjanlahden poikki käy Ruotsihin tie
Sinn' höyrylaiva lainoen minua vie
Kuin laivamme satamasta lähteepi vaan,
Hyvästi tuttavat huutaa viel' saan.

Suomenmaan rantoja enää silmiini näy
laivamme ympäri laineet vaan käy
Ja siintääpi ranta tuon vierahan maan,
Pian Tukholman kuuluisan nähdä jo saan.

Tukholman satamaan saavuttihin
Ja toisehen laivaan me muutettihin,
Kuin Tukholmasta lähdettiin etiä päin,
Niin saavuttiin Göteborin kaupunkiin näin.

Ruotsista ja Norjasta oli jo heit'
Siirtolaiskansaa kuin odotti meit'
Me Engelsmanni laivahan astuttihin,
Kuin iloisna meitä johdatti laivoissakin.

Pohjanmeren yli nyt käypi taas tie,
Joka Göteporista Englantiin vie,
Kun Pohjanmeren helmoissa häilyimme tääll'
Simeän taivaan ja aaltojen pääll'.

Maailman suurimpaan kaupunkihin,
Temsen suu'n, Londonin saavuttihin,
Voi ihmisvirtaa, pyörivää, rannalla tuoll'
En matkallani nähnyt viel' satamass' muoll'.

Kuin laivasta maalle me astuttihin,
Mikä jyry ja huuto oli rannalla siin',
Ei ihmetell', eikä myös laulaakaan saa,
Vaan kiireesti täytyy mun asemall' menn'.

Nyt lähden rautatietä matkustamaan,
Halki Britanian mannerta kulkemahan
Ja valtameren rannalle saavuttihin
Englannin, Liverpolin kaupunkihin.

Siell' linjalaiva suuri jo vartoisi meit',
Joka monen perhekunnan tavaroit' veit
Kuin meidän nyt eroitti Eurooppahast',
Vie siirtomaiden perille Amerikaan ast'.

Tuo Valtameri aava nyt edessämme on
Jota laivamme lähteepi lainomahan,
Ja laiva se eteenpäin kiitäpi oi,
Matkalaiset nauraa, viel' pelikin soi.

Piampa alkaa nyt ankarast' tuull'
Ja saatihin pranninkin pauhinaa kuull'
Julmasti myrsky nyt riehuupi niin
Näin valtameri kauhunsa näytti meill' siin'.

Hirmuisen suuria aaltoja tuo
Valtameri laivaamme vastahan luo,
Vaan uljaasti laivamme vastusti vain
Aaltojen voimaa, kulki eteenpäin ain'.

Meritauti hirmuinen vaivasi meit',
Epätoivon sumukin sydämen peitt',
Vuorokautta kolme myrsky raivosi, oi,
Vihdoinkin asettui tuuli ja tyvenen toi

Nyt ilma oli tyven ja ihana niin
Valtameri taivaan kautta kuvasti siin,
Kuin aurinko säteensä merehen liitt'
Niin nuoret ja vanhatkin luojaansa kiitt'.

Ah! Amerikan manner jo siintääpi tuoll'
Ei matkalaisten silmät nyt ehdikkään muoll'
Kuin etäällä merellä loistaapi vaan,
Kaupungin tornit joita katsella saan.

Laivamme kiitääpi mannerta päin,
Onnellisest' pääsimme perille näin,
Kuin hyvällä vauhdilla satamahan
Laivamme sisälle laski nyt vaan.

New Yorkin kaupungin rannalla tuo
Laivamme, matkustaja joukkonsa luo,
Suomalaiset rannalla vastass' oli meit'
Tuhansilla terveisillä kohtelimme heit'.

Nyt kaupunkia katselen hetkisen vain,
Sitt, sisämaihin rautatiellä matkustaa sain,
Kuin olemme maassa jo Amerikan
Niin laulamasta lakata minäkin saan.

I'll say my farewell oh land of my birth!
I'm off to America for all I'm worth!
I'll cross the many countries and the waves of the sea;
I'm just like a migrating bird flying free.

Over the Baltic a steamship does ply.
It will carry- me to where Sweden does lie.
As we sail from the harbor all my friends near and dear,
They shout to me "Farewell! Good luck to you there!"

Out on the Baltic the shore slips away.
And everywhere around us are waves and cold spray.
We travel over waters till a shore comes in sight;
We now see Stockholm with much joy and delight.

To Stockholm's good harbor we come at last.
Then to another ship we are thereafter passed.
With Stockholm in the distance we now head on our way;
And come then to Gothenburg where we can stay.

From Norway and Sweden, emigrants all
Are waiting for their passage from that port of call.
The captain he is English and he shows us on board,
And takes us around to each deck aft and forward.

We're headed from Gothenburg by the sea,
And then to Eng-land we do sail directly.
We rock on the billows of the great Northern Sea,
O'er dark wave and sky we sail intrepidly.

The Thames River greets our ship that's now come,
to the great city that is known as London.
Its shores are all crowded and with people do teem,
For me it is something I never have seen.

When we arrive there and walk round about,
Amid all the racket, the noise and the shouts,
There's no time in the fracas to wander or sing,
For off to the station ourselves we must bring.

The railroad it takes us from that grand place,
To travel across England at feverish pace.
We cross the mighty country as the train goes around,
And then it comes to stop at Liverpool town.

A great ocean-liner's waiting for us,
It carries all families without a fuss.
We travel in that steamer off from Europe's great shore,
To come o'er the sea to America's door.

The Atlantic mighty before us stands,
And crossing that- ocean is in all our plans.
The ship she pushes forward and she speeds on her way;
The travelers laugh as they dance and they play.

But things they go sour, a strong wind does stir.
And now we see lightning and hear the thunder.
A storm how it rages and lashes us mean,
And now at its worst this great ocean we've seen.

The storm sets upon us with wind and waves.
The onslaught of the ocean our vessel now braves.
But through the great tempest our good ship does ride
And moving straight forward takes storm winds in stride.

Sea sickness hits us, and suffering does cause.
And then a great fog comes and forces a pause.
For three days the tempest our seamen must fight,
But then comes a calm wind and sets us up right.

The end of that weather we now have seen.
And now spreads the ocean so blue and serene.
The sun peacefully shining warms all souls on board,
And many a passenger thanks the good Lord.

America's mainland now comes in sight.
It fills all our eyes with such tears of delight!
And there on the horizon a fine city I see,
With buildings and towers shining beautifully.

Our ship rushes forth to reach the mainland.
And fortunate feel we to reach that fair strand.
We boldly push ahead with a full head of steam,
And then comes the moment when off we all stream.

We've come to New York, the city so fine.
We stand and we look as the sun it does shine.
A crowd of happy denizens are milling about,
And thousands of greetings the Finns there do shout!

The sights of the city, fading now fast.
As off to the Midwest by train we have passed.
And now that we are done with our journey so long,
I can now stop singing this traveling song!

9. Ameriikkaan aikovan hyvästijättö
The Goodbye Song of the American Traveler

Nyt su-rul-la a-lo-tan lau-lu-ni tään, teill' van-hat mun ys-tä-vä-
Now sor-row-f'lly, will I this my song be-gin, For all of my old friends back

ni. Ja tie-dok-si an-nan mun ri-vi-ni nää, ja su-rui-sen
there; My feel-ings I'm gi-ving in these lines here-in, For my heart does

sy-dä-me-ni. Mä ys-tä-vät tei-tä niin pet-tä-nyt oo-n ja
great sor-row bear. My friends, I de-ceived you, your trust I be-trayed, - And

it-se-ni saat-ta-nut tur-mi-jo-on. Vaan an-teeks' mul' an-ta-kaa
led my-self ver-i-ly in-to harm's way. But friends, please for-give me, I

kui-ten-kin ne, Et-tei___ meit luo-jam-me ran-kai-se.
beg you in-deed That in the here-af-ter from Judg-ment I'm freed.

Nyt surulla alotan lauluni tään,
Teill' vanhat mun ystäväni.
Ja tiedoksi annan mun rivini nää,
ja suruisen sydämmeni.
Mä ystävät teitä niin pettänyt oon
ja itseni saattanut turmijoon.
Vaan anteeks mul' antakaa kuitenkin ne,
Ett'ei meit luojamme rankaise.

Mun sydämmen suuresti murheissa on,
Ja eloni huoltuu nyt pois
mää näjen ne murheen päivät nyt jo,
Joit' ikään en näkevän sois,
ei kyyneleet silmistän lopu nyt enää,
Kun suren ja murehdin ystäväin perään.
Ja näjen jo itseni hyljätyks taas,
Ei ystävii ollenkaan ole mull' maas'.

Jää hyvästi armas mun syntymämaan,
sen kummut ja kukkulatkin,
mun siskon aikoo kans Amerikaan.
Ja on mulla kumppanikin,
niin aivomme matkustaa vierasten valtaan.
Riita ja tora mun matkalle saattaa,
pois kyyneleet katkerat kasvoiltani,
sää kirottu entinen ystäväni.

Sen tähdetkin taivaalla todistavat,
Ett' rivini vakavat on,
sun sanas ain makavat sydämmen all',
kun lupasit, sinun nyt oon,
Ja ystävä valallas vannoit sen viel'.
Mää totuutta koskaan sulta en kiell'
vaan monastihan sinä sen rikkonut oot,
sen käytökses todistaa tuomijol'.

Nyt hyvästi sanon ja lopetan pois,
mää takaisin koskaan en tuu.
Jos sinussa elävä henki vaan on
sen todistaa oma mun suun,
sun kuolemas koska mun korviini soi,
niin silloin mää riennän Suomehen pois,
jos aalloissa vain ei hautani oo,
mun sieluni ainakin Suomessa on.

From the broadside collection "Seitsemän kaunista nuorten laulua" [Seven beautiful songs of youth] Published in Tampere in 1891. The song is presented here in abbreviated form, with somewhat altered melody. Melody specified on the broadside: "Kukkaisten keskellä kukkulalla."

Now sorrowfully will I this my song begin,
For all of my old friends back there;
My feelings I'm giving in these lines herein,
For my heart does great sorrow bear.
My friends, I deceived you, your trust I betrayed,
And led myself verily into harm's way.
But friends, please forgive me, I beg you indeed
That in the hereafter from Judgment I'm freed.

My heart it is breaking in sorrow and pain,
My cares they are eating me whole!
I see now my punishment day coming plain,
That troubles and worries me so.
The tears from my eyes they will never subside,
For I am here suffering, no friend at my side.
I feel I'm deserted and so I will be,
No friend here to cheer me in all this country.

My leave did I take of my loving homeland,
Each hill and each knoll bid adieu.
My sister would join me to reach the new land,
My love she was coming as well.
Together we'd planned to start up a new home
But arguments led me to set off alone.
My tears they are bitter, the memory will last
Of you the most cruel of friends of my past.

The stars in the heavens bear witness so true,
My lines are not telling a lie;
Your heart seemed so honest and I trusted you,
When you said you'd always be mine.
Your promise of faithfulness I did believe,
You promised me you would me never deceive.
But you broke your promise and did me betray,
But I'll leave your reckoning for Judgment Day.

My farewell I say as my song I do end,
I'll never come back there to you.
This witness my soul does now unto you send,
If by chance there's life still in you.
Your death knell, if ever it reaches my ears
Then I'll come back to Finland after the years
And unless I drown in completing my quest,
My soul back in Finland at least will find rest.

10. Amerikaan siirtolaisen laulu
The Song of the Immigrant to America

A - me-riik-ka Suo-men poi-kain mie - le-hen nyt kään - tyy, Voi! kun rak - as
Thoughts of men are - turn-ing e - ver, toward A-mer - i - ca far a-way. They so yearn for

ko - tin - sa näin kau - vas jät - tää täy - tyy.
that ad-ven - ture, from dear Fin - land now to stray.

Ameriikka Suomen poikain
Mielehen nyt kääntyy,
Voi! kun rakas kotinsa näin
Kauvas jättää täytyy.

Valtameri lavealta
Silmissämme siintää,
Suomen poikain silmät vuotaa
Eron kyyneleitä.

Ameriikka Suomen poikain
On nyt paras turva,
Kun ei saata veljellänsä
Oleskella orja.

Pappan talo vahvistettu
On mun veljelläni,
Amerikkaan kuuluu täältä
Suomen poikain ääni.

Ameriikkaan Suomen pojat
Tuhansia seilaa,
Ameriikan kultamaassa
Rikastua meinaa.

Ameriikan kulta on niin
Maailmassa mainittuna
Suomen pojat Ameriikan
Matkalle hankittuna.

Ameriikan kulta on niin
Loistavata lajia,
Kaikki Suomen neitosetkin
Ameriikkaan naidaan.

Matkustamme vierahalle
Ameriikan maalle,
Vaikka siellä siirtolaisna
Majaella saamme.

Monta kertaa mielehemme
Suomi vielä muistuu
Kun nuo aallot laivan eessä
Kohisee ja truiskuu.

Höyry vaan kuin voimallansa
Propellia vääntää
Eikä meidän enää salli
Takaperin kääntää.

Piljetit on lunastettu
Ameriikkaan asti,
Eronhetki kyynelillä
Poskiamme kasti.

Eipä tässä itkeminen,
Parempi on laulaa,
Ehkä sydän kuumempi kuin
Masuunissa rauta.

Hyvästi jää sä Suomen maa
Sä kallempi kuin kulta,
Et sä taida ikänänsä
Unhoittua multa.

Kasvakohon kankaillasi
Vapauden kukka,
Valmistukoon hedelmäsi
Tasarvoisuutta.

Että saisi suomalaiset
Täällä sekä siellä
Toisiansa kätellä he
Veljeksinä vielä.

Eläköhön tasa-arvo,
Kuolkohon raha-valta,
Sitten eivät Suomen pojat
Lähde kotomaalta.

From the broadside collection "Nuorison lauluja" [Songs of youth] compiled by Frans Juho Järwinen of Eura. Published in Rauma in 1893. Melody from *Suomen kansan sävelmiä II. Laulusävelmiä*. Ed. Ilmari Krohn. Helsinki 1904–1933. Melody no. 1062, collected from the area of Pori 1889. Original melody unknown.

Thoughts of men are turning ever,
Toward America far away.
They so yearn for that adventure,
From dear Finland now to stray.

In our eyes we do see the ocean,
Stretching out so vast and blue,
But with tears and deep emotion
We consider leaving you.

America there's no other
For a Finnish man young and brave,
There you're not stuck with your brother
Having to work as his slave.

Father's place so fine and strengthened
It is now my brother's home.
So my travels now have lengthened
To America I'll roam.

To America we're sailing,
Hoping there to strike it rich.
Thousands strong in hope unfailing,
Heeding all the freedom pitch.

We've heard tell of that land golden,
Through the world its fame is known;
Now in droves with hearts emboldened
Anxious to see we are grown.

Like a golden land it does shine
Its allure is known everywhere.
Even maidens they do so pine
To be married over there.

So our dreams how far they'll take us,
With such hope we have been sent.
Though the journey it will make us,
Live as lowly immigrants.

Often are the memories drifting,
back to us of our native land.
As beneath the seas are shifting
Till we reach that distant strand.

Steam it strongly does propel us
Boldly onward it pushes so.
Its strong drive it does convince us
Backwards now we cannot go.

Now we have our tickets on us,
To America they are bought.
Sorrow comes hard now upon us
Tears well at each parting thought.

Waste no time with words of yearning
Singing's better for desire.
Even if your heart is burning
like an iron in the fire.

Now to my Finland farewell I say.
You are dearer to me than gold.
In my heart your memory will stay,
Ever there its power hold.

Ever more in your fields abounding
Let the flower of freedom be.
Grant in harvest so resounding
Fruit of true equality.

So that Finns both there and here
Can have hearts that are understood,
And reach out with goodwill clear
Embracing noble brotherhood.

Let equality find a footing
Let the power of money die.
Then we Finns will not be needing
From our native land to fly.

11. Kaarlo ja Alma
Kaarlo and Alma

I - ha-nan koi-vun al - la au-ring-on las-keis-sa, sai Al-ma sul-hol-tans-sa sor-
Be neath a love-ly birch tree be-neath the set-ting sun, sweet Al-ma and her true love their

muk - sen sor-meen - sa. Se sor-mus o - li kul - taa ja kak-si-rin-ki-nen. Kun
court-ship long had run. He placed up - on her fin - ger a pret-ty ring of gold. And

Al - mal-len - sa an - taa nyt Kaar-lo-ni - mi - nen.
Al - ma gave her heart to that Kaar-lo good and bold.

Ihanan koivun alla
Auringon laskeissa
Sai Alma sulholtansa
Sormuksen sormeensa.

Se sormus oli kultaa
Ja kaksirinkinen
Kun Almallensa antaa
Nyt Kaarlo-niminen.

Kuuleppas ystäväni
Almani ihana,
Mä lähden Amerikkaan
Kokoomaan tavaraa.

Sä odottele täällä,
Kun tulen takaisin
Sä olet omanani
Oleva ainiaan.

Alma se lupas' uottaa
Kaarletaan kotona,
Kaksi tai kolme vuotta
Sulhoaan odottaa.

Vaan kolmantena vuonna
Sai Alma piletin.
Kaarlen nimen kautta
Matkustaa käskettiin.

Vaan kuules kuinka kävi
Tää oli kavaluus
Kaarlonsa tuttavalta
Petos ja viekkaus.

Tullut ol' tuttavaksi
Kaarlelle siellä niin
Asiat kaikki tiesi
Kuin Kalle itsekin.

Kun Kaarle kotiin lähti
Almaansa omaamaan,
Petturi Alman käski
Ain Ameriikkahan.

Hyväst Alma jätti
Suomensa suloisen,
Hän oli nuori, nätti,
Ja kaunis kasvoiltaan.

New Yorkin kaupunkihin
Saapuen toivossa
Kohdata Kaarletansa
Jonk' piti vartooman.

Vaan Kaarle kotiin saapui
Toisessa laivassa,
Mielensä täytti kauhu
Kun poissa Almansa.

Tuumasi tuossa hetken
Niin seikat selveni,
Kuultua Alman retken
Näin Kaarlo takaisin.

New Yorkin satamassa
Almata vartosi
Se vieras kavaltaja
Kun Alman veivasi.

Hän Alman heti tunsi
Kun valokuvansa
Jo nähnyt kertaa kuusi
Oli hän Kaarlolla.

Nyt Alman tuttavaksi
Esitti itsensä,
Kun Alma turhaan etsi
Armasta Kaarloaan.

Vaan eipä kosto viivy
Petturi poloisen
Kaarlella jolla kiiruu
Rientää kuin lintunen.

Alman kättä pyytää
Petturi parallaan
Kun Kaarle rintaan sysää
Veitsensä kosijaan.

Petturi maahan vaipuu
Virtaen verensä,
Näin oli palkka saatu
Kavalustyöstänsä.

Presented with melody as in Huugo Värälä's edited collection *Laulelmia vanhoista vahakansivihoista* [Songs from old oilskin notebooks]. Published in Kangasala in 1981.

Beneath a lovely birch tree
Beneath the setting sun
Sweet Alma and her true love
Their courtship long had run.

He placed upon her finger
A pretty ring of gold.
And Alma gave her heart to
That Kaarlo good and bold.

"Now hear my words my honey,
my lovely bride Alma,
I need to earn some money,
Off in America.

"You wait for me on this side,
And when I have come back,
You'll be my loving true bride
And joy we shall not lack."

So Alma vowed with such tears
Her Kaarlo to await.
It might take two or three years,
Before their wedding date.

But after three years' waiting
A ticket came by mail,
And also a note stating
That she should thither sail.

But oh! The cruel betrayal!
This ticket was not true.
A scheming misportrayal
Of one of Kaarlo's crew.

This man became acquainted
With Kaarlo's plans in life,
And by this scheme so tainted
He would procure a wife.

As Kaarlo left for Finland
His bride at last to meet
Petturi called to his land
The faithful Alma sweet.

So Alma took her leave now
Of Finland then and there
The letter she believed now
She was so kind and fair.

She came to New York City
The trip she did not mind.
This faithful maiden pretty,
Her Kaarlo for to find.

But Kaarlo he had traveled
Back home upon a ship.
And found his dream unraveled
For Alma far did slip.

He was in consternation
And then it all came clear.
He heard her destination
And rushed to find her there.

In New York the deceiver
For Alma he did wait.
He met the sweet believer
Confused about her fate.

He knew her by her picture
That he had often seen.
He meant now to ensnare her
With his deceiving scheme.

He made her sweet acquaintance
And told her then his name,
As Alma searched with patience
For Kaarlo without blame.

Revenge it does not take long
Or so you may have heard.
For Kaarlo traveled headlong
As swift as any bird.

Petturi is proposing
In courting manner best,
When Kaarlo comes imposing
And stabs him in the chest.

Petturi falls down bleeding
And writhes upon the ground.
His punishment proceeding,
his wage he now had found.

12. Ameriikkaan lähtö
Going to America

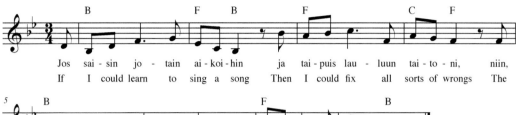

Jos sai - sin jo - tain ai - koi - hin   ja tai - puis lau - luun tai - to - ni,   niin,
If   I   could learn   to   sing   a   song   Then   I   could   fix   all   sorts of wrongs   The

yh - tyis vie - lä ym - mär - rys,   kät - ket - ty sii - hen kä - si - tys.
world would see   and   un - der - stand   What's go - ing on   in   this here land.

Jos saisin jotain aikoihin,
Ja taipuis' lauluun taitoni,
Niin, yhtyis' vielä ymmärrys,
Kätketty siihen käsitys.

Tuo Ameriikka tukala,
Se on liika ja hankala,
Aina tulen tuiman sytyttää
Tuon maasta muuton yllyttää.

Ei ole onni kaikilla
Ameriikan raitilla,
Vaikka hylkivät pukunsa
Antavat ylön sukunsa.

Rientävät sinne innolla,
Voiton suuren tunnolla,
Ei pyri maahan luvattuun
Raamatuissa kuvattuun.

Äl' heitä vitsaa vihassa
Ei asu totuus lihassa,
On synnin jänteet jälillä
Matkassamme ja välillä.

Syy on siihen syntisen
Itsepäisyys ihmisen,
Heitä ajelee ahneus,
Kauhistava kateus.

Kun Engesmanni ennätti,
Sanoman hän lennätti,
Löyttyänsä kultamaan,
Minn' siirtolaiset kutsutaan.

Mies pääsee sinne rahallaan,
Niin, Siperiaan tahallaan,
Kultamaata kaivamaan,
Niit' ahneuden hautojaan.

Mitäs sä teet nyt kullalla
Kun peityt mustall' mullalla,
Käyt' kohti kuolemaa
Josta tulee kutsut tuonelaan.

He vasta huutin tietävät
Kun ruukista ruukkiin rientävät,
Kuinkas täällä jaksetaan
Milläs kyytinsä maksetaan.

Tuohan on Suomelle surkeaa,
Että monta on kulkijaa.
Joilla olis isänmaa
Ja kotomaassa olla saa.

Hannus hautamestari
Ruhtinas ja pestari,
Heitä sinne saattelee
Jotka mammonasta aattelee.

Saatan anteeksi anoa
Amen lauluuni sanoa
Jos olen väärin vääntänyt
Ja sanat nurin kääntänyt.

Broadside written by Juho Marjakangas, published by Herman Hangasmaa of Ylivieska. Published in Oulu in 1893. Sung to the tune of "Voi kuinka kauan kestänee tuo sota suuri ja Ankara." Melody from *Suomen kansan sävelmiä II. Laulusävelmiä*. Ed. Ilmari Krohn. Helsinki 1904–1933. Melody no. 1881, collected in Pieksämäki in 1886. The only known song that seems aimed at dissuading emigration.

If I could learn to sing a song
Then I could fix all sorts of wrongs.
The world would see and understand
What's going on in this here land.

America can be so tough
And getting there can be so rough.
It seems to me once finally there
That everyone just does not care.

The money does not grow on trees
And life for them is not a breeze.
But they all say they say goodbye
And families they stay and cry.

And off they go excitedly
Just hoping to earn big money.
They do not think of God's grand plan
The Bible's words, the Promised Land.

Don't flash your eyes and show anger
The truth may hurt, but is no slur.
We aren't perfect, we sometimes sin.
Along this trip, and times therein.

They're drawn to leave because of sin
And headstrong ways they're mired in.
A lust for gold consumes their thoughts
And plagued by greed the heart it rots.

The Englishman, he took a chance.
He sent back word after one glance.
He'd found a land made up of gold
Where everyone can come it's told.

A man arrives with some money.
He might head north, deliberately,
To dig for gold in frozen land
Where graves of greed and tombstones stand.

What do you do with all that gold
When at your death you're set in mold?
You'll walk with Death and wait your turn
To leave this world, your fate to learn.

They know no shame those greedy men.
From mine to mine they ask again.
"Is there still gold beneath this land?
Keep digging boys for riches grand!"

For old Finland it is so sad.
So many gone, so many lads,
Who here would have, a home so fine,
A bed to sleep, a place to dine.

Mean Hannus he buried them all,
Spoke words so sweet and had the gall
To take them to a foreign place
In search of gold, silver, and lace.

I ask for you to forgive me
And say Amen that is my plea.
If what I've said is all a lie
Words turned around and gone awry.

13. Lähtölaulu
Departure Song

Melody notated by Aatos Rinta-Koski from farmwife Kerttu Talvitie (born 1912) of Kauhajoki.
Collector's archives. No. 552, 1974.

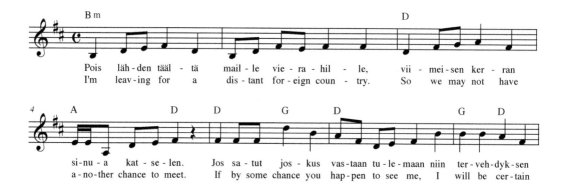

Pois lähden täältä maille vierahille.
Viimeisen kerran sinua katselen.
Jos satut joskus vastaan tulemaan,
niin tervehdyksen saat sinä minulta.

Kättä sinä annoit mulle pilkalla.
Sinä pidit minua vain illan hupina.
Sinä valloitit mun nuoren sydämen,
ja ryöstit vielä ensirakkauden.

Niin monta kertaa kysyin sinulta
miksi et enää minua rakasta?
Syy lienee ollut minun köyhyytein.
Oi senkös tähden hyljäsit sä mun?

Jää hyvästi, sä lausuit minulle.
Voi kuin se koski nuoreen sydämeen.
Vaivuin silloin syliis' tainnoksiin,
enkä tiennyt koska siitä heräsin.

Yhtä vain pyydän poika sinulta.
Käythän mun haudallani kesäiltana?
Tuo seppel tuore mulle muistoksi
ja laske päälle kylmän hautani.

Ei ole mulla muuta ystävää,
ei ole myöskään mailman kunniaa.
En aijo sitä paljon kootakkaan
sillä rakkaus vie minut hautahan.

I'm leaving for a distant foreign country.
So we may have another chance to meet.
If by some chance you happen to see me,
I will be certain you heartily to greet.

You paid attention but went and deceived me.
You played your wiles and captured me with your art.
My true devotion then you took from me,
Turning my head and stealing away my heart.

So many times I asked you please to tell me
Why you no longer loved me like you did.
Could it be maybe my hard poverty?
Was that the thing that left me so jilted?

You touched my heart as you did bid me farewell.
Kind-sounding words they hurried me on my way.
Then in my sorrow in your arms I fell.
I would there gladly with you forever stay.

One thing of you, love, humbly I am asking,
One summer evening dutifully visit me.
Unto my cold grave lovely garland bringing,
There with fondness you can remember me.

I have nobody who will now befriend me.
From my distress not anyone me will save.
In my dishonor nothing else can mend me.
Your cold heart has driven me to my grave.

14. Laulu
Song of an America-Widow

Broadside "Yksi hauska laulu" [One pleasant song] composed by America-widow Elisa Valkama of Kauhajoki. Published by Antti Koivumäki, in Kristiina in 1905. Melody notated by Aatos Rinta-Koski from farmwife Kerttu Talvitie (born 1912) of Kauhajoki. Collector's archives. No. 300, 1972.

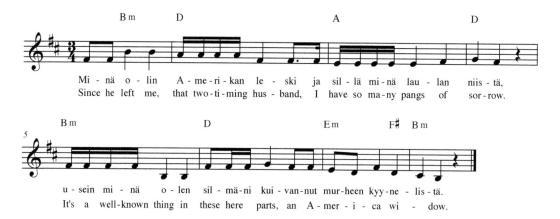

Mi - nä o - lin A - me - ri - kan le - ski ja sil - lä mi - nä lau - lan niis - tä,
Since he left me, that two - ti - ming hus - band, I have so ma - ny pangs of sor - row.

u - sein mi - nä o - len sil - mä - ni kui - van - nut mur - heen kyy - ne - lis - tä.
It's a well-known thing in these here parts, an A - mer - i - ca wi - dow.

Minä olin Amerikan leski ja sillä minä laulan niistä,
usein minä olen silmäni kuivannut murhen kyynelistä.

Jos se on sitte vihitty vaimo taikka nuori likka,
niin ei saa päästää ystäväänsä ikänä Amerikkaan.

Voi kuinka monen pariskunnan välin on Amerikka pahentanut.
Ja moni vaimo on sentähden kunniansa alentanut.

Ei Amerikan siihen syytä ole, kyllä se on turha tuuma.
Paremmin se on Linnaksi, kun siellä on leskein ruuma.

Mutta ne miehet kirotut, jotka viekoittelee vaimot,
Kun ne turmelee ne pahemmin kuin kylmä halla laihot.

Minä olen yksi Amerikan leski muttei te tiedä kuka,
Kun minä laulan itsestäni, niin on mulla siihen lupa.

Mun mieheni on kanssa Amerikassa ollut kahdeksantoista vuotta.
Ja se on aikaa jo mun hyljännyt ja se hyljätyksin mun saattoi.

Ompa se ollut jo enemmänkin, se yhdeksättä toista,
niin on mulla ollut sillä aikaa muresta jo monen moista.

Eikä ole mun surustani tiennyt, muut kun taivaan Luoja.
Kun ei mieheni laittanut mulle rajuilman suojaa.

Itsiäni minä hyppyisilläni elätellä koitan.
Ja mieheni on mun Amerikassa se on Jaakko Matinpoika.

Erokirjan se mulle lähetti, sitte on kolme vuotta.
Niin sen minä tiedän ettei mun sovi siihen nyt enää luottaa.

Lujalla olen ollut Maailman käsis'. On puhuttu rumiaki,
Kun on mun sanottu valanehen eläviä kuviakin.

Väärin minä olen kärsiä saanut, mutten piittaa mitään,
Muttei sellaista miestäkään sovi omanani pitää.

Täs varoitan teitä Amerikan lesket, että viinaa ei saa juoda
ei saa kulkia joukoissa, eikä joukkoja kotia tuoda.

Älkää te Amerikan lesket uskoko viekottelijoita,
jos se on sitten isäntä tai komian talon poika.

Minä olen jäänyt miehestäni, mutta anoppiani kiitän.
Ja ne on sitte hukalla, jos ihmiset tietää siitä.

Ja minä olen niin pahan ämmän tyttö, ettei pahempia ole.
Ja minä olen Valkamasta ja laulan vallan toden.

Kyllä se on ikävää, kun hyljätyksi tulee,
mutta tuomiolla se maksetaan mitä perhe Suomessa suree.

Ajatelkaa te Amerikan lesket, jotka olette viattomia,
ettei te usko ikänä niitä miehiä meikkosia.

Ja oikeenpa ne miehet onki pirulta riivatuita.
Joilla on itsellä emännät ja ne viekoittelee muita.

Miehet on saattanut linnahan niin monta vaimo raukkaa.
Ja kantavat itse kunnian. Ja mitä se niitä auttaa.

Since he left me, that two-timing husband, I have no pangs of sorrow.
It's a well-known thing in these here parts, an America widow.

If you are a good upstanding wife or a happily engaged young girl,
Never let your husband take to the road, or go traveling to the New World.

Many couples are no longer happy, it's all because the man's gone away.
America's call has captured men's hearts, while he left his wife there to stay.

Do not say it's America's doing, there's all too many wives left behind
Ignominy places them in a prison, there to face censure unkind.

How I curse all those deceitful men whose ever-faithful brides' hopes are lost.
Coldly they destroy their wives' tender hearts just like a crop bitten by frost.

I am just such an abandoned widow, but I will never tell you my name.
My experiences I will relate, yes my own fate I will proclaim.

My dear husband he has gone and left me, he's been away for eighteen long years.
For America he jilted me, oh he has left me to my tears.

He's been gone my scoundrel of a husband, it's coming up now on year twenty
He has left me weeping, all alone, with my cares and sorrows plenty.

No one else but God has heard my complaint, or looked upon my deep dejection.
I have had no man stand at my side, from life's storms my first protection.

In these times I'm all alone and trying just to find a way to get on.
Matti Jaakko's son is my husband's name who to America is gone.

Divorce papers well he sent them here and I got them three years ago well nigh,
When they came to me I could plainly see that I could not on him rely.

My fate has been placed in the world's hands and gossipers have made suggestions.
All my conduct has been scrutinized and of me there's been cruel questions.

I have suffered all these many hardships, accustomed to them all I have grown.
I can tell you now a man like him I would never keep as my own.

Oh you women who've been jilted so, never visit friends or just socialize.
Never drink a drop, never have friends home, or you'll sure face slander and lies.

Oh you jilted, never let some man with his smooth talk and his ways you beguile.
Never take his bait though a farmer great, or a young man with looks and style.

That man left me mournfully a'pining, his dear sweet mother has helped me out.
By my side she's stayed she would be ashamed if ever people they found out.

I'm the daughter of a mean old crone, I can truly say no worse there can be.
I'm from Valkama and of my old man, I am telling things so truly.

All the suffering we abandoned women we will boldly read on Judgment Day.
For these many woes we must undergo, they will surely then have to pay.

Heed my counsel you forsaken women you who have been so blameless and wise.
If you want to be from such trouble free, never fall for all such men's lies.

It's the devil who ensnares good husbands and causes them their wives to betray.
With a wife at home there's no need to roam or to lead another astray.

Many men they'd lock away their wives, they'd soon forget their poor wives so true.
They put on fine airs for the world to see, but what good does their pretense do?

II. Perillä. Arrived.
Songs 15–31.

Emigration shattered any sense of predictability in the lives of Finnish emigrants and their families. Where Finnish songs tend to depict village life as staid, constricting, and thoroughly predictable, the emigrant's life in the New World is depicted as having few such limitations or boundaries. A person, the songs suggest, could strike it rich or die in obscurity. Whether in the songs or in real life, family members and friends back home in Finland—people accustomed to daily contact with the people they knew and loved—had to content themselves to wait for the occasional letter from America and the news it would bring. As they processed the emotional and experiential disjunction that emigration entailed, people on both sides of the Atlantic found solace and release in musical expressions. This section of the anthology looks at songs created or related to the initial experiences of migration. As with songs of departure, these songs of arrival are far from historical records or ethnographic evidence: rather, they present imaginative renderings that reflect the ways in which Finns of the late nineteenth century viewed the migrations that were becoming more and more common in their day.

The Story Continues (Songs 15, 16)

Song 15 "Amerikan laulu/Song of America," published by J. Eskelinen in Tampere in 1895, picks up the narrative of emigration where the travelogue songs of Section I leave off. Here we see a male persona, one who describes himself at the end of the song as young, unmarried, and lonely, as he first arrives in New York, full of vigor and anticipation. Already by the third stanza, he is passing into the social interactions and language of the new country, as forward women and English vocabulary push their way into his world. The singer uses *soluuna* ("saloon") for what in Finland would have been called a *kapakka* or *kievari*, and *treini* ("train") for what in standard Finnish was called *juna*, and what in **Song 6** was called *vaunu* ("train car/coach"), and in **Song 8** *rautatie* ("railroad"):

> Sitten tytöt meitä haastoi
> Että käykkäät Soluunahan
> Niin siellä saatte kohdata
> Jo monta tuttavaa
> Vaan me vastasimme heillen
> Ei me joudu Solunaahan,
> Sillä meidän täytyy reisata
> Treini jo odottaa.

—
And the girls made a point to invite us
With them to have a drink
Our old friends would recognize us
At the saloon they did drink.
But we said to them most truly
"The saloon, it is out, that's plain.
For though we could go so happily
We must right now board our train."

Later in the song, when the singer and his companions have plunged into the dark and dangerous life of mining, English loanwords appear for the technical terms associated with mining equipment (*kelsi* for mine elevator, *leveeni* for level). Here we see the classic dichotomy of English loans in immigrant Finnish, as identified by Pertti Virtaranta in his thorough study of Amerikansuomi[1]. On the one hand, in words like *kelsi*, Finnish speakers seem to have simply seized upon an English word because the Finnish term for an object or concept they were meeting in America was simply unknown to them. In many cases, Finns met with new technology in North America that they had no knowledge of before immigrating. On the other hand, as with *treini* or *soluuna*, Finnish Americans may have used an English word because their experience of an object or concept in the United States so differed from what they knew back in Finland that the equivalent Finnish word did not seem apt. Thus, Virtaranta suggests, Finnish Americans come to talk of *vamili*—"family"—instead of *perhe*, reserving the old Finnish term for the more extended, intergenerational families back in the Old Country, and using the English-derived term for the Finnish immigrants' version of the American nuclear family. Here in **Song 15**, we get hints at the novelty of experience that led the singer to describe train rides and saloons using English terms: America is a land of technological innovation as well as social laxity of a kind completely unfamiliar to life back home. One wonders what the effects of these instances of linguistic play and narrative detail would have been on audiences in Finland, where many a young woman might be contemplating with some anxiety the temptations that lay ahead of their boyfriends when they headed off to New York. Tellingly, the singer in this song decorously avoids the women's company, although he does admit to drinking freely in saloons later in the song. And by the end of the song he declares himself in thoroughly pitiable terms:

Vaan tahdotteko tietää
Kuka laulun tehny on
Se oli poika nuori
Köyhä ja arvoton
Joka on tänne tuotu
Eikä ystävätä ole luotu
Vaan yksin täytyy oleskella
Maalla vieraalla.

—
But do you finally want to know now
Who has made up this here song?
It's a guy who has suffered misery,
Lived impoverished for so long.
He's a young man with no friends near
Nor any place to find some rest,
He's got no companions living here
But just stays alone out west.

---

1 Virtaranta 1993

If **Song 15** suggests the temptation of American women, **Song 16** "Amerikan tytöt/America's Girls" makes their wiles unmistakable. A jocular broadside published in Mikkeli in 1909, the song catalogues the allure and finery of American girls, from their fancy hose to their ticking wristwatches to their coiffed hairdos and ample perfume:

> Hajuvesipullo on taskussa
> Jolla ne luussia kasti ja kasti
> Että ne tuoksuisi poikien nokkaan,
> Jo kilometrin päästä asti.
> —
> Right inside their pockets they keep perfume.
> And spritzing themselves they do spray, they do spray,
> So the boys they will smell them a'coming
> Even a mile away.

Again, as in **Song 15**, the song does not aver that the singer has fallen for such women, but he certainly displays detailed impressions of their appearances and ways.

Making a Living (Songs 17, 18, 20, 22)

Most Finnish men came to North America with the intention of becoming landowners and thereby gaining prosperity through farming and livestock husbandry. Through the vagaries of life in the New World, however, many found themselves in the ranks of unskilled labor, particularly in the timber and mining industries, while women found employment as domestic servants. With few specialized skills and limited English, Finns joined the bottom ranks of the American labor pool.

Song 17 "Rosenberg Amerikassa/Rosenberg in America" is written like a letter home. Its main character, Rosenberg, tells of working in manual labor, but announces his plan to buy a sawmill of his own:

> Olen, näet, aikonut mä
> Laittaa suuren sahan,
> Sillä sitten kuristelen
> Toisten ihramahan.
> —
> Got a plan and it's mighty good,
> a sawmill I will buy.
> With that outfit running fine,
> well those fat cats I'll defy.

In lines both jocular and sometimes bitingly ironic, the character boasts of the confidence local bankers have in his word even while he contemplates ditching responsibilities to abscond to Australia. Most centrally, however, he seems to want to convince his friend—the inscribed reader of the letter—to join him:

> Kuuleppas sä velikulta:
> Tule sinä tänne!
> Heittääkää jo hiiteen siellä
> Laiha elämänne.
> —

Come my friend, now come over here,
and listen as I tell
Kiss that old meager life good bye
and say it can go to hell.

The singer adds that he will pay for the friend's ticket. As Mark Knipping notes in his study of Finnish immigration to Wisconsin, about a third of Finns paid for their passage overseas out of personal or familial savings, while another third obtained loans from banks or individuals. A final third received their tickets from friends and family members[1]. The singer seems to indicate that the ticket will simply be a good investment for him: with a friend along, the two men can prosper more easily. In addition, the gnawing loneliness voiced in **Song 15** can be avoided. Rosenberg's jocular confidence contrasts with the actual oppression many Finnish immigrant laborers experienced in an American society increasingly distrustful of immigrant labor from mysterious foreign tracks like Finland.

Song 22 "Lumperijätkän laulu/The Lumberjack's Song," recorded at Kaustinen in 1947 from Oskari Tastula, who learned it from oral tradition, depicts the teamwork, acquired skills, and occasional rivalry of a Finnish American lumberman's life. The song also reflects the abundant borrowing of English terminology that characterized Finnish American trade jargon. The singers who created the song, and who identify themselves at its end as the sawyers Frankki, Jalmari, and Oskari from Kajaani, seem to delight in displaying their specialized knowledge of the various duties and work crews involved in lumber camps of the Upper Midwest[2]. We hear of the work of *lumperijätkät* ("lumberjacks"), *sahurit* ("sawyers"), *natsarit* ("notchers"; also called "buckers"), *laatarit* ("top-loaders"), the *seinipoika* ("chain boy"; "ground mole"), the *timstari* ("teamster"), and *vampparit* ("swampers"). Some of the crews appear dominated by a particular ethnic group: the *laatarit* ("loaders") appear to be mostly French-speaking or French Canadian:

Ranskan pojat täällä ovat laatareina
He varttia vaille huutavat kämpälle kämpimään.
—
Frenchmen here are the loaders, that's the job they do,
Quarter to the hour and they just say that they are through.

The lines hint at a labor world of sometimes striking segregation and inequity, in which Finns found employment only in the most physically demanding and dangerous jobs. The work day described is demanding but satisfying, ending at six o'clock:

Iltasella kello kuus' kun kämppätorvi huus!
Silloin ne pojat metsästä vaan korjailevat luuns'.
—
When at six o'clock work's over then the horn does blow
Then the guys they shake their bones, back to the camp they go.

If songs depict the lumber industry as a life of teamwork and comradery, other songs portray life in the mines as darker and more dangerous. Finns became an important part of the labor forces in the copper country of Michigan's Upper Peninsula and iron range of Minnesota and Wisconsin[3]. Although mining also became an important industry back in Finland, many of the songs present Finnish immigrants as becoming aware of the life of a miner only once they have

1   Knipping 2008, 10
2   Knipping 2008, 13
3   Knipping 2008, 13

arrived in North America. In **Song 15**, described above, the singer tells of learning about mining jobs while on board a train headed west:

> Sitten Insinöörit
> Haastoit meitä työhön kultaruumaan
> Niin siellä saatte oppia
> Ja kultaa kaivamahan.
>
> —
>
> Then the engineers they urged us
> On mining we were soon sold
> Training us they said would be no fuss
> And soon we'd be mining gold.

Mining and the gold rush are fused into a single entity in the song, preparing the immigrants for an exciting and lucrative adventure which they soon discover is monotonous and depressing. The California Gold Rush of 1848–55 was long since over by the time Finnish immigration was reaching its height in North America, although the Klondike and other related Alaska gold rushes of 1896 through 1910 certainly did attracts Finns, who not only participated but sometimes played major roles in the events that transpired[1]. Gold rushes also occurred in northern Finland in the late nineteenth century.

In **Song 18** "Mainarin laulu/A Miner's Song," sung by Kalle Takala in 1946, the miner is presented as nearly as carefree as the lumberjack:

> Maan alla syvällä metallit makaa,
> Siellä ne masiinat puhkuen hakkaa.
> Siellä minä höylään, ja leipäni löyrän
> Ja iloinen olen vaan enkä sure milloinkaan.
>
> —
>
> Deep underground where the metal is found,
> There the machines they do grumble and sound,
> I rest my heels as I earn all my meals
> And I'm feeling oh so happy and sad I'll never be.

The singer describes his work as grimy, sweaty, and backbreaking and suggests that miners sing to cheer themselves in the face of their grim existence. Nonetheless, the song ends with a strong statement of personal dignity: "Mä herra olen vaan, mä herra olen vaan" ("I know I am a man, yes, I know I am a man").

Despite the song's seemingly cheerful demeanor, it was uncontested that the life of a miner was dangerous. Knipping[2] notes that between 1900 and 1913 in just one county in the Upper Peninsula there were some 146 fatal mining accidents. In **Song 20** "Kauhea tapaturma kaivannossa/Tragic Mine Accident," printed as a broadside in Viipuri in 1899, the events of a New Year's Day mining accident are recounted in detail:

> Jalkaa viisitoista vaan
> Enää oli pinnall' maan
> Kun käi kone kallelleen
> Syösten miehet syvyyteen.
>
> —

---

1   Olin 1998, Olin 2013
2   Knipping 2008, 13

Fifteen feet was all that lay
between the men and light of day
When down in lurching, thund'rous din
the lift fell crashing, men within.

Each of the dead is commemorated in a stanza that names his place of birth and circumstances, revealing the South Ostrobothnian preponderance at the mine. It is noteworthy that the broad-side was printed in Viipuri during the same year as the founding of the Finnish Social Demo-cratic Party, a party that would become more explicitly Marxist by 1903[1]. The failures of worker protection and rights, even in the land of supposed opportunity across the sea had powerful motivating effects among Finns on both sides of the Atlantic[2].

Labor Activism (Songs 19, 21)
The growing rise of Finns in socialist, communist and Industrial Workers of the World (IWW) organizations in North America gave rise to a vast array of songs. **Song 19** "Kaivantomiehen lau-lu/The Digger's Song" was composed by Santeri Mäkelä and originally published in the socialist songbook *Työväen laulukirja* (Songbook of the Working Class), printed in Hancock, Michigan, in 1909. Here the miner's existence, treated in lighthearted manner in **Song 18**, is revisited in tones decidedly less jocund. The song opens:

Niin musta on, musta on ikuinen yö
Ja kellot lyö kaksitoista.
Vain torkkuen toverit istuskelee,
Hikikarpalot kulmillansa.
—
Oh, black is the night, it is blacker than hell
As the twelve o'clock bells do sound.
The dog-tired laborers sit for a spell
As the sweat of their brow trickles down.

The stanza's "torkkuen toverit" (translated here as "dog-tired laborers") more literally means "drowsing comrades," and uses the term that Finnish socialists and communists used to translate the Russian tovarisch/comrade. The song presents a conversation between a miner and his con-cerned wife, in which the man's ruined health and impending young death are his rewards for his hard work as a wage slave. The song has parallels in IWW favorites, like the English "Blackleg Miner," frequently included in the IWW's *Little Red Songbook*. The final stanza of that song ex-horts the beleaguered miner to join the union before its too late:

So join the union while ye may
Don't wait till yer dyin' day
'Cause that may not be far away
Ye dorty blackleg miner. [3]

Song 21 "Kulkuripojan laulu/The Young Tramp's Song," originally published in the collection *Proletaarilauluja* (Proletarian Songs) in Duluth, Minnesota, in 1918, illustrates the idealism and determination of many of Socialist songs. The song depicts the present situation of hoboes riding the rails and the better life they'll have one day when justice comes about:

---

1   Lindström 2003, 19
2   Knipping 2008, 14
3   IWW 1995, 68

Vaikka nyt nylkyrit sortaa meitä
Kun heillä on suuri kassa,
Vielä me kerran itsekin istumme
Vallan satulassa.

—

Oh even though they bleed us dry
as they steal our hard-earned money,
There'll come a day fine when we'll take
what is ours and seize liberty.

Homesick (Songs 23, 24, 25, 26, 27)

While the novelties of life in American society could beguile and entertain the temporary traveler, immigration entails longterm cultural adjustment. In that situation, scholars of migration
often note the development of negative feelings and frustrations regarding the host culture, the
phenomenon of culture shock. Finnish immigrants, cut asunder from the familiar linguistic and
cultural environment in which they had grown up, could grow homesick and depressed. Not
only were customs and ideas different in America, but the immigrant could begin to notice that
circumstances were driving a wedge between the immigrant and family and friends back home.
Major events occurred without the opportunity to share in them personally: elders died, new sib-
lings were born, friends and neighbors married, moved, and progressed in life. Many of the songs
produced in the era of mass emigration provide poignant depictions of these fraught experiences,
presenting emigration as traumatic and sometimes tragic.

Song 26 "Kotimaan ikävä/Missing the Homeland," performed by Laina Rinta-Koski (b.
1895) of Kauhajoki, presents a grim depiction of the Atlantic crossing and the fatalities that can
occur. The singer declares:

Ja siks' tämän maailman merellä
Niin monta on onnetonta.
Siks' monelle täällä on elämä
Niin synkkää, niin ilotonta.

—

That's why there are so many people so sad
Who ventured their fortunes at sea
In tempests and storms they've lost all they had
So joyless, so hopeless they be.

On one level, the song describes in very concrete terms the harrowing experience of a storm at
sea. On another level, however, the storm appears a metaphor for other experiences of migration:
the risks undertaken by emigrants, often with insufficient information, and the all-or-nothing
nature of attempts to make a new life in America.

Song 23 "Kotimaani ompi Suomi/My Homeland is Finland," was composed in the United
States by Jooseppi Riippa and was brought to Finland in the repertoire of Matti Penttilä, a
Finnish emigrant who returned to the village of Kaustinen in 1909, after some years in America.
(For more details on such return migrations, see discussion below.) The version presented here
was performed by Martta Puumala and Bertta Valo—Matti Penttilä's daughters—in 1974. The
song provides lyrical descriptions of an idealized Finnish landscape, focusing on its peacefulness,
unhurried rhythms, and beauty. The singer includes descriptions of plants unusual in a North
American context, including *tuomi*, the bird cherry:

Kotimaani ompi Suomi
Suomi on mun kotimaa.
Siellä valkolatva tuomi
Järven rannalla tuoksuva.

—

My homeland is Finland
Finland is my dear homeland.
There the white-tipped fragrant cherry
Stands upon the lake-shore strand.

The homeland here is not depicted as constricting or backward, as in songs included in Section I. Nor is the singer's departure described as motivated by hopes of self-realization and adventure, but rather, by compulsion, exile, and sorrow. The song ends with the singer's hope that either his remains will find their way back to Finland, or that a surrogate grave for him there will be graced by a flowering bird cherry tree. The image is repeated almost exactly in **Song 24** "Petetyn pojan laulu/The Betrayed Boy's Song," published in Ashtabula, Ohio, in 1904, in a pamphlet entitled *Kansanlauluja* (Folk Songs):

Kotimaani ompi Suomi
Kiiruhdan sen kummuillen.
Haudalleni valkotuomi
Kerran kylvää kukkasen.

—

My homeland is beautiful Finland,
There my spirit longs to be.
At my graveside, in that old land,
There will grow a cherry tree.

The song performed by Laura Ahonen (b. 1910) of Kauhajoki, **Song 27** "Vieraalla maalla/On Foreign Land" evinces a similar nostalgia for the distant homeland, according it not only beauty and peacefulness but even sacrality. The song enjoins the listener to embrace love of homeland as a sacred duty, even when circumstances have led to relocation in a distant America:

Muista armas Suomen miesi, kallein tehtäväsi vaan,
Pois on armas kotiliesi, kun sä jätät kotimaan.

—

Men of Finland, always treasure, keep it ever in your mind,
Far away now lies your homeland and the hearth you left behind.

Song 25 "Vieraalla maalla/On Foreign Land" illustrates the complex transnational migrations some of these songs of homesickness depict. The song is a translation of an Estonian choral piece *Võõrsil*, composed by Johannes Kappel (1855–1907) with lyrics by Ado Grenzstein, and based originally on an Estonian folksong. The Finnish version became popular in the United States, where it was heard by, among others, the Finnish activist, diplomat, and newspaper editor Aaro Johannes Jalkanen (1875–1960), who created his own Savo dialect lyrics for the melody under the title *Kallavesj*. Jalkanen's song has become a favorite in Finland ever since. In the immigrant song presented here, the singer laments a life of exile, where the comforts of native land and language are lost. Speaking of language (be it Estonian or, in translation, Finnish), the singer declares:

Kyynelin, kyynelin
Vierahissa kuljeksin.
Täällä ei äidin kieli kaiu,
Huuliltaan ei laulut raiu;
Kaukana on äidin kiel'
Äidin kiel', äidin kiel'.

—

Shedding tears, shedding tears,
Wandering these new frontiers.
Mother tongue here does not ring,
From their lips, no songs they sing;
Far away the mother tongue,
Mother tongue, mother tongue.

Affairs of the Heart (Songs 24, 28, 29)

In late nineteenth-century Finland, romantic love was well but rather recently established as the major focus of courtship[1]. Finding a lifelong partner to marry was a prime topic of popular song. Ideas of marrying for family advantage, or for wealth, may have played a part in many courtships of the time (as, one could argue, in courtships of today) but such was not generally acknowledged, except perhaps among the wealthiest strata of society. **Song 28** "Suomen neito/Maiden of Finland," performed by Heikki Kentala (Finnin Janne) of Kaustinen in 1947, depicts the encounter of a virtuous Finnish maiden with what appears to be a richer but less scrupulous man. In the dialogue of the song's stanzas, the maiden rebuffs her suitor's advances, despite the wealth and position such a pairing (if honorable) would entail. The song ends with the singer enjoining emigrant men to write to their girlfriends back home, implying that the song is meant to dramatize the temptations and pressures a woman could face in the absence of the man she loves:

Sen sanon teille nuoret,
Lähteissänne viel'
Et kirjoitatta neitosille
Tietoja sielt'.
Kun pojat ovat nuoria,
Ja juuri parhaillaan
Silloin he lähtevät
Valtameren taa.

—

Listen all you men who leave,
Sailing from this land.
Oh write to all the girls who grieve,
Write them in your hand.
When worthy boys are young and strong,
And at their very best,
Saying only "so long,"
They leave for the west.

While physical and personality attributes may have played important roles in the ways men and women selected spouses, the most common feature of a true love in the emigrant songs is *faithfulness*: a man or woman needs to show absolute constancy, and often considerable patience, when one's partner heads for foreign shores. **Song 24** "Petetyn pojan laulu/The Betrayed Boy's

1   Virtanen and DuBois 2000, 73–75

Song," discussed above, narrates the wounding experience of a man whose intended bride finds another during his absence in America. The man returns to Finland, eager to be reunited with his true love, only to find her married to another:

Toisen sormus sormellansa
Välkkyi hurjan neitosen.
Toisen suukko huuliltansa
Poies poltti entisen.

—

Then I saw the ring on your finger,
That revealed the awful fact.
Someone else's kiss had broken
Our former lovers' pact.

The singer's lack of prior awareness of his former girlfriend's marital situation before his return to Finland speaks ill of his letter-writing skills: one can imagine that in real life, a fiancé, as well as family members and friends, would certainly have passed along such crucial information as it was unfolding. In the dramatic narrative of the song, however, the betrayed man vows never to venture his heart again, a theme familiar in international popular music, and a cornerstone of the Blues genre so popular during this same era in North America.

The wry **Song 29** "Amerikasta/From America," published as a broadside in Tampere in 1898, purports to be a letter home from a man who has just learned that his girlfriend has been unfaithful. During his time in America, the lowly farmhand Jaska has become a rich and influential "Mister Matson." His plans to send for Liisapet and welcome her to his fine home (described using the English-derived term hausi for what a Finnish peasant of the time would have called a *tupa* or *talo*) are foiled by Liisa's fickle nature: she has taken up with "Torpan Tommi" ("Tommi the crofter" translated in the anthology as "Tom from out of town"), betraying her vows of faithfulness and love. In the song's final stanza, a vindictive Jaska declares:

Saat jäädä Kitusuomehen
Silakan kylkeen kai;
Syö Matson leivän vehnäisen,
Nyt sanon vain: "ku pai."

—

On herring bones you can be fed
In Finland live and die
While I partake of fine whitbread
And tell you now "ku pai"

Liisa can stay in "Kitusuomi" ("Finland of deprivations") while Jaska enjoys his big house and wheat bread in his new life in America, a life he would have gladly shared with her. Now, however, there is nothing to say to his former sweetheart but to end their relationship with the finality and coldness of an English *Goodbye*.

Headed Back to Finland (Songs 15, 30, 31)
In the imagined migration experiences of popular music, emigration tends to happen only once, with the emigrant definitively establishing a new life in America and eventually sending for his faithful true love or financing the subsequent migration of friends. Return migration—heading back to Finland after years or months in America—appears relatively seldom in the songs, even if it represented the actual experience of a substantial portion of Finnish emigrants. Such is

noteworthy, since many of the songs discussed in this and in the previous section (e.g., **Song 3**) specifically describe the journey to America a planned sojourn intended to earn money for subsequent life in Finland. Given the harsh realities and economic pressures of America, return migration could prove a wise and welcome course of action, as perhaps reflected in the case of Matti Penttilä of Kaustinen, the singer of **Song 23**, discussed above. Emigrants could return to Finland, perhaps materially richer, but also certainly wealthier in terms of life experiences and sophistication. In **Song 15**, also discussed above, the singer imagines the popularity he and his fellow emigrants would enjoy if they did return to Finland. He imagines the excited women who would greet him, eager to hear details of life in America:

> Voi kuinka täällä on kauvan
> Saanut odottaa
> Kuinkas olet voinut
> Siellä pitkällä matkallas
> Sano missä olet ollu
> Ja kuinka on reisus käyny
> Minä vastaan teillen
> Hurskaalla luonnolla nyt täs.
>
> —
>
> "Oh how long I have waited
> For you to come back home!
> For so long you've been anticipated
> Tell me everywhere you've roamed!
> Tell me of your great adventures
> I will listen so intent,
> I know you're here as a blessing
> And that you are heaven sent."

Song 30 "Vitikon Jani/Jani Vitikko" purports to be the firsthand account of one such returning migrant, one F.E. Takala of Vimperi. In a Finnish laced with English terms, the singer recounts his character's travels and economic experiments in America, where he worked in agriculture, got into a fist fight with a brawling Massachusetts Irishman, and spent money and time in saloons. In one such establishment, Jani counsels his friends to return to Finland, and his words form the closing stanza of the song:

> Kesän hämyiset yöt,
> tytöt vanhan maan,
> ja kirkkaus sinisen taivaan,
> Pojat hemmetti soikoon,
> ostetaan tiketti jo ensi laivaan.
>
> —
>
> "Sunlit summer nights,
> and the sky so blue,
> and the girls, well, there's no doubt
> Boys, let's buy us a ticket home,
> on the next ship out."

Song 31 "Suomen pojan huvilaulu kotiin tullessa Amerikasta/The Finnish Boy's Amusement Song on His Way Home from America," a broadside published in Tampere in 1895, recounts a home migration in a manner that exactly inverts the events of the travelogue songs discussed in Section I. Here, the singer tells of his excitement boarding a ship bound for Europe and the mounting anticipation as he arrives in Hull. Although some apprehension creeps in as the singer arrives in Finland, his arrival and catching sight of his true love turns all to joy:

> Ja rantahan kun päästihin niin hypyt toimitettin,
> Ja tuskin kata paiskittiin kun kohta pyörähdeltiin.
> Sun fralla rallalla sun fralla rallalla
> Sun rati riti rati riti rallalla lei.
>
> —
>
> Oh, when we finally got to Finland, I jumped off the boat
> I hugged you right away and then I sang a pretty note.
> Your fralla rallalla your fralla rallalla
> Your rati riti rati riti rallalla lei.

The song ends with the singer exhorting his listeners never to venture away from Finland for the false promises of America. In the next section, we examine the songs that Finns back home created about the America so often discussed and imagined, a world of potential and danger and ideals, and a place that deeply affected the emotional life and relations of Finns left behind.

15. Amerikan laulu
Song of America

From the broadside collection "Kaksi laulua" [Two songs] published by J. Eskelinen in Tampere in 1895. Melody from *Suomen kansan sävelmiä II. Laulusävelmiä.* Ed. Ilmari Krohn. Helsinki 1904–1933. Melody no. 4693, collected in Taivalkoski 1902. The same melody was used for this song in Isokyrö. The song has also been sung to the melody of "Meripojan laulu" [Song of a son of the sea].

Ke - sä - kuun kuu - des päi - vä läh - dim - me ko - dis - ta, reis -
On the sixth day of June we par - ted, for to reach A - mer - i - ca. On our

saa - maan A - me - rik - kaan kau - kai - seen maa - han. Vaan tah - dot - te - ko
trip we__ bold - ly__ start - ed to that land so far a - way. I can tell you of our

tie - tää kuin - ka on me - ri - luon - to, tai - si ol - la ker - ta__ vii - mei -
sail - ing, the waves tossed our ship to and fro; It__ was the last time e_____

nen, kun__ nä - in syn - tymä maan.
ver we would see the land we know.

Finnish American terminology used in this song:
Treini = train
Soluuna = saloon
Kelsi = mine elevator
Leveeni = level in a mine

Kesäkuun kuudes päivä
Lähdimme kodista
Reisaamaan Amerikkaan
Kaukaiseen maahan
Vaan tahdotteko tietää
Kuinka on meriluonto
Taisi olla kerta viimeinen
Kun näin syntymämaan.

Reisumme kävi hyvin
Ylitse Atlantin
Se oli kaunis aamu
Kun tultiin New Yorkkiin
Siellä seisoo tyttöjä rannas
Jotka viittas meillen kättä
Ja huusivat: Hurraa, Hurraa!
Te Suomen poikaiset.

Sitten tytöt meitä haastoi
Että käykäät Soluunahan
Niin siellä saatte kohdata
Jo monta tuttavaa
Vaan me vastasimme heillen
Ei me joudu Solunaahan,
Sillä meidän täytyy reisata
Treini jo odottaa.

Kello oli kymmenen
Kun Treiniin astuttiin
Ja kuusi vuorokautta
Vielä siellä ajettiin
Sitten Insinöörit
Haastoit meitä työhön kultaruumaan
Niin siellä saatte oppia
Ja kultaa kaivamahan.

Vaan silloin silmät aukes
Kun kelsin astuttiin
Kolmatta sataa syltä
Maan alle laskettiin
Vaan illall' puoli kuusi
Niin kapteenimme huusi
Että tulkaa poijat leveenillen
Kaikki syynihin.

Vaan moni poika katuu
Kun tänne tulikaan
Ja jätti rakkaan ystävänsä
Kotiaan suremaan
Vaan kun me täältä tuumme
Rakkaaseen kotimaahan
Niin siellä sanoo likat meillen
Terve tultuan.

Voi kuinka täällä on kauvan
Saanut odottaa
Kuinkas olet voinut
Siellä pitkällä matkallas
Sano missä olet ollu
Ja kuinka on reisus käyny
Minä vastaan teillen
Hurskaalla luonnolla nyt täs.

Reisumme on käyny
Pohjois-Amerikas
Ja välistä huviksemme
Käyty Soluunas
Kun rahaa aina on ollut
Eikä puutetta ole tullut
Vaan mitä on ollut liijalti
On juotu Soluunas.

Vaan tahdotteko tietää
Kuka laulun tehny on
Se oli poika nuori
Köyhä ja arvoton
Joka on tänne tuotu
Eikä ystävätä ole luotu
Vaan yksin täytyy oleskella
Maalla vieraalla.

On the sixth day of June we parted,
For to reach America.
On our trip we boldly started
To that land so far away.
I can tell you of our sailing,
The waves tossed our ship to-and-fro.
It was the last time ever
We would see the land we know.

As we crossed the wide Atlantic,
Our passage it was fine.
With delight we were almost frantic
When New York came into sight.
On the shore stood many women
They greeted us with waving hands
And they shouted "hurrah, hurrah!
Welcome boys come from Finland!"

And the girls made a point to invite us
With them to have a drink
Our old friends would recognize us
At the saloon they did drink.
But we said to them most truly
"The saloon, it is out, that's plain.
For though we could go so happily
We must right now board our train."

It was ten when we left the train station
And headed on our ways
As we traveled across the nation,
We went six nights and six days.
Then the engineers they urged us
On mining we were soon sold
Training us they said would be no fuss
And soon we'd be mining gold.

When we stepped on the mine elevator
Our eyes were opened fast.
We sank to a depth that was greater
Eighteen hundred feet went past.
But when it struck five-thirty,
Our captain called it a day.
Around him we did congregate
For we'd earned then our day's pay.

Oh many a lad does regret
That he left home to come here.
For a girl does worry and fret,
For her missing true love dear.
But if ever we should go back
The homeland that we know
Then oh will we get attention
For the girls will love us so.

"Oh how long I have waited
For you to come back home!
For so long you've been anticipated
Tell me everywhere you've roamed!
Tell me of your great adventures
I will listen so intent,
I know you're here as a blessing
And that you are heaven sent."

To America I've made entry
And seen what there's to see
Throughout this gigantic country
I have earned lots of money.
And as dollars there were plenty,
I have spent them in saloons.
There's been drink enough for all my friends
As we sang our drinking tunes.

But do you finally want to know now
Who has made up this here song?
It's a guy who has suffered mis'ry,
Lived impoverished for so long.
He's a young man with no friends near
Nor any place to find some rest,
He's got no companions living here
But just stays alone out west.

16. Amerikan tytöt
America's Girls

From the broadside "Hauskoja kuplettilauluja I" [Pleasant couplet songs] composed by "K. L-nen."
Published in Mikkeli in 1909. Melody supplied by Simo Westerholm from memory, from the song
"Konstantinnoopelin portin päällä" [At the gates of Constantinople]

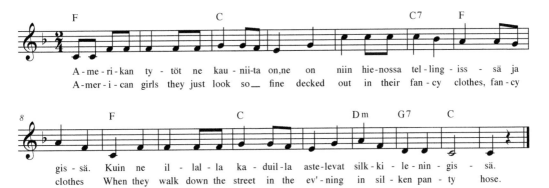

Amerikan tytöt ne kauniita on,
Ne on niin hienossa tellingissä ja gissä.
Kuin ne illalla kaduilla astelevat
Silkkileningissä.

Hivukset on parturi piipannut
Ne on otsalla kähärässä ja rässä.
Että ne kelpaisi poikain riijuksi
Iltahämärässä.

Hajuvesipullo on taskussa,
Jolla ne luussia kasti ja kasti
Että ne tuoksuisi poikien nokkaan,
Jo kilometrin päästä asti.

Kasvot on floorilla peitetty
Ja renkaat ne korvissa kiiltää ja kiiltää.
Kuin niitä kaduilla vastaan sattuu,
Niin poikain sydäntä viiltää.

Kello on tellätty kettinkiin,
Joka ranteessa raksuttelee ja telee.
Siitä saa katsoa tunnit ja vartit,
Kun riijailemaan menee.

American girls they just look so fine
Decked out in their fancy clothes, fancy clothes.
When they walk down the street in the evening
In silken panty hose.

They have spent their days at the beauty salon
Their bangs are all curled to delight, to delight.
So the boys will have something to look at
In the evening twilight.

Right inside their pockets they keep perfume.
And spritzing themselves they do spray, they do spray
So the boys they will smell them a'coming
Even a mile away.

They've got faces covered with lots of make-up
Rings in their ears that do shimmer, and shimmer
When they pass any boys on the street, those
Guys' blood starts to simmer.

On a pretty chain they have hung a clock:
On their wrists it keeps ticking and tocking.
So they know the hour and the minute
While they are a'walking.

17. Rosenberg Amerikassa
Rosenberg in America

Broadside "Uusi laulu" [New song] associated with the writings and thoughts of David Rosenberg, contained in a letter by Rosenberg to a friend in Finland. Melody from *Suomen kansan sävelmiä II. Laulusävelmiä.* Ed. Ilmari Krohn. Helsinki 1904–1933. Melody no. 2181, collected in Kivennapa in the 1840s. Similar to folksong "Ei nyt enää, ei nyt enää kesämarjat auta." The melody was published already in 1849 in H. A. Reinholm's collection Suomen kansan laulantoja [songs of the Finnish people].

Ei nyt e - nää, ei nyt e - nää Ro - sen - berg oo tääl - lä, mut - ta A - me - ri - kas
Ro - sen - berg, oh Ro - sen - berg just ain't no long - er here, no. He is gone to A - mer - i -

on hän i - loi - sel - la — pääl - lä.
ca and li - ving with good cheer, oh.

Ei nyt enää, ei nyt enää
Rosenberg oo täällä,
Mutta Amerikas' on hän
Iloisella päällä.

Ystävälleen Suomenmaahan
kirjoitti hän siitä,
Ett'ei Suomen kitupiikit
häntä varmaan kiitä.

Näin hän kertoo:
Luuletko sä veli, että suren;
Sillä täällä taaskin minä
hyvät moskat puren.

Amerikalaiset ovat
vähän viisaampia,
Kun nuo Suomen kollot kovat,
mutta mull' on sija.

Suomen rahoilla mä ostin
talon, joka loistaa.
Se, se, näet, armon tuopi,
Epäilykset poistaa.

Viisaalle ei vahinkoa
koskaan juuri tule,
Kun ei ensimmältä vallan
varomatta kule.

Eihän sitä uskaltaisi
panna paperille,
Mutta vakuutettuna tää
ei mee vierahille.

Olen, näet, aikonut mä
laittaa suuren sahan,
Sillä sitten kuristelen
toisten ihramahan.

Pankistakin täältä sain jo
rahaa koko lailla.
Kaksisataatuhatta on
taskus' vähää vailla.

Puita on jo ostettu ja
saha kohta hurraa;
Kannattaako tämän pojan
paljon enää surra?

Yhdysvallat luottaa minuun
kun mä täällä hummaan.
Luulevat vaan Suomeen tehnein
pienen velkasumman.

Kun nuo Suomen herrat eivät
uskaltaneet nostaa
Oikeudess' kysymystä
milläpä ne kostaa.

Sitten kun mä kaikki saan mua
uskomahan täällä.
Luistan poies niinkuin lehti
liukkahalla jäällä.

Australian mantereella
nousen taas kuin honka,
Silloin huutaa Amerika,
missä mies nyt onkaan!

Kuuleppas sä velikulta:
tule sinä tänne!
Heittäkää jo hiiteen siellä
laiha elämänne.

Minä tiedän, että eivät
teitä enää usko.
Mutta täällä koittais teille
uusi aamurusko.

Hyvästi nyt ystäväni
tee vaan kuten käsken,
Vakuudeksi vielä sanon:
Rahat nostin äsken.

Toista sitten ottaisimme,
ei ne meiltä kiellä;
Muuan vuosi rehellisnä
oisimme kuin siellä.

Yhdessä kun toimimme, niin
saadaan juuri summa.
Sanotaan vaan sitten että:
vedäppäs nyt humma.

Näin ne sitä huhueli
kai se lienee totta.
Viimeks' sitä kertoeli
"Parantaja" Lotta.

Rosenberg, oh Rosenberg,
Just ain't no longer here, no.
He is gone to America,
And living with good cheer, oh.

He wrote to his friends back home
That there is no Finnish cheapskate
Who would hear what goes on there
And it appreciate.

He told them, "listen up my friends,
Maybe you think that I'm sad?
I've got plenty of good eats and such,
So I am quite easily glad."

I have found as I look around,
Fewer knuckleheads do I see.
There's more clever working men around,
Yet still there is work for me.

I put down on a house,
 I found some hard Finnish cash in a hurry.
And I bought me a home so fine
And banished every worry.

Wise folks they never have to fear
For accidents or trouble.
It's us foolish working stiffs
Who come over here on the double.

To write down all the things I've found
Is not a thing that I'd dare.
But I'm certain that my letter here
You my trusted friend will not share.

Got a plan and it's mighty good,
A sawmill I will buy.
With that outfit running fine,
Well those fat cats I'll defy.

All the banks in this country here
Treated me so well I confess.
I've got two hundred thou' just now
Or maybe there's a bit less.

Lumber's bought and soon up I'll start
My sawmill in a hurry.
And with every little thing so fine,
What for should a man need to worry?

A square deal I got in this land,
In me they place their trust.
Oh imagine a Finland
Where the wages were so just!

Justice for working men back home,
Yhe wealthy Finns do not care.
To consider giving them a break
Those rich old men do not dare.

Once I get all the folks 'round here
To set their faith in me, nice!
I'll skedaddle like a leaf
That's blown across a sheet of ice.

Way down south in Australia,
Just like a young pine I will sprout.
"Where, oh where, has that rascal gone?"
In America they will shout.

Come my friend, now come over here,
And listen as I tell.
Kiss that old meager life good bye,
And say it can go to hell.

They don't see any worth in you,
That's what all of the rich men jeer.
But a new day would dawn for you,
If you would just come over here.

Say farewell and make your way,
Without any trouble or care.
I will add this guarantee,
I've raised for you the fare.

Better living we will find,
No one can that deny.
We'll have us a better year that's clear,
To you I would never lie.

If we work as a team my friend,
Oh such good dough we'll be bagging
We will snicker at those doubters then saying,
"Let's put to rest that old nagging."

Then at last maybe they will see,
And spread a new sort of story.
And those busybody neighbor gals
Will finally tell of our glory.

18. Mainarin laulu
A Miner's Song

Sung by Kalle Takala in 1946, published in Härmän laulukirja [Härmä songbook] song no. 448.

Maan al - la syv - äl - lä me - tal - lit ma - kaa, sie - llä ne mas - ii - nat
Deep un - der ground where the met - al is found, there the ma - chines they do

puh - ku - en hak - kaa. Siellä mi - nä höy - lään ja, lei - pä - ni löy - rän ja
grum - ble and sound.___ I rest my heels as I earn all my meals and I'm

i - loi - nen o - len vaan en - kä su - re mil - loin - kaan.
feel - ing oh so___ hap - py, oh sad I'll ne - ver be

Maan alla syvällä metallit makaa,
siellä ne masiinat puhkuen hakkaa.
Siellä minä höylään, ja leipäni löyrän,
ja iloinen olen vaan enkä sure milloinkaan.

Siellä minä hikoilen päiväni ja yöni,
raskas ja vaikea kyllä on työni.
Ei kaukana vaara, kun puskemme kaaraa,
laulamme vaan, siitä rohkeutta saamme.

Laulusta saarahan intoa uutta,
ei muisteta koko maailman vaikeutta.
Surut ei paina, vaan iloista on aina,
kun ollaan nuoria, niin ei ole huolia.

Mitä minä huolin, suotta mä surra,
kun leipäni tienaan, saa huoleta purra.
Ei arvoni lankee, on selkäni kankee,
mä herra olen vaan, mä herra olen vaan.

Deep underground where the metal is found,
There the machines they do grumble and sound.
I rest my heels as I earn all my meals
And I'm feeling oh so happy, oh sad I'll never be.

All of my days I'm at work grimy, sweaty
Labor that's backbreaking, pushing the mine cart.
Danger is near, and the work it is heavy
We sing to be courageous, we sing just to take heart.

Songs they do raise spirits down in the dark mine,
Cares fade away from the world in a hurry.
No sorrows reach us, there we are just fine,
Because we are so young we just never need worry.

There is no point in grumbling and groaning,
Life's pretty good when there's grub in my tin pan.
Though my back's stiff and my aches have me moaning,
I know I am a man, yes I know I am a man.

Finnish American terminology used in this song:
Kaara = car or, in this case, mining cart

19. Kaivantomiehen laulu
The Digger's Song

From a sound recording of Erkki Rankaviita, Karijoki, made by Antti Hosioja. in 1975. The song was originally written by Santeri Mäkelä of Vimpeli and published originally in a seven-stanza version in *Työväen laulukirja*, published in Hancock, Michigan, in 1909.

Niin mus-ta on, mus-ta on i-kui-nen yö ja kel-lot lyö kak-si-toi-sta_____
Oh, black is the night, it is black-er than hell as the twelve o'-clock bells do sound__

__ Vain tork-ku-en to-ve-rit is-tus-ke-lee hi-ki-kar-pa-lot kul-mil-lan-
__ The dog tired la-bor-ers sit for a spell and the sweat of their brow trick-les

sa._____ Vain
down,_____ Oh

Niin musta on, musta on ikuinen yö
ja kellot lyö kaksitoista.
Vain torkkuen toverit istuskelee,
hikikarpalot kulmillansa.

Niin musta on, musta on manalan sy'än
josta mä leipäni haen.
Kapitaali mun orjakseen ostanut on
käsivarteni ja verenkin.

Oi armaani, armaani, kalpea oi,
mi syömmeni sykkimään sait.
Nyt valkeella vuoteellas lepäjät kai,
iki-vuori mun peittävi vain!

Oi Luoja, oi Luoja, sua kiroa en;
en kiroa kohtaloain
Minä kiroan valtoja tyrannien
ja vapauttain ikävöitsen.

Minä ikävöin vapautta ihmiskunnan
proletaarien sorrettujen
Minä ikävöin taistohon tuimimpahan
veriruusuja katsomahan.

Oh, black is the night, it is blacker than hell
As the twelve o'clock bells do sound.
The dog-tired laborers sit for a spell
As the sweat of their brow trickles down.

Oh, blacker than night is this deep underground
I toil here for my daily bread.
With capital they've made me their wage slave
And they own me from toe up to head.

"Oh, pale you are, pale you are, my dear husband
Oh, how you did make my heart pound
Now lie down on this bed, you need not stand,
My eternal rock, try to rest sound."

Oh, God, my dear God, I don't curse you at all
I don't blame you for what befell me.
I will curse them big shots that make us all crawl
And I miss how it feels to be free.

Oh, I crave the freedom of humanity
The crushed working class is near dead.
I look to blood red roses so longingly
And prepare for the battle ahead.

20. Kauhea tapaturma kaivannossa
Tragic Mine Accident

Ei - pä tah - do tau - o - ta kum - main___ kuo - loin kai - un - ta. Tä - män
Let the mem' - ry long re - sound, of those dear men that Death has found. On New Year's

vuo - den a - lul - la, jot'___ ei kuul - la hal - ul - la.
Eve they lost their lives and so made wi - dows of their wives.

Eipä tahdo tauota
Kummain kuoloin kaiunta,
Tämän vuoden alulla,
Jot' ei kuulla halulla.

Kaivannosta suuresta,
Ameriikan juuresta
Sieltä tieto tullut on
Sanoma suur', iloton.

Kaivos, jossa miehiä,
Lie suuria ja pieniä,
Syväss' on maan pinnalta
Kuudes osa virstasta.

Viime vuoden lopulla,
Vuoden uuden aattona
Kuusi suomalaista on
Siirtynyt siell' kuolohon.

Tapaus on kauheaa,
Jota taasen kuulla saa,
Mutt' miss' on syy tään ihmehen?
Laulaja saa päättää sen.

Syvyydessä kaivosten
Miehet nostokoneeseen
Kävivät ja ylös siin'
Nousta aikoivat he niin.

Mutt' kun kone kohosi,
Ryski se ja peloitti;
Miehet huomas kyllä tään
Vaipuin muotoon synkimpään.

Jalkaa viisitoista vaan
Enää oli pinnall' maan
Kun käi kone kallelleen
Syösten miehet syvyyteen.

Nostokoneen päällä tään'
Kuului olleen yhdeksän;
Miehiä vaan kolme siin'
Tarttui sivurautoin kiin'.

Siten pelastuivat he,
Kuolema men ohitse,
Nyt he syömmin sykkivin
Yhtyy kiitosveisuihin!

Kuus' vain aukon pohjahan
Suistui ammottavahan,
Jolloin kurja kuolema
Kohtais heitä raukkoja.

Miehet, jotka kuolivat,
Iältänsä olivat
Kolmannellakymmenell',
Kaikk' siis ijäll' miehuuden.

Nimet heidän oli näin
Lausun jos tuo käisi päin:
Kauhavalta Suomesta
Alfreed Siivo-vainaja.

J. W. Paavokallio
Pohjois-Suomen urho tuo,
Ylistaron luota hän
Amerikkaan töihin män.

Johan Heikki Kujanpää
Mies ol' vaimotonna tää,
Alahärmän puolelta,
Pohjanmaalta Suomesta.

Kustaa Wilhelm Härmänmaa,
Myös ol' liki Kauhavaa,
Näki lasna iloiten
Suomen sulopäivyen.

Matti Tammi taitava
Syntyi Ilmajoella,
Kätkeä nyt hänet saa
Ameriikan kultamaa.

Sitten Jaakko Mikkola,
Merijärven tienoilta.
Nämä kuusi ne siis on,
Jotka joutuivat kuolohon.

Vaimot, lapset, heidän nyt
Suremaan on yhtynyt,
Muistain ijän kaikensa
Kummallista kuoloa.

Originally printed as the broadside "Jälkikaikuja kaksoismurhasta Inkilässä ja kauhea tapaturma Amerikan kaivannossa, jossa kuusi suomalaista sai surmansa" [Reverberations of a double murder in Inkilä and a terrible accident in an American mine, in which six Finns lost their lives] Viipuri 1899. Melody from Jaakko Kivirinta's 1961 rendition of *Keisarin murhayritys* [Assassination attempt of the czar] 1880, Alavuden laulukirja no. 159. The tragic event commemorated in the song took place in Ishpeming, Michigan, on December 31, 1898 (Päivälehti 1898).

Let the memory long resound,
Of those dear men that Death has found.
On New Year's Eve they lost their lives
And so made widows of their wives.

From a mine both deep and low
Now come the tidings full of woe.
Of those good miners in their prime
And their sad deaths at New Year's time.

Five hundred feet beneath the ground,
They met their deaths with crashing sound.
Those men did perish, one and all
Death took the short men and the tall.

It was on that fateful day
That should have been a holiday.
Six men of humble Finnish birth
Six men of valor and of worth.

'Twas a mournful sight to see
And of the things that came to be.
We're left with questions to this day
Of why it happened in this way.

Deep inside the depths below
The miners were all set to go.
As in a lift they planned to ride
Up to the surface, up topside.

As the lift it made to rise
A sudden crash it gave surprise.
And those good men sank in the gloom
As the mine shaft became their tomb.

Fifteen feet was all that lay
Between the men and light of day.
When down in lurching, thund'rous din
The lift fell crashing, men within.

Of their number there were nine
A lucky three did safety find.
They caught ahold of safety line,
And found escape from that dark mine.

Those three men got out safely
And fickle death it let them be.
They lived to see their later days,
And sing a grateful hymn of praise.

Of the six that did remain,
They hurdled down in fear and pain.
Their tragic death could not avoid,
Their hope and lives were fast destroyed.

They were young and in their prime,
Of full-grown age and happy time.
In their mid-thirties were they all,
Yet to their deaths they now did fall.

On our lips their names must stay,
as oft we think on that sad day.
Oh, Alfreed Siivo, he was one,
From Kauhava this man had come.

The late J. Paavokallio,
From Ylistaro did he go.
From northern Finland had he come,
And worked his best till life was done.

Johan Heikki Kujanpää,
Oh never time for marriage had.
Alahärmä had been his home,
From Ostrobothnia he had flown.

Kustaa Wilhelm Härmänmaa,
He also haled from Kauhava.
Back home in Finland verily,
He had lived life so joyfully.

Matti Tammi, man of might,
In Ilmajoki first saw light.
Now after all his hard life's toil,
He rests in American soil.

Jaakko Mikkola, last one,
From Merijärvi he did come.
Those are the six who met their fate,
On that horrendous New Year's date.

Wives and children now are left
Who of their loved ones are bereft.
Now they sit mourning for them all,
Who lost their lives in that great fall.

21. Kulkuripojan laulu
The Young Tramp's Song

From the book Saunio-Tuovinen, *Edestä aattehen* published in Helsinki in 1978. Originally published in the collection *Proletaarilauluja* [Proletarian songs] Duluth, Minnesota, 1918.

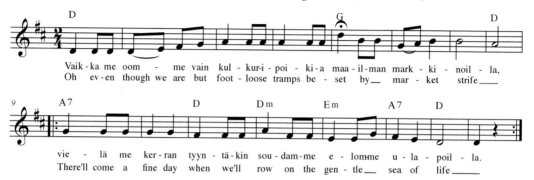

Vaik - ka me oom - me vain kul - kur-i - poi - ki - a maa - il-man mark - ki - noil - la,
Oh ev - en though we are but foot - loose tramps be - set by— mar - ket strife

vie - lä me ker - ran tyyn - tä - kin sou - dam-me e - lomme u - la - poil - la.
There'll come a fine day when we'll row on the gen - tle— sea of life

Vaikka me oomme vain kulkuripoikia
maailman markkinoilla,
vielä me kerran tyyntäkin soudamme,
elomme ulapoilla.

Vaikka vaan orjan osa nyt meillä
ja kahleita kantelemme,
vielä me kerran piiskureille
potkuja antelemme.

Vaikka nyt hoopoina "kaaran" katolla
lauluja laulelemme,
vielä me kerran "Pulmannin" vaunussa,
haikuja vetelemme.

Vaikka me oomme kulkuripoikia,
kodin hoivaa vailla,
vielä me kerran palatseissakin
istumme herrain lailla.

Vaikka nyt nylkyrit sortaa meitä,
kun heillä on suuri kassa,
vielä me kerran itsekin istumme
vallan satulassa.

Oh even though we are but footloose tramps
Beset by market strife.
There'll come a fine day when we'll row
On the gentle sea of life.

Oh even though it is a terrible lot
As we slave for a poverty wage.
There'll come a day fine when we'll beat
Evil bosses in our rage.

Oh even though we are hobos that sing
As we ride these railway cars
There'll come a day fine when we'll smoke
In the Pullman porters' bar.

Oh even though we are footloose tramps,
With no place that we can call home
There'll come a day fine when we'll rest
In a palace of our own.

Oh even though they bleed us dry,
As they steal our hard-earned money,
There'll come a day fine when we'll take
What is ours and seize liberty.

Finnish American terminology used in this song:
Kaara = railroad car

22. Lumperijätkän laulu
The Lumberjack's Song

Sung at Kaustinen by Oskari Tastula in 1947. Archived at the Finnish Literature Society. Origin unknown. Melody used for a number of different couplets, including "Vedenpaisumus" and "Noaakin arkki" produced by Iivari Kainulainen in 1912.

Nyt aivon laulun laulella noista lumperijätkistä,
vaan eikä heidän vertaistansa löydy laisinkaan.
Sahurit ne vetelee vaan hieman koukussaan,
joka katkon kohdalla pistää tupakan.

Sahurit ne metsässä mennä jungertaa
kiilat heillä kaulalla vaan kilvan helähtää.
Natsari se työnsä tietää, kuinka natsataan,
kuinka lyödään parkkimerkki, kuinka mitataan.

Vampparit ei murehdi, ei sure päiviään
he risut paaliin pailaavat, laulavat laulujaan.
Ranskan pojat täällä ovat laatareina,
he varttia vaille huutavat kämpälle kämpimään.

Seinipoika pailin päällä seiniä vetelee,
"Hoppaheijaa" timstarille sieltä huutelee.
Timstarit ne aamusella ylös ajetaan,
ensitöiksi heillä ompi tiimit haarnestaa.

Lantinkilla miehet ompi jäässä ainiaan,
he naputusta tanssiivat ain tukin tyven pääll'.
Iltasella kello kuus', kun kämppätorvi huus!
Silloin ne pojat metsästä vaan korjailevat luuns'.

Kun me tullaan kämpälle niin ryhdytään pesemään,
kuin on pesty, pyyhitty, niin sitten syömähän.
Isäntiä täällä ompi kolme kaikkiaan,
laatareille sahureille sekä vamppareill'.

Jos joku tahtoo kysyä tään laulun tekijää,
niin tämän laulun lauloivat nuot herrat sahurit.
Yksi niistä Frankki oli ja toinen Jalmari,
ja kolmas oli Kajaanista, nimi Oskari.

Finnish American terminology used in this song:
Haarnestaa = to harness
Laatari = loader
Lantinki = place of collection of lumber
Lumperijätkä = lumberjack
Natsari = notcher, bucker
Pailata = to bale
Sahuri = sawyer
Seini = chain
Seinipoika = chain boy, ground mole
Tiimi = team (of horses)
Timstari = teamster
Vamppari = swamper, branch collector, brush man

Well now a little song I'll sing of those timber-cutting men,
No, there's no others in the world who can compare to them.
Just a little crooked go the logs under the saw,
After every cut there's time for a smoke or chaw.

Oh sawyers through the woods will walk with a wedge dangling from their necks.
And buckers know to measure and to mark and cover specs.
Each one has a skill that they have learned and now know best.
Every day the job it puts that know-how to the test.

Oh swampers do not worry, they never say anything is wrong.
No they just spend the day collecting, singing out their song.
Frenchmen here are the loaders, that's the job they do,
Quarter to the hour and they just say that they are through.

A ground mole sets the chain, so he can haul up a load of wood.
And "Hoppaheijaa teamster there" he shouts out oh so good.
Every morning early they set out upon their ride.
Harnessing up horses those teamsters take in stride.

Oh cold as ice it always seems just to stand there upon a stump.
And so to keep the circulation they will dance and jump.
When at six o'clock work's over then the horn does blow.
Then the guys they shake their bones, back to the camp they go.

When we have gotten back, well we all want just a little scrub.
Then clean and dry we can at last just sit and eat some grub.
There are three straw bosses there who tell us what to do.
One for sawyers, one for loaders, one for swampers too.

If anyone would like to ask who has made this here little song,
Then you can say the sawyers and you won't have got it wrong.
One of them was Frankki, and then there was Jalmari,
And a third was from Kajaani, he was Oskari.

23. Kotimaani ompi Suomi
My Homeland is Finland

Published in Life and Letters of Joseph Riippa 1868–1896. Finnish American Historical Society of the West. Vol. 9 no. 1. April 1974. Ed. Walter Mattila. According to notes in that edition, Jooseppi Riippa composed this song himself. The publication does not however mention the source of the words, i.e., whether they were taken from a manuscript etc. The melody included in that publication was borrowed from Finland. The melody provided here is from Kaustinen, as sung by Martta Puumala and Bertta Valo in 1974. Their father Matti Penttilä had brought the song home from America in 1909. Conserved in the collection of the Kansanmusiikki-instituutti.

Kotimaani ompi Suomi
Suomi on mun kotimaa.
Siellä valkolatva tuomi
järven rannalla tuoksuva.

Ahon laidat armahimmat
mansikoista punertuu.
Ruusut siell' on kaunihimmat
Siell' on kirkkahampi kuu.

Siellä äiti hymyhuulin
tuuti pientä kehdossa,
Siellä ensi kerran kuulin
lintuin laulun lehdossa.

Siellä myöskin ensikerran
lempi syttyi sydämeen.
Liekö ollut tahto Herran,
kun se päättyi kyyneliin.

Synnyinmaani heitin silloin
huolissani huokaillen.
Milloin taasen näen oi milloin
Suomen sulopäivyen.
Suomen sulo päivän sen.

Kotimaani ompi Suomi
sinne riennän poloinen.
Haudalleni valkotuomi
toki kylvää kukkasen.

My homeland is Finland
Finland is my dear homeland.
There the white-tipped fragrant cherry
Stands upon the lake-shore strand.

At the edges of the clearing
The strawberries turning red
Roses fragrant sweetly blooming
And the moon shines overhead.

There a mother smiles calmly
As she rocks her infant child.
In the forest I heard sweetly
Songbirds trilling free and wild.

There it was the first moment
That my heart felt pangs of love.
But 'twas tears the good Lord sent
'Twas a sign from up above.

Sailing from my only homeland
Sighing so with misery.
When will I again see Finland,
And my country's true beauty?

My homeland is Finland,
There my soul will always be.
At my graveside, in that old land,
There will grow a cherry tree.

24. Petetyn pojan laulu
The Betrayed Boy's Song

Originally published in the pamphlet Kansanlauluja [folk songs] published in Ashtabula, Ohio. The pamphlet is undated but cannot be earlier than 1904. This song contains verses similar to those that Matti Penttilä brought back to Finland in 1909 (see **Song 23**). Both works may be modeled on another unknown publication. The song seems to be a combination of **Song 23** and the well-known broadside of the 1890s Petetty [betrayed] or Petetyn pojan laulu [Song of the betrayed boy]. Melody from *Suomen kansan sävelmiä II. Laulusävelmiä.* Ed. Ilmari Krohn. Helsinki 1904–1933. Melody no. 1403, collected in the vicinity of Oulu in 1900.

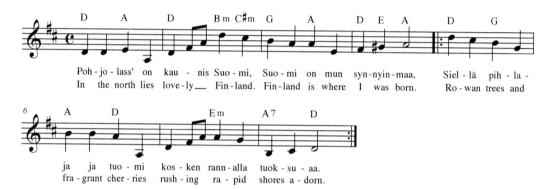

Poh-jo-lass' on kau-nis Suo-mi, Suo-mi on mun syn-nyin-maa, Siel-lä pih-la-
In the north lies love-ly Fin-land. Fin-land is where I was born. Ro-wan trees and

ja ja tuo-mi kos-ken rann-alla tuok-su-aa.
fra-grant cher-ries rush-ing ra-pid shores a-dorn.

Pohjolas' on kaunis Suomi,
Suomi on mun synnyinmaa,
Siellä pihlaja ja tuomi
Kosken rannalla tuoksuaa.

Ahon laidat armahimmat
Mansikoista punestuu.
Siell' on immet ihanimmat,
Siellä kirkkahampi kuu.

Siellä myöskin ensi kerran
Lempi syttyi sydämiin,
Vaikka lie se tahto Herran,
Kun se päättyi kyyneliin.

Huolissani huokaelin,
Silloin jätin synnyin maan.
Nyt taas jääköön huvitukset
Kotia kun pääsen vaan.

Kotimaani ompi Suomi,
kiiruhdan sen kummuillen.
Haudalleni valkotuomi
Kerran kylvää kukkasen.

Muistat kai, sä neito, vainen
Ajan, jolloin lemmittiin,
Jolloin suukko polttavainen
Saattoi tunteet hurmeisiin.

Muistat kai, kun kesäilloin
Lehtoteitä kuljettiin,
Kuinka maa ja taivas silloin
Syleilyymme suljettiin.

Muistat, kuinka kulkeissamme
Ne illat kului hupaisaan,
Muistat, kuinka huuliltamme
Valat virtas tulvinaan.

Kun mä lausuin: "Kauas lähden
Vaan sä mua muistat kai,"
Silloin vannoit sä luojan nähden:
"Sua lemmin kuollessain."

Vieri viikot, vuodet luisti,
Kotimaille matkustin,
Vielköhän armas muistat
Ajan, ajattelin mä.

Taaskin koito kullan luoksi
Riensin vastaan riemuiten,
Mutta, mutta minkä vuoksi
Kalpenit sä armaani?

Toisen sormus sormellansa
Välkkyi hurjan neitosen.
Toisen suukko huuliltansa
Poies poltti entisen.

Voi, niin silloin sydän sortui,
Päivä sammui rinnastain,
Silloin sielu raukka murtui.
Ikihaavan sinne sain.

Se oli silloin, kun ma vannoin,
Etten lemmi konsanaan,
Koska sekin, jolle annoin
Ensi lemmen, petti vaan.

In the north lies lovely Finland
Finland is where I was born.
Rowan trees and cherries fragrant,
Rushing rapid shores adorn.

At the edge of the pretty clearing,
Strawberries grow full and red.
Maidens in the evening they sing
And the moon shines overhead.

There it was the first ever moment
That my heart felt pangs of love.
But 'twas tears that the good Lord sent
'Twas a sign from up above.

In my grief and my troubled worries,
I left my native country.
But since I have crossed the great seas
Homeland memories they please me.

My homeland is beautiful Finland.
There my spirit longs to be.
At my graveside, in that old land,
There will grow a cherry tree.

Can you recall my lovely maiden,
A time when we were in love?
All it took was a kiss, just one,
And suddenly we sailed above.

Can you recall walking slowly,
Down long winding summer paths?
Earth and sky they witnessed truly,
Love that none could e'er surpass.

Can you recall filling long nights,
With our words of love and trust?
Vows of faithfulness we did plight,
As this country, leave I must.

When I said to you that I must go
"Please always remember me."
You swore to God your love would grow,
"I'll always love you tenderly."

Weeks they rolled by, years went so quickly,
To Finland I finally came.
Did you recall your vow to me,
When anxiously I called your name?

As I ran I shouted your name out.
I came smiling to your door.
But why did your face fill with doubt,
When our love was finally sure?

Then I saw the ring on your finger
That revealed the awful fact.
Someone else's kiss had broken
Our former lovers' pact.

On that day I was brokenhearted.
My world turned from light to dark.
Feeling like my soul departed,
Wounding me with lasting mark.

On that day I swore I would never
Words of love again dare say.
My first love she took another,
And my heart she did betray.

25. Vieraalla maalla
On Foreign Land

On the basis of the verse structure, set to the melody of "Kallavesj-laulu" [song of Kallavesj], itself based on an Estonian folk melody. The composer of "Kallavesj-laulu" was Aaro Jalkanen, who worked as the editor of the newspaper *Siirtolainen* [The Migrant] in Hancock, Michigan.

Yk - si - näin   yk - si - näin   täy - tyy pois mun rien - tä - mäin,   sil - män täyt - tää
All a-lone,   all a-lone   I must flee   a - way from home   bit - ter tears do

kyy - nel kar - vas   loi - stos jäi mun maa - ni ar - mas,   kau - vas kal - lis syn - nyin - maan,
fall so sad - ly   I will al - ways love my coun - try   far   a - way dear na - tive land,

Yksinäin, yksinäin	All alone, all alone,
Täytyy pois mun rientämäin,	I must flee away from home.
Silmän täyttää kyynel karvas;	Bitter tears do fall so sadly.
Loistos jäi mun maani armas,	I will always love my country.
Kauvas kallis synnyinmaan,	Far away, dear native land,
Synnyinmaan, synnyinmaan.	Native land, native land.
Synnyinmaan, synnyinmaan,	Native land, native land,
Konsa taas sun nähdä saan,	When shall I see you so grand?
Konsa kumpus' mulle loistaa,	When will countrymen there greet me,
Sylis' hellä huolet poistaa,	Their embrace remove my worry?
Kaipaavalla kyynelin,	Longingly I'm shedding tears,
Kyynelin, kyynelin.	Shedding tears, shedding tears.
Kyynelin, kyynelin,	Shedding tears, shedding tears,
Vierahissa kuljeksin.	Wandering these new frontiers.
Täällä ei äidin kieli kaiu,	Mother tongue here does not ring.
Huuliltaan ei laulut raiu;	From their lips, no songs they sing.
Kaukana on äidin kiel'	Far away the mother tongue,
Äidin kiel', äidin kiel'.	Mother tongue, mother tongue.
Äidin kiel', äidin kiel',	Mother tongue, mother tongue,
Lemmekäs kuin äidin miel',	Comforting both old and young.
Vieras kiel' on outo vento,	Foreign language is so strange.
Tuosta taukos laulu lento	Songs of home, they seem to change.
Vieras ään' on lemmetön,	Foreign voices show no love,
Lemmetön, lemmetön.	Show no love, show no love.
Pohjolain, Pohjolain.	In my North, in my North,
Siell' on hauska vaeltain,	Gladly would I wander forth.
Siellä vienot lauluin liikkuu,	Gentle does that singing sound,
Kukka silmikolla kiikkuu	Flowers swaying, on the ground.
Päällä niittyin loistavain,	Lovely meadows bursting forth,
Pohjolain, Pohjolain.	In my North, in my North.

26. Kotimaan ikävä
Missing the Homeland

As sung by Laina Rinta-Koski (b. 1895) of Kauhajoki. Melody notated by Aatos Rinta-Koski no. 98, 1972. Original melody unknown.

Ne tuu - let ne myr - skyt niin myl - vi - en käy ja toi - vo-jen ran - ta on
The winds and the storms, they come thun-der-ing down. The shores of our hopes they are

tuol - la. Niin kau-ka-na et - tei pur-te-hen näy, on tuu-li - en tuol - la puol - la.
hid - den. They're not to be seen from this ves-sel's crown as by these fierce waves we're dri - ven.

Ne tuulet ne myrskyt niin mylvien käy
ja toivojen ranta on tuolla.
Niin kaukana ettei purtehen näy.
On tuulien tuolla puolla.

Ja sinne sen rantahan toivojen,
Jok' ainoan matkan on määrä.
Vaan pursi kun vallas on myrskyjen,
vie monta, niin monta se väärään.

Ja siks' tämän maailman merellä
niin monta on onnetonta.
Siks' monelle täällä on elämä,
niin synkkää, niin ilotonta.

The winds and the storms, they come thundering down.
The shores of our hopes they are hidden.
They're not to be seen from this vessel's crown,
As by these fierce waves we're driven.

To far-away new shores of hope do we go,
The place that we're longing to be.
The vessel is blown by storms to and fro,
And many will find their graves at sea.

That's why there are so many people so sad,
Who ventured their fortunes at sea.
In tempests and storms they've lost all they had,
So joyless, so hopeless they be.

27. Vieraalla maalla
On Foreign Land

Sung by Laura Ahonen (b. 1910) Kauhajoki. Melody notated by Aatos Rinta-Koski no. 1041, 1972.
Original unknown.

Kau - nis on tää ke - sä - il - ta, il - ta ar - mas sun - nun - tain. Täh - det tuuik - kii
Sun - day eve - ning, warm and love - ly, in the peace - ful — sum - mer - time. Stars are shi - ning

tai - va - hal - ta, is - tuis - sa - ni — yk - sin vain.
in the sky a - bove, all a - lone I — pass the time.

Kaunis on tää kesäilta, ilta armas sunnuntain.
Tähdet tuikkii taivahalta, istuissani yksin vain.

Ihaelen tähtösiä, taivahalle katsahtain.
Muit'en kohtaa ystäviä vierahissa kulkeissain.

Muistoni nyt hiljaa liitää metsän korpeen Pohjolaan,
missä järven pinta siintää korven kuuset humuaa.

Siellä luonto kesäilloin kansallensa kirkkaan suo.
Siellä linnut laulaa kilvan iloa se rintaan tuo.

Siellä lehdet liehuu puissa viljapellot lainehtii.
Kiitos kallis uhkuu noissa Luojan luokse kiirehtii.

Siellä hongat huminoivat Suomen laulut kajahtaa.
Niityn kukat vihannoivat, luontoa tää kaunistaa.

Kuule kaunis Väinön kansa, kuule kuinka hiljalleen,
koivu kuiskaa kummultansa, näin hän kuiskaa kansalleen.

Muista armas Suomen miesi, kallein tehtäväsi vaan,
Pois on armas kotiliesi, kun sä jätät kotimaan.

Sekä neito valkotukka, kukoistat sä kauniisti,
niinkuin kaunein ruusun kukka, kasvat kotimaassasi.

Oi sa maani Suomi kallis, kasva, kartu, ainiaan.
Viihdy niinkuin rannan tuomi, saavutat sä kunnian.

Sunday evening warm and lovely, in the peaceful summertime.
Stars are shining in the sky above, all alone I pass the time.

I admire all the night stars as I gaze up at the sky.
But I see no friends about me, as I go wandering by.

Recollections slowly take me to the woods of my homeland,
Where the lakes and all the rivers shine, and the spruces calmly stand.

There the sun gives light to people, every summer all night long.
There the birds sing, bringing beauty, as they trill out in lovely song.

There the leaves of every tree wave, nature is so adored.
From the people, voices rise in thanks as they praise their one true Lord.

All the pine trees they are silent, song of Finland ringing out.
And the flowers in green meadows, they are blooming all about.

Hear my words you Väinö's people listen just how quietly
The trees whisper to our people, as they sing so beautifully.

Men of Finland, always treasure, keep it ever in your mind.
Far away now lies your homeland and the hearth you left behind.

Finnish maidens, hair so golden, in your homeland living free
Like a rose you flower sweetly, ever growing more lovely.

Oh my Finland, thrive and prosper like the cherries on the shores.
Like the forests, growing stronger, glory will be ever yours.

28. Suomen neito
Maiden of Finland

Sung by Heikki Kentala, also known as Finnin Janne (1878–1957) in Kaustinen in 1947. The song is apparently an abbreviated version of a longer work, explaining gaps in the plot. Conserved in the archives of the Finnish Literature Society. The phrase *Suomen neito*, "Maiden of Finland," can refer to the country of Finland itself, which is said to resemble a woman in outline on maps.

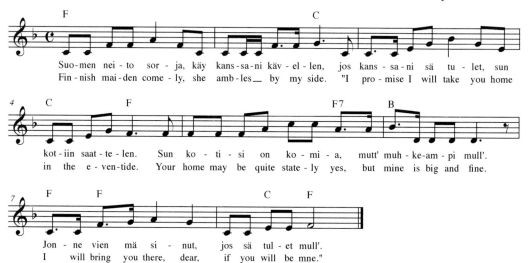

Suo-men nei - to sor - ja, käy kans-sa-ni käv - el - len, jos kans - sa-ni sä tu - let, sun
Fin-nish mai-den come - ly, she amb-les— by my side. "I pro - mise I will take you home

kot - iin saat - te - len. Sun ko - ti - si on ko - mi - a, mutt' muh - ke-am - pi mull'.
in the e - ven-tide. Your home may be quite state - ly yes, but mine is big and fine.

Jon - ne vien mä si - nut, jos sä tul - et mull'.
I will bring you there, dear, if you will be mne."

Suomen neito sorja,	Finnish maiden comely,
käy kanssani kävellen,	She ambles by my side.
jos kanssani sä tulet,	"I promise I will take you home,
sun kotiin saattelen.	In the eventide.
Sun kotisi on komia,	Your home may be quite stately,
Mutt' muhkeampi mull'.	But mine is big and fine.
Jonne vien mä sinut,	I will bring you there, dear,
jos sä tulet mull'.	If you will be mine."
Kiitos herra kunnian,	"Thank you for your praise so kind
ma lausun herra teill'.	I'll not come my lord.
En tule minä koskaan,	Oh, never will I change my mind,
asumahan teill'.	Take your room and board.
Kun teidän käytös herran	Because, my lord, you have no shame,
on aivan arvoton.	And act unworthily.
Luuleekos herra sellaiseks'	Fancy ways you aim,
neitosen tään.	You'll not conquer me."
Sen sanon teille nuoret,	Listen, all you men who leave,
lähteissänne viel'	Sailing from this land.
et kirjoitatta neitosille	Oh write to all the girls who grieve,
tietoja sielt'.	Write them in your hand.
Kun pojat ovat nuoria,	When worthy boys are young and strong,
ja juuri parhaillaan.	And at their very best.
Silloin he lähtevät	Saying only "so long,"
valtameren taa.	They leave for the west.

29. Amerikasta
From America

Jaakko Matti's son's letter to his old sweetheart. From the broadside collection "Kolme huvittavaa ja kaunista laulua" [Three entertaining and beautiful songs] edited and published by "J. K." in Tampere in 1898. The melody provided here is taken from the unpublished song of Frans Juho Järvinen of Eura, entitled "Egyptinmaan maaherrana" [As the lord of Egypt], as with **Song 22**.

Nyt o - tan pän - nän kä - te - hen ja kir - jeen kir - joi - tan täält
Oh now I take my pen in hand and write you this let - ter here

ta - kaa mai - den, mer - i - en mä kät - tä o - jen - nan. Vii -
from a far and dis - tant land, hope it finds you bet - ter. I

mei - sen ker - ran ter - veh - dän sua näi - llä ri - veil - lä; min -
write these lines to your ad - dress and ques - tion pose to you: How

täh - den van - han ys - tä - vän noin saa - toit hyl - jä - tä?
could you leave me in dis - tress, your one love good and true?

Nyt otan pännän kätehen
Ja kirjeen kirjoitan,
Täält' takaa maiden, merien
Mä kättä ojennan.
Viimeisen kerran tervehdän
Sua näillä riveillä;
Mintähden vanhan ystävän
Noin saatoit hyljätä?

Sun tähtes olen raatanut,
Sun tähtes, Liisa — niin,
Sun muotos olen muistanut,
Kun mainiin painuttiin.
Vaan älä huoli! Omakses,
Ottaisit vieläkin,
Nähdessäs vanhan sulhases,
Mun, mister Matsonin.

Suomessa olin Jaska vaan
Ja halpa renkimies;
Nyt misteriksi mainitaan,
Se enkelskaa on — yes!
Ja aioin ostaa tiketin
Sun tänne tullakses,
Sun tuoda omaan hausihin,
Vaan petit sulhases.

Se Torpan Tommi tolvana,
Sun riisti rinnaltain.
Saanetko edes kahvia,
Kuin joskus tilkan vain?
Ois mistres olla kelvannut
Sun hyvä Liisapet;
Nyt ompi kaikki muuttunut,
Voi sua, Liisapet!

Saat jäädä Kitusuomehen
Silakan kylkeen kai;
Syö Matson leivän vehnäisen,
Nyt sanon vain: "ku pai."
Saat jäädä Kitusuomehen
Silakan kylkeen kai;
Syö Matson leivän vehnäisen,
Nyt sanon vain: "ku pai."

Finnish American terminology
used in this song:
Enkelskaa = English
Mistres = Mistress, Mrs.
Pännä = pen
Hausi = house/home
Ku pai = goodbye

Oh, now I take my pen in hand,
And write you this letter.
Here from a far and distant land,
Hope it finds you better.
I write these lines to your address,
And question pose to you:
How could you leave me in distress,
Your one love good and true?

For you I've always striven dear,
My Liisa so divine.
Your image in my memory here,
I took into the mine.
But don't you worry, when you see,
This man who was your own.
Now no one "Matson!" barks at me;
By Mister I am known.

Oh, back home they called me Jaska,
I was a poor farmhand.
Here everyone calls me Mister,
It's English and so grand!
I planned to pay the way for you,
And finally have you here.
And bring you to our hausi new,
But you betrayed me dear.

Oh, he stole you away from me,
That Tom from out of town.
Can he offer you coffee?
Or just water, is it brown?
Mrs. Matson they'd all call you,
My dearest Liisapet.
Now look at what it's all come to,
You heartless Liisapet.

On herring bones you can be fed,
In Finland live and die.
While I partake of fine Whitbread,
And tell you now "ku pai."
On herring bones you can be fed,
In Finland live and die.
While I partake of fine Whitbread,
And tell you now "ku pai."

30. Vitikon Jani
Jani Vitikko

Song written by F. E. Takala of Vimperi. Melody by Eero Hautala of Evijärvi, in 1978. The song appears to be based on actual occurrences.

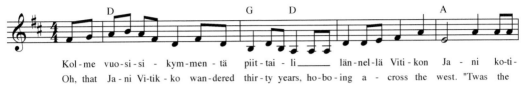

Kol-me vuo-si-si - kym-men - tä   piit - tai - li____   län-nel-lä Viti-kon Ja - ni   ko-ti-
Oh, that Ja - ni Vi-tik - ko wan-dered thir-ty years, ho-bo-ing a - cross the west. "Twas the

i - kävä van-hoilla päi - villä sieltä   Vim-pe-liin tule-maan   pa - ni.
home-sick-ness that pulled him back, Vim-pe-li he liked   best____

Kolme vuosikymmentä piittaili Lännellä Vitikon Jani,
koti-ikävä vanhoilla päivillä sieltä Vimpeliin tulemaan pani.

Hän Kuparisaarilla trammaili teki Arizonaan retken,
ja kääpetsifarmia runnasi Air Iiverin konrilla hetken.

Kun Pasifikin rataa rikattiin kaatui aarniometsä kuin lakoon,
vuoria sitten kun räjäytettiin, ajettiin junalla ampua pakoon.

Yks airesmanni Jania löi Bostonin baarissa kerran.
Jani horjahti, maailma musteni silmissä hintin verran.

Jani liitiin kun vastas, aires huus: "löit lujasti särkyi luutkin,"
Jani nyrkkiä pyyhkien tuumaili; "sitä moittineet ovat muutkin."

Mahkura-Maijan saluuna oli Janille paikka tuttu,
siellä piirilasien ääressä moni syntyi mojova juttu.

Vanhaa maata kun muisteltiin siellä joskus mielin herkin,
Jani leppälantin pöytään löi ja tarjosi kuvillenkin.

Joo pojat, tämä sitä Länttä on, täällä kaikki on suurenmoista,
mutta juhannussaunan veroista, siellä kotona, ei oo toista.

Kesän hämyiset yöt, tytöt vanhan maan, ja kirkkaus sinisen taivaan,
pojat hemmetti soikoon, ostetaan tiketti jo ensi laivaan.

Oh, that Jani Vitikko wandered thirty years, hoboing across the west.
'Twas the homesickness that pulled him back: Vimpeli he liked best.

Well he tramped all the way down to Copper Island and to Arizona he went.
On a cabbage farm on Iver's land, he settled down a moment.

Along the Pacific Trail he cut down the forests and every single tree.
When the coalmines blew the hilltops off, trains they used to flee.

In a tavern in Boston, an Irishman struck poor Jani one day.
Jani's sight went sort of black and dark, and Jani did sway.

And then Jani took a swing at that Irishman, who said "You broke my jaw in two!"
Jani shook his fist and said out loud, "Others have cried that too."

Yes, Maija's old saloon was his favorite haunt of any place around.
As they spun their yarns and traded tales, many a beer did go down.

Every now and again, they would mention Finland, the place they'd left behind.
Jani nodding at the memory, bought a round to unwind.

"Yes boys, living's pretty good, everything's as it should in this land we've found out
west.
But a midsummer sauna back home, that is clearly best."

"Sunlit summer nights and the sky so blue, and the girls, well, there's no doubt.
Boys, let's buy us a ticket home on the next ship out."

Finnish American terminology used in this song:
Airesmanni = Irishman
Hintin verran = a hinting reference
Konri = rural area, region
Kääpetsi = cabbage (Finnish kaali)
Leppälantti = a quarter (the coin. Leppä, alder, implying red color)
Liiti = deal
Piiri = beer
Piittailla = to ramble, ride without a ticket
Rikata = to rig, fix up
Runnata = to run, lead
Trammailla = to tramp around, wander
Air = mister (Finnish herra)

31. Suomen pojan huvilaulu kotiin tullessa Amerikasta
The Finnish Boy's Amusement Song on His Way Home from America

From the broadside "Kaksi uutta laulua" [Two new songs] edited and published by W. H. Toivonen. Published in Tampere in 1895. Melody taken from Nakkila resident Vihtori Grönfors's rendition of the song "Siel on paljon kauniita naisii" [Lots of pretty women there], 1937. Conserved in the archives of the Finnish Literature Society.

Minä olen Suomesta, juuri keskeltä sen napaa,
Vaan en minä Amerikast' aarretta sen tapaa.
Sun fralla rallalla sun fralla rallalla
Sun rati riti rati riti rallalla lei.

Kun minä olen pohjan poika, oikein aika eppa,
En minä rupee tässä maassa pitkältäkään reppaan.
Sun fralla rallalla :,:

Ja kotiin aivon lähteä ja mennä sitä pitää,
Vaikka ei ole taskussakan juuri yhtään mitään.
Sun fralla rallalla :,:

Vaan se on pahin asia ennenkun astun rantaan,
Kun tarttis tuloryypyn Suomessakin antaa.
Sun fralla rallalla :,:

Vaan mitäs kannan murhetta vaan heitän kaikki valtaan,
Kyllähän tuo Astrea laiva mun kotimaahan kantaa.
Sun fralla rallalla :,:

Englannissa poikettihin Hullin kaupungissa,
Jossa sydän iloitsi ja hyppeli kun kissa.
Sun fralla rallalla :,:

Vaan jopa kului hetkinen ja täytyy laivaan astuu,
Vaan eipä tuosta pojan tossut pahastikaan kastu.
Sun fralla rallalla :,:

Vaan taas kun läksin viiltämään tuota isoo Aatlan selkää,
Niin rupesinpa ryypytöinnä pikkuruisen pelkään.
Sun fralla rallalla :,:

Vaan jopa johtui mieleeni armas Suomen ranta,
Että pitääpähän tulotanssi lirusilmill' antaa.
Sun fralla rallalla :,:

Ja rantahan kun päästihin niin hypyt toimitettiin,
Ja tuskin kättä paiskattiin kun kohta pyörähdeltiin.
Sun fralla rallalla :,:

Nyt lopuksi mä nuorukaiset sanon vielä teille,
Eihän pidä matkustella koskaan mieron teille.
Sun fralla rallalla :,:

Älkää panko pahaksenne, vaikka hieman laulan,
Eihän pidä ruveta nyt aivan kovin nauraan.
Sun fralla rallalla :,:

I come from good old Finland, and a tiny little town,
And I have seen America but never its renown.
Your fralla rallalla your fralla rallalla
Your rati riti rati riti rallalla lei.

Because I am a man of the northern country,
I will not stay here for very long, for I'll head back to sea.
Your fralla rallalla :,:

I plan to sail home, to good old Finland I shall go,
Without much money at all, I have less than what I owe.
Your fralla rallalla :,:

But there is nothing worse than arriving so broke to shore,
Wanting to buy a round for the country I adore.
Your fralla rallalla :,:

But why do I take with me all these worries out to sea?
This fine ship will surely back to Finland carry me.
Your fralla rallalla :,:

To grand old England we set forth, in Hull port where we're at,
We are so close to Finland now, my heart jumps like a cat.
Your fralla rallalla :,:

Stretching legs there portside, oh how the time flew by.
When we got back aboard the ship, my shoes they were still dry.
Your fralla rallalla :,:

But when we set sail out upon the great Atlantic sea,
From my flask I took a little swig, just to relax me.
Your fralla rallalla :,:

And then the shores of Finland, yes they flashed before my eyes.
So then I did a happy dance, underneath blue skies.
Your fralla rallalla :,:

Oh, when we finally got to Finland, I jumped off the boat.
I hugged you right away, and then I sang a pretty note.
Your fralla rallalla :,:

Now all you fine young people, listen closely here to me:
Always stay here at home, and promise never go to sea.
Your fralla rallalla :,:

Oh, please let me sit down here, as I sing this little song.
You don't need to laugh so hard, even if I'm singing wrong.
Your fralla rallalla :,:

III. Kotona. At Home.
Songs 32–54.

Amerikan rannan kaupunki
se hopialta hohtaa.
Siellä ne pojat halata saa
hattupäisiä kohta.

City on America's great coast line
How like silver it seems to glitter.
Maidens in fine hats who are good for hugging
Eagerly they'll twitter. (**Song 32**e)

Piirileikit, ring dances, were popular entertainments in Finland during the late nineteenth century and into the 1930s[1]. As players gathered together in a circle, they sang songs made up of four-line stanzas as the musical accompaniment of dances in 2/4, 4/4, or 3/4 time. Although modern performances of ring dances often employ instrumental music supplied by a fiddle or accordion, ring dances in Finnish rural areas in the past often relied on a capella singing of rhymed stanzas. Sometimes during the dance men occupied the center of the ring and women circled around them, choosing a partner for an interval of pair dancing before all participants returned to a unified ring. Then the procedure would reverse, with women moving to the center of the ring and men encircling them and selecting a partner of their choice for the next interval of pair dancing. Sometimes the dance would take the form of a "leski-leikki," in which a lone center dancer would choose a partner from the ring for an interval of pair dancing and eventually return to the outer ring, thus leaving a new dancer as the "widow(er)" in the center. Whatever the particular sequence of such events, the duration of the dancing was determined by the sung verses of the song. In practice, this meant that a participating singer who liked the pairings of any particular moment could prolong that pairing through singing additional verses. Since the songs were usually performed by women, this practice afforded women an opportunity to use their singing strategically to maximize or minimize contact with current or potential suitors[2]. Not surprisingly, as is evident from the songs contained in this portion of this anthology, images of dancing, romantic coupling, and the gaining or loss of a partner figure prominently as topics in the songs performed in such dances. Significantly, however, as these songs also demonstrate, ring dance songs often address aspects of migration, be it the emigration of eligible men or women

---

1   Rausmaa 1981, 167
2   Virtanen and DuBois 2000, 165–166

from Finland to America, the fortunes of migrants abroad, or the feelings of the friends, family, and romantic partners such emigrants left behind. Continuing an essentially medieval musical tradition, Finnish ring dance songs of the nineteenth and early twentieth centuries nevertheless often touch on strikingly contemporary issues of their day. By looking at the songs created, performed, and preserved in rural communities during the era of the Finnish migration, we can gain a sense of the viewpoints and voices of people both within Finland and in North America, particularly the feelings and perceptions of those Finns who continued their lives "Atlannin takana," (behind the Atlantic), *kotona*, back home.

While the narrative songs presented in other sections of this anthology often offer portrayals of historical experiences—e.g., the travels by boat and train that brought Finnish emigrants to the New World, the work conditions in lumber camps, kitchens, and mines that immigrants experienced, the occasional return of migrants to their homeland—ring dance texts tend to offer fewer such details. Terse and witty, and occasionally wistful, they suggest in the manner of lyric songs more generally the emotions and perceptions of depicted singers/speakers whose circumstances and experiences are portrayed or hinted at in the songs[1]. Often avoiding all but the most essential narrative details, ring songs focus attention instead on spotlighted moments in a migrant's life, sketching with sometimes startling economy a speaker's poignant feelings and perceptions at a particular moment in the migration process, or a speaker's overall emotional situation that resulted from a permanent or temporary separation[2]. Thus, where narrative songs can provide seemingly detailed (but often markedly fictive) historical portraits of migrants' lives, lyric ring songs provide imaginative windows into the supposed or actual emotional worlds of migrants and their loved ones caught up in the momentous experience of trans-Atlantic migration. While recognizing the essentially imaginative nature of these lyrical works, an examination of such song texts can allow us to sense the profound influence the experience of emigration had on the Finnish populace back home in Finland as well as in North America. They suggest some of the wide array of social, economic and emotional repercussions of mass migration in Finnish communities.

Enacting Personas

Although composed and performed in Finland, the ring songs included in this anthology often adopt the confident persona of a person headed off for the New World. Adopting such a persona allowed a singer to depict the feelings of a person in a particular situation and to comment by implication on the personal and interpersonal ramifications of the person's ("speaker's") choices. Narrative events are suggested in such depictions of viewpoint or psychology, but are not the primary focus of songs: instead, the thoughts or feelings of the speaker take center stage. Typical of the depiction of a confident persona is the bold declaration that Ida Wahlroos of Juva includes in her song from 1900 (**Song 33**):

Minä lähden Amerikkaan,
Minnekäs sinä joudut?
Lähde sinäkin Amerikkaan
Rinkitanssin kouluun!

—

I am off to America,
Where oh where will you go?
You can also come along,
Learn a ring dance song.

---

1   DuBois 1995, 239–258; DuBois 2006
2   DuBois 2004

The stanza juxtaposes the verbs *lähteä* ("to leave")—a verb implying volition and ability—and *joutua*,("to wind up, fall into"), a verb that connotes passivity, getting into difficult straits, or winding up in a situation not of one's liking. The speaker of the song's lines, confident of success in America, uses the empowering verb lähteä to describe the planned departure, counselling the person listening to escape the confining situation conveyed by the verb *joutua* by similarly adopting a strategy of leaving: "Lähde sinäkin Amerikkaan" ("You should leave for America as well"). Travel to America is not depicted as a risky or fraught undertaking but rather as a positive alternative to becoming stymied or stranded back in Finland. Emigration, the speaker asserts, will be as easy and as enjoyable as learning to dance. Travel to America is dramatized in the words and the movement of the dance, and in the process, the momentous, life-changing event of migration is rendered light, familiar and exciting. At the same time, the adoption of this jaunty emigrant persona within the song allows a singer to avoid a focus on the emotional frustrations or regrets suggested by the verb *joutua*, and potentially more reflective of the actual experiences of a woman singing such a song to male audience members who might likely choose to emigrate. The final line's mention of learning a ring song dance (going to a "rinkitanssin koulu"—"ring dance school") brings the song back from the more hypothetical topic of possible emigration to the concrete present performance situation of the ring dance, where the song's performer and listeners are united in bodily and social interaction.

In poetically characterizing the thoughts of emigrants, ring dance songs often depict their speakers making confident, and perhaps unrealistic, pronouncements regarding the advantages and thrills of migration. In Alppo Kinnunen's 1901 "Ameriikkalaisen laivan pilli/The Whistle of an American Ship" (**Song 36**), the speaker asserts:

Adopting a female persona in his performance, Alppo Kinnunen employs similar wording in his rendering of "Tytöt lähtee Turun rantaan/The Girls Go to Turku's Shore" (**Song 37**), although his version reverses the pronouns and personas contained in the above song:

> Sinä menet Ameriikkaan,
> mihinkäs minä joudun?
> Lähde heilani Amerikkaan
> rinkintanssikouluun.
> —
> Go my dear to America,
> What is left here for this fool?
> With my love I do you send there,
> I hope you find a dancing school!

Here a listener's impending emigration becomes a taunt: the song's speaker, apparently a woman from indications in the other verses of the song, dismisses her love with the same admonition to go to a "rinkintanssikoulu," a "ring dance school." The speaker is apparently remaining behind in Finland, but her defiant or flippant words avoid any direct expression of sorrow. Only in her use of the verb *joutua* about herself does she intimate to any extent the emotional gravity of her situation or her possible feelings about the impending separation from the listener.

In poetically characterizing the thoughts of emigrants, ring dance songs often depict their speakers making confident, and perhaps unrealistic, pronouncements regarding the advantages and thrills of migration. In Alppo Kinnunen's 1901 "Ameriikkalaisen laivan pilli/The Whistle of an American Ship" (**Song 36**), the speaker asserts:

> Ameriikan maa se on lämpimä maa
> ja sinne mun tekee mieli,
> kun Suomen maa näin nuorelle pojalle
> on reissata liian pieni.
> —
> America, that's the place to be,
> Warm and sunny there.
> Finland it's just too small a country
> To keep me penned up here.

The contrast between America as a supposed land of opportunity and Finland as a place of confinement or stagnation carries over here from the many narrative songs and broadsides discussed elsewhere in this study. In Kinnunen's song, however, the poignancy of leave-taking as a component of emigration is also intimated as the speaker acknowledges the sorrows that will result from separation, even temporary, from a true love:

Voi minä hullu kun piljetin ostin
ja läksin maailmalle.
Heilani jäi mun suremaan
tuonne Helsingin asemalle.
—
Foolishly a ticket I did buy
Passage 'cross the sea.
Left my true love to weep and to cry,
Back home in Helsinki.

Within the broader text of the song, then, the speaker's pronouncements are not presented as historical facts, but rather as depictions of the mindset of a confident emigrant confronting the exciting but difficult prospect of migration.

In portraying the thoughts of emigrants, ring dance songs often depict speakers engaged in economic calculations. A ring song recorded by Aatos Rinta-Koski in 1975 depicts men choosing to emigrate in order to earn cash:

Poijat ne menöö Amerikasta
hakemahan rahaa.
Niin ei sitä tiedä lähteisnänsä
moniko sieltä takaasi palaa.
—
Boys when they're heading for America,
It's money they're going for.
None of those boys know as they're sailing away
How many will come back to this shore.

The risks of their venture are ominously acknowledged in the second couplet of the verse, where the speaker notes the fact that the eventual fate of an emigrant was not always certain or predictable. Some emigrants might reap good earnings in America and return home as rich and prosperous men of substance. But others could end up stranded in the New World, or disappear entirely. In his "Tytöt lähtee Turun rantaan/The Girls Go to Turku's Shore" (**Song 37**), Alppo Kinnunen's speaker states:

Ameriikassa, Ameriikassa
siell' on lysti olla.
Siellä sahat, siellä myllyt
käyvät kalliolla.
—
In America if you please
Lots of fun times can be found.
Sawmills there and factories
They're covering the rocky ground.

Here the sources of employment migrants are likely to find are listed as pull factors for men considering emigration. Where the dream of gaining farm land remained an important factor in many Finnish emigrants' decision to journey to North America, the realities of wage employment in factories and mines is acknowledged here as an economic niche for men who find themselves in areas with poor agricultural prospects, such as Michigan's Upper Peninsula or the mining belts of Wisconsin or Minnesota.

The characterization of men's economic decision-making is sometimes depicted in terms of food metaphors, adding a lively further dimension to the portrayal of the psychology of male emigrants and the women they leave behind. **Song 32a** declares:

> En mä tiedä poijes tulost'
> Siell' on niin helppoa työtä.
> Rusinoita ja omenoita
> saa siellä pojat syödä.
>
> —
>
> Don't be sure your boyfriend's gonna
> Leave his good job behind.
> Loads of raisins, pecks of apples
> Are what the boys there find.

A man who has emigrated to America is likely to remain there, the song's speaker suggests, because of the plentiful earnings and easy life he will find. Plans of an eventual return to Finland may thus fail to materialize. Alppo Kinnunen incorporates much the same lines into a statement addressed at male emigrants themselves (**Song 37**):

> Lähde heilani Ameriikkaan
> Siell' on helppoa työtä.
> Rusinoita ja veskunoita
> Ameriikassa syödään.
>
> —
>
> Head to America my dear
> Gainful work you will there do.
> Sweets and raisins you will taste there
> It's such a life that waits for you.

In a similar use of food metaphors to characterize economic decision-making **Song 32d** employs an image of America as a land of peaches in comparison to Finland as a land of blueberries. The comparison plays on the familiar Finnish proverb "Oma maa mansikka, muu maa mustikka" (one's own country [i.e., Finland] is a strawberry; any other country is but a blueberry), demoting Finland to the less desirable status of the smaller berry:

> Amerikan maalla persikat kasvaa
> Suomessa mustikoita.
> Amerikan maalla taaloja vuollaan
> mutta Suomessa kolikoita.
>
> —
>
> Farmers in America grow peaches
> While in Finland there's just blueberries.
> Pockets full of dollars are what they've got
> While here just coins one carries.

The song's lines present a double entendre: America is both a place of higher wages (dollars over coins), and also a place of greater wealth more generally, just as a dollar is greater than a coin, or a peach greater than a blueberry. The fact that peaches grow in carefully tended orchards and Finnish blueberries in semi-wild forest clearings add further dimensions to the verse's images and their portrayal of a speaker seemingly confident in the superiority of the country to which he is headed.

Where ring dance songs often focus on the economic decision-making of men, the fact that most ring dance songs were performed by women leads to their occasional inclusion of female personas and depictions of women's decision-making in relation to emigration. Kerttu Talvitie's **Song 50** depicts the frustrations of a woman wanting to emigrate but finding herself consigned to a servant's station instead:

> Piian pestin mä ottanu olen,
> ja palvella sen meinaan vaan.
> Enkä minä vielä tänä vuonna—
> Atlannin merellä seilaakkaan.
>
> —
>
> I have found me a job in a big house,
> Oh, as a serving girl I must toil.
> No Atlantic trip is slated for me—
> I'll have to stay here on Finnish soil.

The speaker in the song plans to make the most of her limited life in Finland, finding as many boyfriends as she can to make up for her ignoble existence taking orders and cleaning chamberpots. Another of Kerttu Talvitie's songs, **Song 51**, expresses the regrets of a woman who has turned down a landed suitor, leading to his eventual decision to head off to America:

> Taloo oli komia ja poikaki niin soria
> ja molemmat mä olisin saanu.
> Sitä hommas paappa ja sitä touhus mamma
> mutta minä kun en rakastanu.
>
> —
>
> Grand was the house they offered, handsome the boy they proffered,
> Nicely I would be married.
> But though parents both they did urge me on,
> For him no love I carried.

Where economic factors could and did motivate decisions to emigrate, ring songs suggest, emotional factors also could play a role. America could be the place for jilted lovers to make a new start, putting behind them the sorrow and possible humiliation of a romantic rejection.

Spotlighting Techniques

Because of their limited number of lines, and also because of their aesthetic norms as lyric rather than narrative works, Finnish ring dance songs typically avoid the blow-by-blow characterization of narrative events evinced by some of the songs presented in other sections of this anthology. Instead of minutely detailed narrative sequences, ring dance songs often tunnel an entire migration experience into just one or two vividly described moments. **Song 39** of 1907 describes the boarding of a train and ship as devices for depicting the pain and sorrow of young lovers separated by the act of emigration:

Kun poijat ne astuu masiinahan niin
masiina alla huutaa
hyvästi nyt tämän kylän flikat,
eikä nyt enää muuta,

Kun poijat ne astuu laivahan,
niin laiva se vetehen painuu,
kun flikat ne rannalla itkivät,
jotta vesi se merehen painuu.

—

When boys they all step aboard the carriage,
Loudly the whistle screams.
Farewell girls, there won't be any marriages,
Tears just, and broken dreams.

Then boys they all step aboard the steamship
Ponderously weighted down.
Into the waves salty teardrops drip,
As the girls by the dockside frown.

Here, in a brief song of only two verses, the speaker depicts the intensity of departure, displaying none of the bravado or confidence of songs portraying the viewpoints of prospective emigrants themselves. The song's narrator hovers outside of the minds of the song's characters, focusing both on the feelings of parting lovers and the sounds and appearance of the heartless machines that will accomplish their separation.

Similarly, Alppo Kinnunen's "Ameriikkalaisen laivan pilli/The Whistle of an American Ship" (**Song 36**) spotlights the moment of initial departure, albeit now from the perspective of a man boarding a ship:

Ameriikkalaisen laivan pilli
mun korvihini kaikuu.
Hoikan sorian neiton viereen
tämäkin poika vaipuu.

Ameriikkalaisen laivan mastossa
lippu liehuvainen.
Nuorella pojalla sydän se on
kuin koski kuohuvainen.

—

I can hear the ship's loud whistle blowing—
echoes in my ear.
Time has come, and this lad is going
to leave his girlfriend dear.

I can see the Yankee flag hoisted high,
up on that ship's mast.
like in white water feelings fly, my
heart's a'beating fast.

The sounds and sights of the moment of farewell are captured in touching detail, along with the sounds and sights of boarding a steamship.

Other songs select moments from the trans-Atlantic journey to spotlight. In **Song 49**, Kerttu Talvitie's speaker states:

> Merellä olen minä syntynyt
> Hei himputa rimpun, rimpun pila pila.
> Merellä olen minä syntynyt
> Ja laivalla olen minä luotu.
>
> Amerikan laivan kannella
> Hei himputa rimpun, rimpun pila pila,
> Amerikan laivan kannella
> On ristiäiseni juotu.
> —
> I got my start out on the great blue sea
> Hei rimputa rimpun, rimpun pila pila
> I got my start out on the great blue sea
> Yes, born on a great sailing vessel.
>
> On a ship bound for great America
> Hei rimputa rimpun, rimpun pila pila
> On a ship bound for great America
> Yes there as a baby I was baptized.

Life's experiences are tunneled into the sea passage itself, which becomes equated with the entirety of life. None of the speaker's former life figures at all in the song, as the speaker asserts having been born at sea. In a similar fashion, but with less metaphorical flourish, Kalle V. Rintanen's "Laivan päällä on lysti olla/It Is Fun to Be on the Ship" (**Song 47**) presents a snapshot of the time at sea as a singularly exciting moment in a migrant's life:

> Laivan päällä on lysti olla
> silloon kun se soutuu.
> Mitäs on väliä tällääsen haliun
> millekkä maalle se joutuu.
> —
> It is fun on this ship we're sailing,
> In the waves we are rocking.
> Even if I don't know when we will reach our goal
> Or where at last we'll be docking.

The purposefulness and economic planning of typical emigrants (at least as depicted in other songs) is replaced here with a persona completely at ease with an unbounded meandering on the sea, uncertain of either duration or destination.

Kerttu Talvitie ends her **Song 49** with a description of the moment of happiness and relief embodied in a ship's arrival in New York harbor. Her final verse brings to a close to the spotlighted moments of travel contained in her song:

Amerikan rantaan kun saavutaan
Hei himputa rimpun, rimpun pila pila
Amerikan rantaan kun saavutaan
Niin mastohon nousee lippu liehuvainen.
—

Once in the American harbor safe
Hei rimputa rimpun, rimpun pila pila
Once in the American harbor safe
They hoist up aloft that great Old Glory.

The moments of emigration—leavetaking, travel, and arrival—are each fragmented and portrayed in these musical snapshots of an emigrant's life in ways that draw on the imagistic norms of Finnish lyric and accomplish the rhetorical end of delineating the mind and thoughts of people engaged in migration.

Depicting Separation
Ring dance songs focus often on romantic relations, and a portrayal of emigration thus often includes a depiction of feelings of sorrow or frustration caused by separation. The songs seldom depict a couple emigrating together: rather, one or another partner departs first, either promising to return after a certain amount of time or promising to send a ticket for the partner to follow later. Alternatively, the emigrant's departure may spell the end of the relationship altogether. Such is perhaps the case in **song 32d**:

Heila tuli saattamaan
mua Hangon rantaan asti.
Meitä lähti merten taakse
koko laivalasti.

Laiva tummansininen
se Atlantilla seilaa.
Sillä laivalla tämäkin tyttö
reissaella meinaa.
—

Oh my boyfriend he came with me,
Hanko harbor to see.
And he saw me off with many,
sailing across the sea.

Ship of dark blue
on my passage I will cross the ocean.
Yes to sail on that fine vessel
is this maiden's notion.

Here it appears that a woman has chosen to emigrate, and she is escorted to the harbor by her boyfriend, who will remain behind in Finland. The song makes no prediction of what the woman's life will be like in the new land, other than to note the separation from family and lover that her departure will bring. Nor does the song intimate whether the boyfriend may someday follow. In Maija Mäenpää's 1946 ring dance song (**Song 40**) a woman is depicted choosing to leave Finland after a failed romance:

Jonsen mä saa sitä sellaasta poikaa,
jota minä toivottelen,
niin astun Amerikan laivahan
ja mennä hoilottelen.

Jonsen mä saa sitä sellaasta poikaa,
josta mä itte tykkään,
niin astun Amerikan laivahan
ja merehen sieltä hyppään.

—

If I can't get the boy that I dream of,
him that my heart does fancy,
I'll make my way to lands faraway,
and make that passage chancy.

If I can't get the boy that I dream of,
The boy who is my only one,
To America I'll go with no love,
And jump into the ocean.

The short song portrays America as a place to go if one's romantic life in Finland fails. And in **Song 48**, the number of women who have taken this step is described as numerous, so that men back in Finland are anxious to follow:

Mennähästä poijat me Amerikkahan
flikat on menny jo aikaa.
Niiden on siellä ikävä
ja meitä ne sinne kaipaa.

—

Boys, America is calling us,
don't you know the girls they all have gone there.
They are all waiting there just for us,
oh those girls are feeling so forlorn there.

Where songs such as these present separation as a regrettable but inevitable element of migration, other songs assign blame to characters for the misery caused by separation. In Irja Kuoppala's **Song 52**, a female speaker expresses her outrage at being asked to wait for an extended period for her boyfriend to either send for her or to return himself to Finland:

Heila on menny Amerikhan
ja flikka on Amerikan-leski.
Vaikka se olis sielä viisitoista vuotta
niin orotella mun käski.

—

My true love's gone away and left me behind,
a widow's life, no debating.
He told me to patient be if
fifteen long years I'm waiting.

Tiila Ilkka's 1950 **Song 41** depicts a woman half-way through such a waiting period, as she wonders whether or not the wait will result in the promised marriage:

Ja heila meni Amerikkaan,
ja minä jäin kun leski.
Kaksitoista vuotta minun vartoella käski,
sun rallalalei, rali, rallalalei, pojat narrailee.

Ja kuusi vuotta on kulunut,
ja se on toinen puoli.
Enkä minä sillä välin varaheilasta huoli,
sun rallalalei, rali, rallalalei, pojat narrailee.
—
Passage 'cross the sea my lover boldly he has taken
And I'm left behind just like a widow, sad, forsaken.
"Wait for me for twelve years, oh our love will be unshaken!"
Sun rallalalei, rali, rallalalei, oh the tricks boys play.

Six long years have passed and I've not taken me another,
Twelve years is a sentence that is not like any other.
I am stuck at home just with my father and my mother.
Sun rallalalei, rali, rallalalei, oh the tricks boys play.

Song 32c presents a similar situation, in which the singer recounts having received a letter that asks her to wait fully fifteen years:

Heila kirjeen kirjoitti
Ja käski odotella.
Viisitoista ajastaikaa
Käski vartoella.

Kuusi vuotta kulunut
On vasta toinen puoli.
Enhän mina vielä tänä vuonna
Varaheiliä huoli.
—
My boyfriend wrote me,
asking me to wait for him a while oh.
He said just wait fifteen years
and then we'll be together
and that has just cramped my style, oh.

Six years have now passed
and I know I'm only halfway there, woe.
But I'm still not gonna find a temporary boyfriend
But my, how the time goes slow, oh.

The song inserts a surprising happy ending however in its final stanza, in which the wayward boyfriend is depicted finally sending a ticket so that his bride can join him:

Heila mulle tiketin laittoo
Amerikan maasta.
Käski lähtiä seilaamahan
Hangon satamasta.
—

My boyfriend sent a ticket
for my passage to that land, oh.
Now I'm headed for the high seas and I'll be a'sailing
From Hanko harbor strand, oh.

Feelings of longing are natural in protracted separations, and these yearnings find frequent portrayal in the ring songs. Typical is **Song 46**:

Voi kun mä saisin ne Atlannin aallot
yksin luetuksi,
että mä saisin sen oman kullan
sylihini sulietuksi.
—

Oh, if I could only go cross the Atlantic
to where my true love is living,
Then I could finally show my devotion
Hugs and kisses I would be giving.

In **Song 45**, Miina Takala's speaker counsels her listeners not to dwell on such sorrow, which is now irreparable:

Mitäpä surulla viettäisimme,
näitä nuoruuren aikojamme.

Kun kahren puolen Atlannin merta,
on meiränkin heilojamme.
—

Why should we give our hearts to sorrow
We're young and we are living?

We're by an ocean separated
but why should we be mourning?

Collected in 1946, the song seems to acknowledge a sense of normalcy regarding separations occasioned through temporary or permanent emigration. Losing one's lover through migration is neither unexpected nor entirely cataclysmic so long as one is still young and has time and means of finding enjoyment. Songs like these could easily have played roles in helping people process the strains and complexities of prolonged separation, particularly in a Finland in which open discussion of feelings still could be regarded as improper or uncomfortable.

The Dance Hall Beckons

A feature common to many ring songs included in this anthology is their description of American dance halls. As Ellen Luoma shows[1], the American dance hall offered Finnish migrants an

---

1   Luoma 1979

entirely novel means of conducting courtship. Sustained couples dances like the waltz or polka afforded a different degree and mode of physical intimacy than what had been common in ring or set dances in Finland[1]. At the same time, dance halls also provided a different context for the initiation of romantic relationships, freed of the Old World considerations of landedness, inheritance, social status and family reputation. In the public dance hall, potential partners could appraise each other openly and choose partners on the basis of criteria like charm, appearance, and dancing ability[2]. A couple that enjoyed dancing together might eventually marry in a social system based not on landed title but on cash earnings, personal work, and individual choice. Ring songs collected in Finland signal an awareness of the license and liberation afforded by the American dance hall and the new norms of self assertion and enjoyment they provided.

Dance halls are seldom described in detail in ring songs, apart from mention of floors painted yellow, perhaps a reference to the ostentatious gilding of urban dance hall interiors in wealthy venues like New York City, or the novel floor coverings that were replacing wooden floorboards in many such establishments. Typical is the description included in **Song 32d**:

Amerikan rannass' on tanssimalava
se on maalattu keltaiseksi.
Siellä on moni mammanpoika
ruvennu herraiseksi.

—

Dance halls in America are so fine
And they've all been a'painted yellow.
Many mama's boys they have sampled those joys
And they are fine fellows.

Tiila Ilkka includes a similar description in her **Song 42** of 1950:

Amerikan likkajen tanssilava
se on maalattu keltaiseksi.
Ja en oo ittiäni sanonukkaan
heilani vertaiseksi.

—

American girls on a floor for dancing
that is prettily painted yellow.
A'dancing we did go, I don't know
Am I a worthy fellow?

Ilkka's song continues to detail the kinds of courtship activities that could take place there:

Ja minä se heitin vanhan kullan
aivan muiren haltuun.
Ainakin niin kauvaksi
kun juoruämmät talttuu.

—

Dancing with my girl with a reckless twirl,
I let someone else there have her.
She then danced away the night
over nosy ladies' jabber.

---

1   Virtanen and DuBois 2000, 165–175
2   Luoma 1979, 36

The practice of changing partners—a compulsory part of the ring dance but not of more modern couples dances—has led the speaker to underestimate the forwardness and confidence of his girlfriend. As the song details, she has taken the opportunity of changing partners in a dance to explore new social relations, even to the point of attracting the gossip of nosy onlookers. In the new dance hall context, courtship success depends not only on family connections or status, but also on attentiveness to one's partner and skill in dancing. The importance of dancing skill for a man is underscored in Tiila Ilkka's "Amerikan polkka/American Polka" (**Song 43**):

Amerikan polokkan tahtia
ei sitä kaikki tairakkaan.
Joka ei taira polokan tahtia,
ei sitä likkaa nairakkaan.

Ollahan vain iloosia,
kun ei meill oo suruja.
Eikä joka poian vieres
taharo aika kulua.
—

Yankee polka has a rhythm that will
make many good feet falter.
If a man cannot do a good polka
he'll never reach the altar.

Let's be glad and cut the rug happily
we don't have any sorrows.
not every fellow's good on the dance floor
there are some sorry fellows.

Her song's speaker makes it clear that competence in dancing is a key avenue for winning a girl's heart, and that a man who can't dance is going to have troubles getting married. The fun of such a remark, of course, derives directly from the fact that one hears it while dancing, or attempting to dance, in the ring dance. That the imagined dance floor of the song is actually far away in America reflects the ways in which young people in Finland dreamed of a life far away from home, in the exciting and novel America that they knew of through songs and letters.

If America is a place where dance takes a more openly amorous form, it is also a place of moral compromise and danger. In **Song 42** we hear of the heavy drinking that goes on in American "hotels," a euphemism for the bars, saloons, and eventual (during Prohibition) speak-easies in which men might spend part or all of their hard-won earnings:

Ja varsa se sirottihin renkaaseen,
se koriasti hörähteli.
Poijat ne joivat Amerikan hotellissa,
lasit ne helähteli.

Ryyppyni ryyppään ja lauluni laulan
ja elän niin kuin tahron.
Kukas mua tämän kylän ämmät
elämänsä lahjoo.
—

What a fine strong foal there was tied to a pole
as we sat in a Yankee saloon.
The horse it neighed so lustily
as we clinked our glasses in tune.

I sing my song and I drink my fill
I just do as I am pleasing.
Who knows how many maidens fine
on a guy such as me are seizing?

Similarly, **Song 48** describes hotels open at all hours for carousing, a notion that must have both startled and intrigued rural Finns as they imagined life far away across the ocean.

The libertine potential of life in America is boisterously extolled in some songs, such as **Song 34**, recorded in the village of Korpela and preserved in the folklore archives of the Finnish Literature Society:

Amerikan flikkain huulet
on kuin syltynrasva.
Fiikunoita, rusinoita
Amerikas' kasvaa.
—
Ruby red lips, oh so lovely
On the pretty girls there.
Such tasty fruits that there await me,
I will sample everywhere.

Adapting the food metaphor found in other ring dance songs to a description of women, America is said to offer girls with lips like "syltynrasva" (the fat of head cheese) whom the speaker regards as "fiikunoita, rusinoita" (figs, raisins), just waiting to be sampled.

Within this wide-open society of dance, drink, and cavorting, the songs also make occasional reference to interracial encounters, sometimes exoticized and racist. **Song 38** mentions "neekerityttöjä" (Negro girls) as one of the delights of the new land:

Voi, kun mä saisin Amerikan rannalla
Ristipäädyss' asua.
Omenapuita ja neekerityttöjä
Amerikass' kasvaa.
—
Oh if I could be living there in that country,
far away from this native land of mine.
Apple trees there grow, girls are black there head to toe,
It's a land where the living is so fine.

The specification of race here and in other songs appears a means of signaling loose morals. **Song 35** states that the singer will find a "neekeriflikan" ("Negro girl") to marry. And in **Song 47**, Kalle V. Rintanen also employs the image, switching the sex of the Finn involved from male to female:

Eikä mun pappa eikä mun mamma
oo mua tuuritellu,
vaikka musta tulis Amerikas
neekeripojalle hellu.

—
No one cares about me here at home
Mom and dad don't me flatter.
But in that foreign land, I'll find for me a man
Blackskinned or white, it won't matter.

Consorting with people of other races figures in such songs as part of a wide array of libertine activities offered in the new country. Singers deftly sketch the mindsets and motives of emigrating youths and seem to revel in images of what was at the time considered to be improper and incautious. For audiences back in rural Finland at the end of the nineteenth or beginning of the twentieth century, the very notion of even meeting people of color must have seemed nearly unimaginable. Such images, of course, bear little relation to actual romances between Finnish immigrants and African Americans in North America, where Finns were neither more prone nor less prone to interracial marriages than other Nordic groups.

Lambasts and Lampoons
While most of the ring songs portray the migration experience in generalized, stereotypical manner, focusing on the feelings of unnamed but seemingly typical male or female speakers, singers occasionally seem intent on describing actual events and persons. Village gossip, adventures, and betrayals come to the fore in songs that reflect the fact that local women improvised song texts during performance. In **Song 54**, for instance, a song pieced together from verses supplied by Tiila Ilkka and Kerttu Talvitie, the speaker asks:

Oottakos te kuullu kuinka Kannuksen likkoja on
Amerikas onnestanu.
Ja yhyrell on tytär, ja toisell on poika,
ja kolomas ei oo viälä saanu.

Sellaisia terveisiä kun Peräkorven Jukka oli
Misikaanin valtiosta tuonu.
Kun hän ei ollu rahojansa hukanteille antanu,
oli saluunassa pelannu ja juonu.
—
Did you hear the news about the Kannus girls,
Now they've left their homeland here for another?
Oh, one she has a daughter, and one has a son,
And the third one she is not yet a mother.

That is what that Jukka Peräkorpi said when he came back
From the lumber camps in north Michigan. Oh,
What little money he still had in his pack,
It was what he had not given the barman.

Miina Takala has similarly saucy words about people she names in **Song 44** of 1946:

Mitähän se Kivimäen Jaska
ajatella mahtaa,
kun se tuon Huhtalan Ventlan
asemalle tahtoo.
—

Oh there goes Jaska Kivimäki,
courting he's a'headed.
It's that fine Ventla from Huhtala
to whom he'd get wedded.

The song depicts the unfaithful Jaska leaving Ventla behind with a newborn baby as he arrives in New York to start a new life, presumably without her:

Kivimäen Jaska se sanoo,
että voi voi herran tähären,
kun kehto rupiaa soutumahan,
niin Amerikkaan lähären.

Kivimäen Jaska, hoikka poika,
näitä lauluja laulaa,
kun ei se enää vetää saa
sen Huhtalan Ventlan kaulaa.
——
Now they have a little baby sleeping
in a cradle rocking.
Jaska's to America headed
in New York he's docking.

Jaska Kivimäki's boldly singing,
manners so appealing.
But poor Ventla knows his ways better
No more her heart he's stealing.

A similar tell-all strategy appears in **Song 53**, in which Irja Kuoppala sings of a dastardly Jussi Viitukka:

Viitukan Jussi se Amerikkaan
väärillä kirjoilla seilas.
Yhren flikan tuli paha olla,
että perähän se mennä meinas.

Jussi se sano sillen flikallen,
että hyvästi, ja voi vaan hyvin.
Viitukan Jussin raikas ääni kuulu
Härmän joen yli.
——
Viitukka's Jussi he went off to America
Falsified the papers for sailing.
Left behind a girl in such difficulties, she was
after him loudly wailing.

Jussi he gives that poor girl a sweet farewell, as
parting words he does deliver.
Jussi Viitukka his voice it does so cheerfully
sound over Härmä river.

It is difficult to know for certain whether such songs refer to actual people or verifiable transgressions. To some audiences the names and deeds may have been well-known, while to others they have been merely amusing details in a song performed during the ring dance. In any case, songs like these sketch once again the psychology and motivations of emigrants, depicting the intense feelings of betrayal or outrage that could sometimes accompany an emigrant's departure for America.

Metaphorical Flourishes

While often employing stock images as part of lines improvised and performed while dancing, ring songs sometimes display vivid natural imagery that seems to indicate a longer or more careful composition. In **Song 52**, Irja Kuoppala sings:

> Niin kun se vesi siellä kiehuvas koskes
> kiven ympäri kiertää,
> niin mun nuori syrämmeni
> maailmalle rientää.
>
> —
>
> Just like the water in the rushing rapid
> Flows 'round and 'round the rock,
> So is my young heart guided
> Alone in this world to walk.

Vivid images intensify the weightiness of the emotions depicted in the song, as the audience glimpses a speaker's subjective perceptions of the world, colored by powerful feelings. An equally striking image is provided in **Song 46** by Kalle V. Rintanen:

> Niinkuin ne kivet kylmiä on
> siellä järvessä jäitten alla,
> samanlainen se sydän on
> sillä pojalla reissaavalla.
>
> —
>
> Oh, like the stones lying cold under lake ice
> Emigrant boys uncaring
> Head to the sea and they think not about us,
> Leaving girls in their wake despairing.

In **Song 50**, Kerttu Talvitie waxes poetic with the stanza:

> Ruusut, ruusut, tulipunakukat,
> eikä ne kuki talavella.
> Eikä sitä viitti yhtä poikaa
> koko ikänsä palavella.
>
> —
>
> Roses red they just bloom in the spring;
> you won't find them blooming in winter time.
> And you'll not find me just one boy loving,
> I will not serve him a whole lifetime.

The metaphor here helps characterize a speaker who refuses to be limited by the situation in which finds herself. Like roses that refuse to bloom in winter, so she will refuse monogamous attachment to a single lover in a world in which men are both mobile and untrustworthy. In **Song 48**, Kerttu Talvitie presents a more pensive speaker, who recounts:

Mettän polokuja kulukeissani tuli vastahani kivi.
Siihempä oliki kiriootettu sen uuden ja vanhan nimi.

Ja mettän polokuja kulukeissani tuli vastahani mänty.
Ei mikää oo sen lämpöösempi kun oman kullan sänky.
—
Walking down the shady forest path suddenly an old stone looms before me.
Initials carven there, I can just make them out, old yet new they implore me.

Walking down the shady forest path suddenly an old pine looms before me.
Nowhere is warmer than lying by my true love, no nothing else restores me.

Poetic turns of phrase capture in fleeting and momentary images the enduring emotional strains and sorrows of a life marked by emigration. At the same time, rendered brief and pithy, and performed as part of social dance, such lyric images seem to mitigate feelings of sorrow, dismissing them as minor, while reminding an audience of fellow dancers of the fun-loving and adventurous nature of youth, abroad or *kotona*, back home.

32a. Piirileikkisikermä
Ring Dance Medley 1

The following medley of the most common ring dances collected in Alavus, Eura, Härmä, Kauhajoki, Kaustinen, Lapua, Ruotsinpyhtää, Saarijärvi, and Veteli. Melody from *Suomen kansan sävelmiä II. Laulusävelmiä.* Ed. Ilmari Krohn. Helsinki 1904–1933. Melody no. 1844, collected in Veteli, 1905.

Läh - te - käät - te   A - me - rik - kaan,   mi - nä läh - den   kans - sa.   Ei - kä ne   lai - vat
Head-ing   for A - mer - i - ca?   Well,   I   may tag a   long ___   Take it   from me, they're

tal - vel - la   sei - - - - laa   kun   tie   on   aal - loil - - lan - sa.
not   on   the sea,   when   the   win - ter waves   are   so   strong.

Lähtekäätte Ameriikkaan,	Heading for America?
minä lähden kanssa.	Well, I may tag along.
Eikä ne laivat talvella seilaa	Take it from me, they're not on the sea
kun tie on aalloillansa.	When the winter waves are so strong.
Minä menen Ameriikkaan	To America I will go
sinne menee kaikki.	There we're all headed for
Sokerisannalla sannoitettu	They all say the way's sugarcoated
on Ameriikan raitti.	That leads from here to that shore.
Musta meri avara	See the wide dark open ocean
se siniselle siiluu.	With its waves all of blue.
Englantilaisen laivan täkillä	As I'm standing on the ship deck
kulta Maarillen kiiluu.	I keep thinking of you.
Englannista Ameriikkaan	Clear from England there to State side
on se tervatouvi,	With the smell of ship tar.
jota myöten pojat lamppaa	They are yearning as they're sailing
Ameriikan krouviin.	For'n American bar.
En mä tiedä poijes tulost'	Don't be sure your boyfriend's gonna
siell' on niin helppoa työtä.	Leave his good job behind.
Rusinoita ja omenoita	Loads of raisins, pecks of apples
saa siellä pojat syödä.	Are what the boys there find.
Kun mä pääsen perille	When I get there I will send off
niin preivin sulle lykkään.	A long letter, you'll see.
Kysyn sulta, oma kulta	And I'll ask you how you are doing
vieläkö minusta tykkäät.	And are you still sweet on me?

32b.

Melody notated by Aatos Rinta-Koski no. 584, 1975.

Poi - jat ne me - nöö A - me - rik - ka - han niin fli - kool - len tu - loo su - ru, kun ne
Boys they are head - ing__ for A - mer - i - ca and girls they are feel - ing low.___ For af-

pää - söö At - lan - tin tuol - len puo - len, niin ho - tel - lis - ta lau - lu jo kuu - luu.
ter they cross the At - lan - tic o - cean they'll sing - ing to the ho - tel__ go.___

Poijat ne menöö Amerikkahan	Boys they are heading for America,
niin flikoollen tuloo suru.	and girls they are feeling low.
Kun ne pääsöö Atlantin tuollen puolen	For after they cross the Atlantic Ocean
niin hotellista laulu jo kuuluu.	They'll singing to the hotel go.
Poijat ne menöö Amerikasta	Boys when they're heading for America,
hakemahan rahaa.	It's money they're going for
Niin ei sitä tiedä lähteisnänsä	None of those boys know as they're sailing away
moniko sieltä takaasi palaa.	How many will come back to this shore.

32c.

Melody from Härmän laulukirja no. 306.

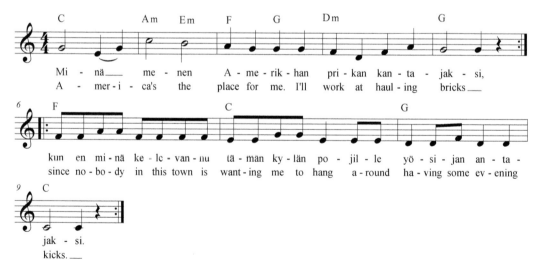

Mi - nä__ me - nen A - me - rik - han pri - kan kan - ta - jak - si,
A - mer - i - ca's the place for me. I'll work at haul - ing bricks__

kun en mi - nä ke - le - van - nu tä - män ky - län po - jil - le yö - si - jan an - ta -
since no - bo - dy in this town is want - ing me to hang a - round ha - ving some ev - ening

jak - si.
kicks. __

Minä menen Amerikhan prikan kantajaksi. Kun en minä kelvannu tämän kylän pojille yösijan antajaksi.	America's the place for me. I'll work at hauling bricks. Since nobody in this town is wanting me to hang around Having some evening kicks.
Minä menen Amerikhan mutten mensi vielä. Enkä mensi ollenkaan mutta henttuni on siellä.	America, ain't a place that I would gladly go. I would not be headed there for any sort of reason Except that my beau said so.
Heila kirjeen kirjoitti ja käski odotella. Viisitoista ajastaikaa käski vartoella.	My boyfriend wrote me, asking me to wait for him a while. He said just wait fifteen years and then we'll be together And live out our life in style.
Kuusi vuotta kulunut on vasta toinen puoli. Enhän minä vielä tänä vuonna varaheiliä huoli.	Six years have now passed and I've still got half the time to go. Well I'm still not gonna find a temporary boyfriend But my, how the time goes slow.
Heila mulle tiketin laittoo Amerikan maasta. Käski lähtiä seilaamahan Hangon satamasta.	My boyfriend sent a ticket for my passage to that land Now I'm headed for the high seas and I'll be a'sailing From Hanko-harbor strand.

32d.

Melody: Malisto-Sonninen: Karjalaisia kansanlauluja Kiihtelysvaarasta [Karelian folk songs from Kiihtelyssaari]. Published in Lappeenranta in 1978.

Han-ko-nie-mes pie-ni lai-va, sii-hen it-te-ni las-taan, Suo-mi ei voi
Han-ko ship is now a-wait-ing. I must soon climb a-board. I'm a child that

e-lät-tää näin köy-hän mam-man las-ta.
mo-ther Fin-land can no long-er af-ford.

Hankoniemes pieni laiva siihen itteni lastaan. Suomi ei voi elättää näin köyhän mamman lasta.	Heila tuli saattamaan mua Hangon rantaan asti. Meitä lähti merten taakse koko laivalasti.
Laiva tummansininen keltainen sen ovi. Sinä rikas minä köyhä, ei me yhtehen sovi.	Laiva tummansininen se Atlantilla seilaa. Sillä laivalla tämäkin tyttö reissaella meinaa.

Hanko ship is now awaiting.
I must soon climb aboard.
I'm a child that mother,
Finland can no longer afford.

Oh my boyfriend he came with me,
Hanko harbor to see.
And he saw me off with many,
Sailing across the sea.

Ship of dark blue, door of yellow,
On that vessel I see.
In your richness I am mindful
Of my great poverty.

Ship of dark blue on my passage
I will cross the ocean.
Yes to sail on that fine vessel
Is this maiden's notion.

32e.

Melody notated by Aatos Rinta-Koski no. 238, 1972.

A - me - ri - kan maa se on läm - min maa, mut - ta Suo - mi on vi - lun ar - ka.
Wea - ther in A - mer - i - ca is so warm but in Fin - land it's of - ten freez - ing.

A - me - ri - kan fli - kat ne sa - no - vat: "Voi, Suo - men poi - ka par - ka!"
"Oh poor Fin - nish boy!" say the mai - dens coy, when they want to be teas - ing.

Amerikan maa se on lämmin maa,
mutta Suomi on vilun arka.
Amerikan flikat ne sanovat
voi Suomen poika parka.

Weather in America is so warm
But in Finland it's often freezing.
"O poor Finnish boy," say the maidens coy,
When they want to be teasing.

Amerikan maahan mennä pitää
ison rahan tähden.
Sitte mä kerran laulelen
kun Suomen maasta lähden.

Travel to America for the pay
And that's why we have got to go.
This is what I'll sing when from Finland I sail
That's the truth I know.

Amerikan rannass' on tanssimalava
se on maalattu keltaiseksi.
Siellä on moni mammanpoika
ruvennu herraiseksi.

Dance halls in America are so fine
And they've all been a'painted yellow.
Many mama's boys they have sampled those joys
And they are fine fellows.

Amerikan rannan kaupunki
se hopialta hohtaa.
Siellä ne pojat halata saa
hattupäisiä kohta.

City on America's great coast line
How like silver it seems to glitter.
Maidens in fine hats who are good for hugging
Eagerly they'll twitter.

Amerikan maalla persikat kasvaa
Suomessa mustikoita.
Amerikan maalla taaloja vuollaan
mutta Suomessa kolikoita.

Farmers in America grow peaches
While in Finland there's just blueberries.
Pockets full of dollars are what they've got
While here just coins one carries.

33. Maailman avaralla
In the Wide World

Singer Ida Wahlroos of Juva, 1900. Conserved in the archives of the Finnish Literature Society/Kontio.

Maa - il - mal - la   a - va - ral - la   saat on - ne - si koit - taa: Saat ot - taa
On   your own in   this wide world oh   you must make your for - tune.   Grab your love

o - man kul - lan,   rai ral - la - la - lal - laa.
give 'em   a   twirl,   rai ral - la - la - lal - laa.

Maailmalla avaralla
Saat onnesi koittaa:
Saat ottaa oman kullan,
Rai rallalalallaa.

Minä lähden Amerikkaan,
Minnekäs sinä joudut?
Lähde sinäkin Amerikkaan
Rinkitanssin kouluun!

Amerikan alusmeri
Sininen kuin savu;
Amerikasta tänne saakka.
Kuuluu kultani laulu.

"Ruususeppel kiehkurainen
Kaunistaa sinun pääsi,
Ensi kesänä tulevana
Vietetään sinun hääsi."

On your own in this wide world,
Oh you must make your fortune.
Grab your love, give 'em a twirl,
Rai, rallalalallaa

I am off to America,
Where oh where will you go?
You can also come along,
Learn a ring dance song.

The Atlantic stretches vastly,
With its waves of dark blue.
From that shore to Finland's door,
Your love's song comes to you.

Wreath of roses, fresh and lovely,
They do crown your sweet head.
And we know how it will go,
Next summer you'll be wed.

34. Amerikkaan mina menen
To America I Go

Melody from *Suomen kansan sävelmiä II. Laulusävelmiä.* Ed. Ilmari Krohn. Published in Helsinki in 1904–1933. Melody no.1607, Teuva, 1889. Conserved in the archives of SKS/S. Korpela.

A - me - rik - kaan   mi - nä me - nen   tu - le   si - nä   kans - sa,   et - tä mam - man
To A - mer - i - ca___ I'll go,   please won't you come a - long? A pret - ty girl like

kau - niit fli - kat   kui - vais ko - ti - an - sa.
you, you know just   shouldn't be left a - lone.

Amerikkaan minä menen
tule sinä kanssa,
että mamman kauniit flikat
kuivais kotiansa.

Amerikkaan minä menen
aivan rahan tähden.
Ja vielä veisun kirkaasen
kun tästä kylästä lähden.

Amerikan flikkain huulet
on kuin syltynrasva.
Fiikunoita, rusinoita
Amerikas' kasvaa.

Amerikan meren yli
on tervattu touvi.
Sitä myöten poiat pyörii
Amerikan krouviin.

Musta meri sininen
ja siniseltä siintää
Amerikan ylävuorilla
Kultamaalilta kiiltää.

Iloisella mielellä
ja nauravaisella suulla.
Jätän minä tämän kylän
vaikkei taitta luulla.

To America I'll go.
Please won't you come along?
A pretty girl like you, you know,
Just shouldn't be left alone.

To America I'll go
Just to earn some money
A lovely song I'll happily sing though,
When I'm headed off to sea.

Ruby red lips, oh so lovely,
On the pretty girls there.
Such tasty fruits that there await me,
I will sample everywhere.

There's a massive, hulking tow rope,
Stretching across the sea.
The boys they follow, filled with such hope,
Then drink in taverns freely.

There the great blue sea is looming,
Shore of riches calls me.
Oh, mountains high, with gold are blooming,
Waiting there abundantly.

With a grin and laughing smile,
And a spirit happy,
I can't believe, in just a while,
I'll put this place behind me.

35. Eikä mun tääl ole hyvä olla
Things Are Not Good For Me Here

Melody from *Suomen kansan sävelmiä II. Lauhusävelmiä.* Ed. Ilmari Krohn. Published in Helsinki in 1904–1933. Melody no. 580, Southern Ostrobothnia, 1889. Conserved in the archives of the SKS/S. Korpela.

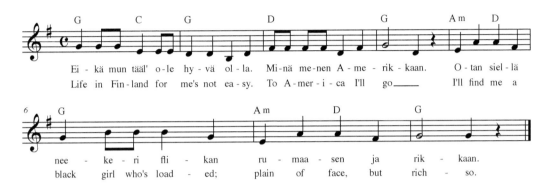

Ei - kä mun tääl' o - le hy - vä ol - la. Mi - nä me - nen A - me - rik - kaan. O - tan siel - lä
Life in Fin - land for me's not ea - sy. To A - mer - i - ca I'll go____ I'll find me a

nee - ke - ri fli - kan ru - maa - sen ja rik - kaan.
black girl who's load - ed; plain of face, but rich - so.

Eikä mun tääl' ole hyvä olla,	Life in Finland, for me's not easy.
minä menen Amerikkaan.	To America I'll go.
Otan siellä neekeriflikan	I'll find me a black girl who's loaded;
rumaasen ja rikkaan.	Plain of face, but rich so.
Amerikan maa se lämmin maa	America is so warm and steamy.
ja Suomi on hallan arka.	Finland it is frozen through.
Amerikan poiat surkenteloo	Yankee boys call "Girl, come on near me!"
Suomen tyttöparkaa.	'cause they're shivering too.
Eikä mua ilahuta hypyt eikä tanssit	Jumping and dancing don't make me happy.
eikä tämän kylän ämmään marsi.	Village strolls aren't in my plans.
Jolsei mua ilahuta henttuni siniset silmät	When my blue-eyed girl's standing by me.
ja lämmin käsivarsi.	We're just holding hands.
Amerikkaan nämä poiat	Boys sail away for to make their fortune.
olis omiansa.	Maidens they are left behind.
Että ne mamman kauniit tytöt	Pretty Finnish girls get no portion.
kuivaas kotiansa.	Wedding feasts won't find.
Amerikkaan nämä poiat	Boys sail away for to make their fortune,
menöö järjestänsä.	Planning for a life that's new.
Eikä ne sinne yksin mee	They don't head off all on their lonesome:
ne vievät ystävänsä.	Friends go with them too.

36. Ameriikkalaisen laivan pilli
The Whistle of an American Ship

Sung by Alppo Kinnunen. Melody from *Suomen kansan sävelmiä II. Laulusävelmiä*. Ed. Ilmari Krohn. Published in Helsinki in 1904–1933. Melody no. 400, Kerimäki, 1901. Conserved in the archives of the Finnish Literature Society/L. Soini.

A - me - riik - ka - lai - sen   lai - van   pil - li mun   kor - vi - hi - ni   kai - kuu,
I   can hear the ship's   loud   whis - tle   blow - ing   e - choes in   my   ear.

hoi - kan   so - ri - an   nei - ton   vie - reen se   tä - mäkin   poi - ka   vai - puu.
Time   has   come,   and this   lad   is   go - ing to leave   his   girl - friend   dear.

Ameriikkalaisen laivan pilli	I can hear the ship's loud whistle blowing,
mun korvihini kaikuu.	Echoes in my ear.
Hoikan sorian neiton viereen	Time has come, and this lad is going,
tämäkin poika vaipuu.	To leave his girlfriend dear.
Ameriikkalaisen laivan mastossa	I can see the Yankee flag hoisted high,
lippu liehuvainen.	Up on that ship's mast.
Nuorella pojalla sydän se on	Like in white water feelings fly,
kuin koski kuohuvainen.	My heart's a'beating fast.
Ameriikkalaisen laivan mastoa	Gently blows the wind on that mast,
tuuli se häilyttelee.	Rocking that fine boat.
Atlantin merellä jo vieterisohvassa	My true love's on the ocean so vast,
heilani keijuttelee.	To reach that land remote.
Ameriikkalaisen laivan kokka on	On that vessel's prow is paint of gold
maalattu keltaseksi.	Glistening like the sun.
Senkös tähden ne tämän kylän likat	Makes me think of those smiles so bold,
on tullu niin herttaseksi.	When girls back home have fun.
Ameriikan maa se on lämpimä maa	America, that's the place to be,
ja sinne mun tekee mieli,	Warm and sunny there.
kun Suomen maa näin nuorelle pojalle	Finland it's just too small a country to
on reissata liian pieni.	Keep me penned up here.
Voi minä hullu kun piljetin ostin	Foolishly a ticket I did buy,
ja läksin maailmalle.	Passage 'cross the sea.
Heilani jäi mun suremaan	Left my true love to weep and to cry,
tuonne Helsingin asemalle.	Back home in Helsinki.

37. Tytöt lähtee Turun rantaan
The Girls Go To Turku's Shore

Song sung, as with **Song 36**, by Alppo Kinnunen. Melody from *Suomen kansan sävelmiä II. Laulusävelmiä*. Edited by Ilmari Krohn in Helsinki in 1904–1933. Melody no. 1346, Kerimäki, 1901. Conserved in the archives of the Finnish Literature Society/L. Soini.

Ty - töt läh - tee Tu - run ran - taan poi - jes poi - ki - a pyy - tään, et - tei noi - ta
Girls are lin - ing Tur - ku har - bor tel - ling boy - friends "Oh please stay!" Fin - nish boys won't

Suo - men poi - ki - a A - me - riik - kaan vie - täis.
tar - ry long - er, they're off to the U S of A.

Tytöt lähtee Turun rantaan	Girls are lining Turku harbor,
poijes poikia pyytään,	Telling boyfriends "Oh please stay!"
ettei noita Suomen poikia	Finnish boys won't tarry longer,
Ameriikkaan vietäis.	They're off to the U S of A.
Ameriikassa, Ameriikassa	In America if you please
siell' on lysti olla.	Lots of fun times can be found.
Siellä sahat, siellä myllyt	Sawmills there and factories
käyvät kalliolla.	They're covering the rocky ground.
Lähde heilani Ameriikkaan	Head to America my dear
siell' on helppoa työtä.	Gainful work you will there do.
Rusinoita ja veskunoita	Sweets and raisins you will taste there.
Ameriikassa syödään.	It's such a life that waits for you.
Syksysellä järven jäällä,	Here the cold and snowy weather,
siell' on hyvä keli.	Freezes waters all through.
Ameriikassa valtameri	There the ocean freezes never,
on sininen kuin peili.	How warmly lap those waves of blue!
Sinä menet Ameriikkaan,	Go my dear to America,
mihinkäs minä joudun?	What is left here for this fool?
Lähde heilani Amerikkaan	With my love I do you send there,
rinkintanssikouluun.	I hope you find a dancing school!

38. Amerikan takana
Beyond America

Conserved in the archives of the Finnish Literature Society/M. Rinta. Isokyrö.

A - me - ri - kan ta - ka - na   At - lan - nin mer - el - lä, siel' on niin   pal - jon   vet - tä.
Far be-yond the sea stret-ches A-mer-i - ca free, the At - lan - tic it comes up in-be - tween.

Amerikan takana Atlannin merellä,
siell' on niin paljon vettä.
Sinne saa mennä sellaiset,
jotka ystävänsä pettää.

Far beyond the sea stretches America free,
The Atlantic, it comes up in-between.
That's the place for folk, who ditch others, it's no joke,
It's the land that all immigrants have seen.

Amerikan heijani valkoista tukkaan
Tuuli huiskuttelee.
Kun se kävelee maata ja vettä
ja mua vain muistuttelee.

There upon the shore walks the one that I adore,
As the breeze brushes gently white-blond hair.
Walking by the sea, does my true love think of me?
Wish I knew if that one for me does care.

Voi, kun mä saisin Amerikan rannalla
Ristipäädyss' asua.
Omenapuita ja neekerityttöjä
Amerikass' kasvaa.

Oh if I could be living there in that country,
Far away from this native land of mine.
Apple trees there grow, girls are black there head to toe,
It's a land where the living is so fine.

39. Kun poijat ne astuu
When Boys Step

Kuortane 1907. Eteläpohjalaisten laulukirja no. 230. Published in Jyväskylä in 1931.

Kun   poi - jat ne as - tuu   ma - sii - na - hanniin ma - sii - na al - la   huu - taa,
When boys they all step a - board the car - riage   loud - ly the whist - le   screams.

hy - väs - ti   nyt   tä - män ky - län fli - kat___   ei - kä nyt e - nää   muu - ta.
Fare - well girls, there won't be a - ny marr - iag - es, tears just and bro - ken   dreams.

Kun poijat ne astuu masiinahan niin
masiina alla huutaa
hyvästi nyt tämän kylän flikat,
eikä nyt enää muuta,

When boys they all step aboard the carriage,
Loudly the whistle screams.
Farewell girls, there won't be any marriages,
Tears just, and broken dreams.

Kun poijat ne astuu laivahan,
niin laiva se vetehen painuu,
kun flikat ne rannalla itkivät,
jotta vesi se merehen painuu.

Then boys they all step aboard the steamship
Ponderously weighted down.
Into the waves salty teardrops drip,
As the girls by the dockside frown.

40. Järven rannalla sorsikkoheinäs
On the Lake Shore in the Duckweed

Singer Maija Mäenpää, 1946. Härmän laulukirja no. 283.

Jär - ven__ ran - nal - la sor - sik - ko - hei - näs lau - le - li sor - san poi - ka.
Out by the lake shore and down by the duck - weed lone - some a duck is cal - ling.

yh - ren__ poi - jan mie - len__ muk - han mi - nä vain ol - la koi - tan.
I want to see that boy that I need, he is the one I'm re - cal - ling.

Järven rannalla sorsikkoheinäs
lauleli suorsan poika.
Yhren poijan mielen mukhan
minä vain olla koitan.

Jonsen mä saa sitä sellaasta poikaa,
jota minä toivottelen,
niin astun Amerikan laivahan
ja mennä hoilottelen.

Jonsen mä saa sitä sellaasta poikaa,
josta mä itte tykkään,
niin astun Amerikan laivahan
ja merehen sieltä hyppään.

Out by the lake shore and down in the duckweed
Lonesome a duck is calling.
I want to see that boy that I need,
He is the one I'm recalling.

If I can't get the boy that I dream of
Him that I'd gladly marry
Off to America I will go,
Here I will no longer tarry.

If I can't get the boy that I dream of
Him that my heart does fancy
I'll make my way to lands faraway
And make that passage chancy.

If I can't get the boy that I dream of
The boy who is my only one
To America I'll go with no love
And jump into the ocean.

41. Juhannuksen aikana
Over Midsummer

Singer Tiila Ilkka, 1950. Alavuden laulukirja no. 244.

Ju - han - nuk - sen   ai - ka - na   on   il - ma   läm - pi - mäm - pi,   vii - ren - tois - ta
Mid - sum - mer   has   come and how   the   sun shines e - ver   bright - er.   Mai - den when she's

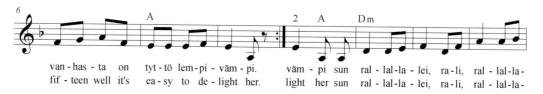

van - has - ta   on   tyt - tö lem - pi - väm - pi.   väm - pi sun   ral - lal - la - lei, ra - li, ral - lal - la -
fif - teen well   it's   ea - sy to de - light her.   light her sun   ral - lal - la - lei, ra - li, ral - lal - la -

lei, po - jat nar - rai - lee.
lei, oh the tricks boys play.

Juhannuksen aikana on ilma lämpimämpi,
viirentoista vanhasta on tyttö lempivämpi,
sun rallalalei, rali, rallalalei, pojat narrailee.

Ja heila meni Amerikkaan,
ja minä jäin kun leski.
Kaksitoista vuotta minun vartoella käski,
sun rallalalei, rali, rallalalei, pojat narrailee.

Ja kuusi vuotta on kulunut,
ja se on toinen puoli.
Enkä minä sillä välin varaheilasta huoli,
sun rallalalei, rali, rallalalei, pojat narrailee.

Ja heila meni Amerikkaan santajunan päällä,
ja santajunan päällä.
Ja pikkulinnut suruissansa laulelevat täällä,
sun rallalalei, rali, rallalalei, pojat narrailee.

Midsummer has come and now the sun shines ever brighter.
Maiden when she's fifteen well it's easy to delight her.
Sun rallalalei, rali, rallalalei, oh the tricks boys play.

Passage 'cross the sea my lover boldly he has taken
And I'm left behind just like a widow, sad, forsaken.
"Wait for me for twelve years, oh our love will be unshaken!"
Sun rallalalei, rali, rallalalei, oh the tricks boys play.

Six long years have passed and I've not taken me another,
Twelve years is a sentence that is not like any other.
I am stuck at home just with my father and my mother.
Sun rallalalei, rali, rallalalei, oh the tricks boys play.

To America my lover headed, oh so gladly
Yes he rode a train there, and he did so, oh so gladly.
While the little birds here they are singing, oh so sadly.
Sun rallalalei, rali, rallalalei, oh the tricks boys play.

42. Amerikan likkojen tanssilava
American Girls' Dance Floor

As with **Song 41**, Singer Tiila Ilkka, 1950. Alavuden laulukirja no. 3.

Amerikan likkajen tanssilava
se on maalattu keltaiseksi.
Ja en oo ittiäni sanonukkaan
heilani vertaiseksi.

Ja minä se heitin vanhan kullan
aivan muiren haltuun.
Ainakin niin kauvaksi
kun juoruämmät talttuu.

Tierän heilani komian luonnon,
se pakkaa paremmille.
Ja monta kertaa on horjahtanu
muakin huonommille.

Ja varsa se sirottihin renkaaseen,
se koriasti hörähteli.
Poijat ne joivat Amerikan hotellissa,
lasit ne helähteli.

Ryyppyni ryyppään ja lauluni laulan
ja elän niin kuin tahron.
Kukas mua tämän kylän ämmät
elämänsä lahjoo.

American girls on a floor for dancing
That is prettily painted yellow.
A' dancing we did go, I don't know
Am I a worthy fellow?

Dancing with my girl with a reckless twirl,
I let someone else there have her.
She then danced away the night
Over nosy ladies' jabber.

She's a pretty girl and I know for certain,
That much better than me she's gotten.
Then again that is how things go.
She has had others just as rotten.

What a fine strong foal there was tied to a pole
As we sat in a Yankee saloon.
The horse it neighed so lustily,
As we clinked our glasses in tune.

I sing my song and I drink my fill,
I just do as I am pleasing.
Who knows how many maidens fine
On a guy such as me are seizing?

43. Amerikan polkka
America's Polka

As with Songs 41 and 42, Singer Tiila Ilkka, 1950. Alavuden laulukirja no. 312.

A - me - ri - kan po-lok-kan tah - ti - a ei si - tä kaik - ki tai-rak-kaan
Yan - kee pol - ka has a rhy - thm that will make ma-ny good feet fal - ter.

Jo-ka ei tai - ra po-lo-kan tah - ti - a ei si - tä lik - kaa nai-rak-kaan.
If a man can - not do a good pol - ka____ he'll ne - ver reach the al - tar.

Amerikan polokkan tahtia ei sitä kaikki tairakkaan. Joka ei taira polokan tahtia, ei sitä likkaa nairakkaan.	Yankee polka has a rhythm that will Make many good feet falter. If a man cannot do a good polka, He'll never reach the altar.
Ollahan vain iloosia, kun ei meill oo suruja. Eikä joka poian vieres taharo aika kulua.	Let's be glad and cut the rug happily, We don't have any sorrows. Not every fellow's good on the dance floor, There are some sorry fellows.
Amerikan laivat seilaa hopiaisella sillalla. Ja poijat ne saa maata panna heilansa viereen illalla.	Yankee ships they sail away far away, Crossing the mighty sea. In the night fellows hopefully, luckily, With their girls will be.
Ja ollahan vaan iloisia, jottei suru voittaisi. Ja mielelläni minä toisen likan heilaa vähän hoitaisin.	Let's be glad and cut the rug happily, Hearts in the dance we'll send. Leave it for sometime off in the morning To deal with an angry boyfriend.
Näiren likkain raikuva rinta on niin heleppo raikumaan. Se saattaa monta mamman poikaa perähänsä vaipumaan.	Lovely girl, she sings a song prettily. Many a fellow'd take her. If a guy could be by her side for the night, Oh, how he'd thank his maker!
Ollahan vain iloisia vaikkei meistä tykätä. Jos ei saara vetämällä, otetaan ja lykätään.	Let's be glad and cut the rug happily, Hopefully then our hearts will meet. But if our looks don't win the day handily, Victory we'll get by fancy feet.

44. Mitähän se Kivimäen Jaska
Wonder What that Jaska of Kivimäki Thinks

Singer Miina Takala, 1946. Härmän laulukirja no. 94.

Mitähän se Kivimäen Jaska
ajatella mahtaa,
kun se tuon Huhtalan Ventlan
asemalle tahtoo.

Kun masiina huuti ensi kerran,
niin Huhtalan Ventla itki,
kun Jaska se lähti ajamaan
sitä rautatietä pitkin.

Huhtalan isoolla Hermannilla
on tytär hoikka ja soria.
Kivimäen Jaska friiarina
pikkuunen ja koria.

Kivimäen Jaska se sanoo,
että voi voi herran tähären,
kun kehto rupiaa soutumahan,
niin Amerikkaan lähären.

Kivimäen Jaska, hoikka poika,
näitä lauluja laulaa,
kun ei se enää vetää saa
sen Huhtalan Ventlan kaulaa.

Oh there goes Jaska Kivimäki,
Courting he's a'headed.
It's that fine Ventla from Huhtala
To whom he'd get wedded.

Loudly blaired the engine whistle
As that Jaska's train was leaving.
Then that fine Ventla from Huhtala's
Heart with fear was heaving.

Down there in the village lives old Herman
Ventla is his daughter.
Little charming suitor Jaska
In his snares he's caught her.

Now they have a little baby sleeping
In a cradle rocking.
Jaska's to America headed,
In New York he's docking.

Jaska Kivimäki's boldly singing,
Manners so appealing.
But poor Ventla knows his ways better,
No more her heart he's stealing.

45. Kun mina olsin kryytimaasta
As I Was from the Door Garden

As with **Song 44**, Singer Miina Takala, 1946. Härmän laulukirja no. 286.

Kun mi - nä ol - sin kryy - ti - maas - ta, kun mi - nä ol - sin kryy - ti - maas - ta ja
Since I was born with - in a gar - den, since I was born with - in a gar - den, oh

kun mi - nä ol - sin kryy - ti - maas - ta se ää - rim - mäi - nen kuk - ka.
since I was born with - in a gar patch I was a pret - ty flow - er.

Kun minä olsin kryytimaasta,
kun minä olsin kryytimaasta
ja kun minä olsin kryytimaasta
se äärimmäinen kukka.

Since I was born within a garden
Since I was born within a garden
And since I was born within a garden,
I was a pretty flower.

Yksi poika muakin varten,
yksi poika muakin varten,
yksi poika muakin varten
syntyny olis hukkaan.

There's just one boy who's meant to have me
There's just one boy who's meant to have me
There's just one boy who's meant to have me
To sorrow he's been fated.

Niin palion kun mua prissattu on,
niin palion kun mua prissattu on,
niin palion kun mua prissattu on
sen yhren poijan tähren.

They dolled me up just for that suitor
They dolled me up just for that suitor
They dolled me up just for that suitor
So that he'd take me gladly.

Kun veret ikään aukenoo,
kun veret ikään aukenoo,
kun veret ikään aukenoo
niin Amerikhan lähären.

Sailing away on the Atlantic
Sailing away on the Atlantic
Sailing away on the Atlantic
I'm off to America.

Mitäpä surulla viettäisimme,
mitäpä surulla viettäisimme,
mitäpä surulla viettäisimme
näitä nuoruuren aikojamme.

Why should we give our hearts to sorrow
Why should we give our hearts to sorrow
Why should we give our hearts to sorrow
We're young and we are living?

Kun kahren puolen Atlannin merta,
kun kahren puolen Atlannin merta,
kun kahren puolen Atlannin merta
on meiränkin heilojamme.

We're by an ocean separated
We're by an ocean separated
We're by an ocean separated
but why should we be mourning?

46. Voi kun mä saisin ne Atlannin aallot
Oh, if I Could Get the Waves of the Atlantic

Singer Kalle V. Rintanen, 1960. Härmän laulukirja no. 361. Additional lyrics noted by Aatos Rinta-Koski from farmwife Kerttu Talvitie (born 1912) of Kauhajoki. No. 1482, 1981.

Voi kun mä sai-sin ne At-lan-nin aal-lot yk-sin___ lu-e-tuk-si,
If I could on-ly go cross the At-lan-tic to where my true love's liv-ing,

et-tä mä sai-sin sen o-man kul-lan sy-li-hi-ni su-li-e-tuk-si.
then I could fi-nal-ly show my de-vo-tion hugs and kis-ses I would be giv-ing.

Voi kun mä saisin ne Atlannin aallot
yksin luetuksi,
että mä saisin sen oman kullan
sylihini sulietuksi.

Voi kun ne Atlannin kuohuvat aallot
veis minun ikäväni.
Jättäisin minä papan ja mamman
ja syntymäpitäjäni.

Eikä ne Atlantin kuohuvat aallot
kasva sinikukkaa.
Moni poika vasituista heilaa
lempii aivan hukkaan.

Eikä ne Atlantin kuohuvat aallot
kasva ruusuja punaisia,
vaikka ne tuutii Amerikan rantaan
poikia tuhansia.

Niinkuin ne kivet kylmiä on
siellä järvessä jäitten alla,
samanlainen se sydän on
sillä pojalla reissaavalla.

Oh, if I could only go cross the Atlantic,
to where my true love's living,
Then I could finally show my devotion,
Hugs and kisses I would be giving.

Oh, how the waves of the deep blue Atlantic
Would wash away my sorrow.
Mother and father I'd gladly abandon,
Finland I would give up tomorrow.

Oh, on the waves of the foaming Atlantic,
Flowers of blue aren't growing.
Many a boy, a girl's heart he has broken,
Callously into the sea throwing.

Oh, on the waves of the foaming Atlantic,
Red flowers don't grow either.
Thousands of boys to the seas they have taken,
They've all caught American fever.

Oh, like the stones lying cold under lake ice,
Emigrant boys uncaring.
Head to the sea and they think not about us,
Leaving girls in their wake despairing.

47. Laivan päällä on lysti olla
It Is Fun to Be on the Ship

Singer Kalle V Rintanen, 1960. Härmän laulukirja no. 301. Additional lyrics from Kustaa Etelämäki, 1962, as published in Härmän laulukirja no. 80.

Lai - van pääl - lä on lys - ti ol - la sil - loon kun se ___ sou - tuu.
It is fun on this ship we're sail - ing, in the waves we are rock - ing.

Mi - täs on vä - li - ä täl - lää - sen ha - li - un mil - lek - kä maal - le se
E - ven if I don't know when we will reach our goal or where at last we'll be

jou - tuu.
dock - ing.

Laivan päällä on lysti olla
silloon kun se soutuu.
Mitäs on väliä tällääsen haliun
millekkä maalle se joutuu.

Alahalta tuomesta oksia taitan,
ja niitä mä istuttelen.
Kaikille tämän kylän hilisuille
minä onnea toivottelen.

Ja luulhan ett on lysti olla,
kun minä aina laulan.
Laulullani minä pienet surut
syrämmeni pohjahan painan.

Eikä mun pappa eikä mun mamma
oo mua tuuritellu,
vaikka musta tulis Amerikas
neekeripoijalle hellu.

It is fun on this ship we're sailing,
In the waves we are rocking.
Even if I don't know when we will reach our goal
Or where at last we'll be docking.

From a branch of a tree at my home,
I will pluck a ripe cherry.
As I leave family, that seed I'll bring with me,
Planting the tree that I carry.

When I sing in this happy manner,
Joyfulness I am faking.
In my song artfully, sorrows you'll never see,
Hiding my heart that is aching.

No one cares about me here at home,
Mom and dad don't me flatter.
But in that foreign land, I'll find for me a man,
Blackskinned or white, it won't matter.

48. Mettän polokuja kulkeissani
When Walking on Forest Paths

Aatos Rinta-Koski from farmwife Kerttu Talvitie (born 1912) of Kauhajoki. No. 1485, 1981.

Met - tän   po - lo - ku - ja   ku - lu - keis - sa - ni   tu - li   vas - ta - ha - ni   ki - vi.
Walk - ing   down the shad - y   for - est path   sud - den - ly   an   old stone looms be - fore me.

Sii - hem - pä   o - li - ki   ki - ri - oo - tet - tu   sen   uu - den ja van - han   ni - mi.
in - it - ials car - ven there,   I can just make them out,   old yet___ new im - plore me.

Mettän polokuja kulukeissani tuli vastahani kivi.
Siihempä oliki kiriootettu sen uuden ja vanhan nimi.

Ja mettän polokuja kulukeissani tuli vastahani mänty.
Ei mikää oo sen lämpöösempi kun oman kullan sänky.

Mennähästä poijat me Amerikkahan flikat on menny jo aikaa.
Niiden on siellä ikävä ja meitä ne sinne kaipaa.

Jos teidän flikat tää paha tuloo olla niin ajakaa te masiinalla.
Kun kuudesta, kuutehen hotellit on auki joka asemalla.

Amerikan rannas' tanssilava se on maalattu keltaaseksi.
Siellä on niin moni mamman poika ruvennu herraaseksi.

Amerikan rannas on tanssimalava, voi jes, kun on hyvä olla.
Eikä mun lauluni kauaa kuulu tämänkylän vainiolla.

Walking down the shady forest path suddenly an old stone looms before me.
Initials carven there, I can just make them out, old yet new implore me.

Walking down the shady forest path suddenly an old pine looms before me.
Nowhere is warmer than lying by my true love, no nothing else restores me.

Boys, America is calling us, don't you know the girls they all have gone there.
They are all waiting there just for us, oh those girls are feeling so forlorn there.

If you girls are feeling out of sorts then you can just head to the train station.
There you will surely find hotels big, ballrooms fine, open at each location.

In America where everything is so fine the dance floors they are yellow.
That is the place where a mama's boy can become oh quite a fancy fellow.

In America where everything is so fine, oh yes, to dance I'm eager.
that is the place for me, village life can't hold me, no more you'll me beleaguer.

49. Merellä olen mina syntynyt
I Have Been Born on the Sea

Aatos Rinta-Koski from farmwife Kerttu Talvitie (born 1912) of Kauhajoki. No. 240, 1972.

Me - rel - lä   o - len mi - nä   syn - ty - nyt hei   him - pu - ta rim - pun,   rim - pun   pi la pi - la
I   got my start out on the   great blue   sea hei   him - pu - ta rim - pun,   rim - pun   pi - la pi - la

Me - rel - lä   o - len mi - nä   syn - ty - nyt ja   lai - val - la o - len   mi - nä   luo - tu.
I   got my start out on the   great blue   sea yes,   born out on a great   sail - ing   ves - sel.

Merellä olen minä syntynyt
Hei himputa rimpun, rimpun pila pila.
Merellä olen minä syntynyt
Ja laivalla olen minä luotu.

Amerikan laivan kannella
Hei himputa rimpun, rimpun pila pila,
Amerikan laivan kannella
On ristiäiseni juotu.

Amerikan laivan maston nenäss'
Hei himputa rimpun, rimpun pila pila
Amerikan laivan maston nenäss'
Ne pummulivillat liehuu.

Siellä ne kuparipellin päällä
Hei himputa rimpun, rimpun pila pila,
Siellä ne kuparipellin päällä
Amerikankahvit kiehuu.

Nuoren meripojan sydän on
Hei himputa rimpun, rimpun pila pila
Nuoren meripojan sydän on
Kuin koski kuohuvainen.

Amerikan rantaan kun saavutaan
Hei himputa rimpun, rimpun pila pila
Amerikan rantaan kun saavutaan
Niin mastohon nousee lippu liehuvainen.

I got my start out on the great blue sea,
Hei rimputa rimpun, rimpun pila pila
I got my start out on the great blue sea,
Yes, born on a great sailing vessel.

On a ship bound for great America,
Hei rimputa rimpun, rimpun pila pila
On a ship bound for great America,
Yes there as a baby I was baptized.

On an American ship's tall main mast,
Hei rimputa rimpun, rimpun pila pila
On an American ship's tall main mast,
That's where the cotton sails they do flutter.

There on that stove of copper coffee boils,
Hei rimputa rimpun, rimpun pila pila
There on that stove of copper coffee boils,
It's warming the American sailors.

Young sailor's heart it is a'racing so,
Hei rimputa rimpun, rimpun pila pila
Young sailor's heart it is a'racing so,
Just like a mighty surging spring river.

Once in the American harbor safe,
Hei rimputa rimpun, rimpun pila pila
Once in the American harbor safe,
They hoist up aloft that great Old Glory.

50. Piian pestin mä ottanut olen
I Have Taken the Position of a Maid

Aatos Rinta-Koski from farmwife Kerttu Talvitie (born 1912) of Kauhajoki. No. 494, 1974.

Piian pestin mä ottanu olen
ja palvella sen meinaan vaan.
Enkä minä vielä tänä vuonna
Atlannin merellä seilaakkaan.

Vaikkei mun poskeni punota,
mutta sen sanon ett' olen ehtaa vaan.
Ja sen minä teille tänkylän poijat
sanua kyllä kehtaan vaan.

Ruusut, ruusut, tulipunakukat,
eikä ne kuki talavella.
Eikä sitä viitti yhtä poikaa
koko ikänsä palavella.

Seitsemänkymmentäseitsemän laivaa
Atlantinmerellä seilaajaa.
Seitsemän kertaa seitsemän poikaa
tämä flikka narrata meinajaa.

Enköstä minä viä tänäkää vuonna
Amerikan rantahan seilaakaan.
Kun jumala on luonu mun piianrompiksi
syrpyskoppia kantamahan.

I have found me a job in a big house
Oh, as a serving girl I must toil.
No Atlantic trip is slated for me,
I'll have to stay here on Finnish soil.

Though my cheeks they are no longer red
I will say I'm young, hearty, and so hale.
That is what I'll say to you village boys
Though from these shores I would gladly sail.

Roses red they just bloom in the spring
You won't find them blooming in winter time.
And you'll not find me just one boy loving,
I will not serve him a whole lifetime.

Seventy-seven ships they will sail,
Far across the mighty Atlantic grand.
That's how many lonely men there are,
That this serving girl she will sure command.

No ticket is a' waiting for me,
Just a serving girl's life that is my lot.
Others they may cross the Atlantic
But I am stuck here changing chamberpots.

51. Pilvet on taivahalla
Clouds Are in the Sky

Aatos Rinta-Koski from farmwife Kerttu Talvitie (born 1912) of Kauhajoki. No. 529, 1974.

Pilvet on taivahalla, tähdet on taivahalla,	Clouds up there in the sky, and stars up there in the sky,
keskellä palaa rurjat.	Those fires they are brightly burning.
Enkä sure henttuni päiviä,	There is no one I will be pining for;
vaikka ne on niin kurjat.	I am for no one yearning.
Se ilta oli pimiä ja taivahalla paloo	Oh how the night was dark although many stars were shining
ne lukemattomat tähäret.	Up in the sky they shone down,
Enkä minä saattanut hyvästiä jättää	When you gave me no chance to say farewell,
kun viimeisen kerran lähärit.	When you were leaving this town.
Taloo oli komia ja poikaki niin soria	Grand was the house they offered,
ja molemmat mä olisin saanu.	handsome the boy they proffered,
Sitä hommas paappa ja sitä touhus mamma	Nicely I would be married.
mutta minä kun en rakastanu.	But though parents both they did urge me on,
	For him no love I carried.
Ne lehdet, jokka syksyllä varisoo	Autumn leaves they are falling, turning so many colors
ne on niin heleveniä.	Orange, and red and yellow.
Ne aijat, joita pois en mielestä saa	Oh those vivid memories linger on,
ne on aikoja mennehiä.	I still can see that fellow.
Poika se lähtöö Amerikkaan	He's headed off across the sea, there's no coming back to me,
ja ei sitä nähärä kauan.	Far away he's travelled.
Surevaaselle heilalleni	And I'm singing for him this mournful song,
tämän lähtölaulun laulan.	All of my hopes unravelled.

52. Niin kun se vesi
Like the Water

Singer Irja Kuoppala, 1975. Härmän laulukirja no. 312.

Niin kun se ve - si siel - lä kie - hu - vas kos - kes ki - ven ym - pä - ri kier - tää
Like rush-ing wa-ter in a swift surg-ing ra - pid round a rock is a' flow - ing,

niin mun nuo - ri sy - räm - me - ni maa - il - mal - le rien - tää.
So my young heart rac - ces ev - er: out in the world it's go - ing.

Niin kun se vesi siellä kiehuvas koskes
kiven ympäri kiertää,
niin mun nuori syrämmeni
maailmalle rientää.

Eikä mun saisi eikä kannattaisi
kolomia rakastella,
kun itte mä oon kun paimenflikka,
ja heilani on kun herra.

Enkä minä viitti työtä teherä
Kyyrän vainiolla,
kun Amerikas on niin hyvä olla
ja heleppo herrastella.

Heila on menny Amerikhan
ja flikka on Amerikan-leski.
Vaikka se olis sielä viisitoista vuotta
niin orotella mun käski.

Like the water in a swift surging rapid
Round a rock is a'flowing,
So my young heart races ever:
Out iln the world it's going.

The one I love he will not think on poor me, no,
None give me contemplation.
I'm a lowly shepherdess, and
He's of a higher station.

I will not spend my time a' breaking my back here,
Toiling here oh so coldly.
When in America they are
Living it up so boldly.

My true love's gone away and left me behind, a
Widow's life, no debating.
He told me to patient be if
Fifteen long years I'm waiting.

53. Viitalan Miinalla
Viitala's Minna

As with **Song 52**, singer Irja Kuoppala, 1975. Härmän laulukirja no. 163. Additional verses as recorded from the same singer in the radio program " Minä Amerikhan lähären" January 1, 1979.

Vii - ta-lan Mii - nal-la ver - ho - ja on___ mut - ta Li - la-pa-kan Lis - sull' on ra - haa.
Mii - na___ Vii - ta-la has got nice dra-per-ies, but Lis-su Li-pak-ka she's got mo - ney.

Tuon - kos tä - hä - ren se Lai - tu - rin To-pun o - li lin - nas___ ol - la pa - ha.
That is why per-haps that To - pu Lai-tu - ri is sad in the pen-i - ten - ti - ary.

Viitalan Miinalla verhoja on
mutta Lilapakan Lissull' on rahaa.
Tuonkos tähären sen Laiturin Topun oli
linnas olla paha.

Viitukan Jussi se Amerikkaan
väärillä kirjoilla seilas.
Yhren flikan tuli paha olla,
että perähän se mennä meinas.

Jussi se sano sillen flikallen,
että hyvästi, ja voi vaan hyvin.
Viitukan Jussin raikas ääni kuulu
Härmän joen yli.

Miina Viitala has got nice draperies,
But Lissu Lipakka she's got money.
This is why perhaps that Topu Laituri
Is sad in the penitentiary.

Viitukka's Jussi he went off to America
Falsified the papers for sailing.
Left behind a girl in such difficulties,
She was after him loudly wailing.

Jussi he gives that poor girl a sweet farewell,
As parting words he does deliver.
Jussi Viitukka his voice it does so cheerfully
sound over Härmä river.

54. Oottakos te kuullu
Have You Heard?

Singer Tiila Ilkka, 1950. Alavuden laulukirja no. 199. Second verse from Aatos Rinta-Koski from farmwife Kerttu Talvitie (born 1912) of Kauhajoki. No. 239, 1972.

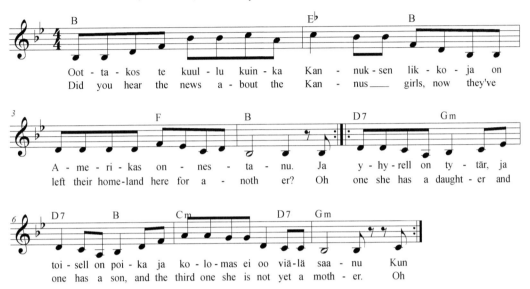

Oot - ta - kos te kuul - lu kuin - ka Kan - nuk - sen lik - ko - ja on
Did you hear the news a - bout the Kan - nus girls, now they've

A - me - ri - kas on - nes - ta - nu. Ja y - hy - rell on ty - tär, ja
left their home-land here for a - noth - er? Oh one she has a daught - er and

toi - sell on poi - ka ja ko - lo - mas ei oo viä - lä saa - nu Kun
one has a son, and the third one she is not yet a moth - er. Oh

Oottakos te kuullu kuinka Kannuksen likkoja on
Amerikas onnestanu.
Ja yhyrell on tytär, ja toisell on poika,
ja kolomas ei oo viälä saanu.

Sellaisia terveisiä kun Peräkorven Jukka oli
Misikaanin valtiosta tuonu.
Kun hän ei ollu rahojansa hukanteille antanu,
oli saluunassa pelannu ja juonu.

Did you hear the news about the Kannus girls,
Now they've left their homeland here for another?
Oh, one she has a daughter, and one has a son,
And the third one she is not yet a mother. Oh,

That is what that Jukka Peräkorpi said when he came back
From the lumber camps in north Michigan. Oh,
What little money he still had in his pack,
It was what he had not given the barman.

IV. Levyllä. On the Turntable.
Songs 55–81.

Westerholm's final section (**Songs 55–81**) is titled "On the Turntable" in reference to the many Finnish and Finnish American performers who recorded music during the first decades of the twentieth century. These performers, most of them men, recorded sentimental songs about the homeland, the lovers, the friends, the families they left behind. They recorded labor songs, shining a light on the terrible working conditions that many Finnish Americans faced. They recorded humorous songs, funny tunes about their lives in the New World that reclaimed the stereotype of the Finnish immigrant as a country rube. They recorded violin and accordion songs to dance to. They sang mostly in Finnish, although the occasional Swedish or German rendition also occurs. Some of these men and women were born in the United States and died in the United States. Others immigrated to the New World only to return to the Old. Still others were Finnish musicians, in the United States simply to tour and record. All of these musicians recorded songs that reflected the immigrant experience for the many Finns who came to the United States, that spoke to the lives they lived and the lives they had left behind. Sampling from the approximately 800 Finnish American songs and tunes recorded for American record labels, the twenty-seven songs that follow demonstrate the lively Finnish American musical tradition that could be found in Finnish communities throughout the United States[1].

Westerholm's songbook is dominated by men and includes only one song by a woman—Viola Turpeinen—perhaps the most popular Finnish American musician of her day. Tupeinen's artistic output was primarily instrumental; the song Westerholm included is one of only a few commercial recordings of Viola Turpeinen singing. It is accompanied in this collection by a second song, this one by penned by Antti Syrjäniemi and recounting the stirring effects of Turpeinen's music. Of course, it is important to note that plenty of women were singing at this time. Alan Lomax and Sidney Robertson, folklorists who conducted fieldwork in the Upper Midwest in the 1930s, recorded several Finnish American women, including Lillian Aho, Ilona Hallinen, Amanda Heikkinen, and Cecilia Kuitunen, to name just a few. Those recordings can now be found at the American Folklife Center at the Library of Congress.

Other women recorded for labels like Columbia, Edison, and Victor. While often avoiding the jocular or melancholic immigrant songs that are featured in this anthology, they frequently focused on classical adaptations of folksongs, patriotic songs of Finland, and even romantic songs in the German Lied style. Artists like Esteri (Ester) Hukari, Katri Lammi, and Elli Suokas re-

---

1   Gronow 1982, 12

corded multiple numbers for Columbia and Victor in the late-1920s and early-1930s and were well-known in their day (Spottswood 1990, 2570, 2582, 2585, 2601–2603). Despite their shared experience as commercially-recorded Finnish American musicians, the lives of Hukari, Lammi, and Suokas took very different paths.

Esteri Hukari (1904–1990) spent much of her childhood and early adult years in her home-town of Fitchburg, Massachusetts (Immigration and Naturalization Service 1930; U.S. Census Bureau 1930). On April 6, 1932, Hukari recorded four songs for Columbia, two of which, "Vanha kirkko" ("The Old Church") and Kesäyö ("Summer Night") were released on the Co 3206-F record (Spottswood 1990, 2570). Around that same time, she moved to New York City along with her sister Ellen (Elli), to pursue a career in music. During the 1930s, the sisters toured the United States, with Ester singing in both Finnish and English and Elli accompanying her on the piano[1].

Katri Lammi (d.c. 1958), née Lamminen, on the other hand, was a working-class immigrant to the United States who became a soprano opera singer[2]. Between December of 1928 and June of 1931, she recorded fourteen songs that were released commercially—ten for Columbia, including "Urali" ("Urals"), "Pikku Äiti" ("Little Mother") and "Syksyn Tuulet-Valssi" ("Autumn Winds Waltz") and four for Victor, including "Soi Viserrys, Soi" ("Sing, Bird, Sing") (Spottswood 1990, 2582). Sometime after her final recording session for Columbia in June of 1931, she and her husband, Jukka Ahti, himself an accomplished singer, immigrated to Soviet Karelia where they founded a Finnish-language theater in the capital city of Petroskoi/Petrozavodsk[3]. She was one of about 6,500 Finnish communist immigrants from Canada and the United States who left North America for Soviet Karelia to assist in building the communist state[4]. In 1938, she was arrested during the Great Purge and sent to Lime Island for hard labor. She is said to have died years later on the island of Valamo in Soviet Karelia[5].

A soprano like Lammi, **Elli Suokas** (1893–1931) was born in Helsinki and began her career as a musician there, before immigrating to the United States in 1915[6]. Settling initially in New York and then moving to Michigan after her marriage to Norwegian American Peter Steinback, Suokas recorded and released seventeen songs for Victor in 1916 and nineteen songs in 1917—twelve for Victor and seven for Columbia—before recording four more songs for Columbia as Elli Suokas Steinback in 1920[7]. For over a decade, Suokas toured the United States performing widely[8]. In 1929, Suokas moved to Detroit where she worked for Ganapol Studios as a singer. Her life was cut short, however, on January 31, 1931, when she died due to complications following an abortion at the age of thirty-seven[9].

The music of these Finnish American women, while often not explicitly narrating the Finnish American experience, inescapably reflects the Finnish American experience. Westerholm's work is an important one in illuminating Finnish American recorded music, but much work remains for future scholars. We hope that this translated anthology will encourage others to seek out the work of the many lesser-known Finnish and Finnish American performers—like Hukari, Lammi, and Suokas—who were a part of that immigrant experience, and who contributed to Finnish American musical traditions in the New World.

A further element of the musical traditions of Finnish America are the many brass bands that performed in Finnish American communities throughout the country. Most likely beginning in the 1870s in Oregon and the Upper Peninsula of Michigan, brass bands spread widely

---

1   *Fitchburg Sentinel* 1937, 7
2   Niemelä 1997b
3   Gronow n.d.
4   Saramo 2014, 49
5   Sevander 1993, 110–111
6   National Archives and Records Administration 1924, Immigration and Naturalization Service 1915; *Fitchburg Sentinel* 1916, 2
7   Michigan Department of Community Health 1918; Spottswood 1990, 2601–2602
8   *Fitchburg Sentinel* 1916, 2; *Monessen Daily Independent* 1917, 1; *Ironwood Daily Globe* 1927, 4
9   Michigan Department of Community Health 1931

in the early 1900s, as Finnish soldiers immigrated to the United States after the dissolution of Finnish army battalions serving in Russia. While military bands did exist, following the Civil War, Finnish American brass bands were, first and foremost, community bands, often with amateur musicians playing alongside professionals, and with members who were usually employed in non-musical professions as well[1]. The popularity of these ensembles reached their peak in the 1920s, possibly due to the rising popularity of radio and ethnic music records[2]. Both brass bands and individual performers toured Finnish America, playing for large crowds at temperance societies, labor societies, church gatherings, and the numerous Finn Halls—gathering places for Finnish immigrants across the continent. Finnish American communities had long brought in talented performers from Finland to perform[3]. In doing so, these communities maintained an ongoing relationship with the popular music of the country they had left behind.

The Finn hall shaped music-making in Finnish American homes as well. Before the turn of the century, commercially available sheet music was hard to come by. At the dawn of the twentieth century, in stepped entrepreneurial immigrants, who, recognizing the importance of music to new communities, began printing and selling sheet music, drawing on the readily available infrastructure for print production in American cities. The idea of selling sheet music for home use helped create the market for eventual record sales as well. With the rise of the phonograph, Finnish immigrants wishing to enjoy popular music were no longer reliant on either attending a performance by a musician or ensemble performing at the local Finn Hall or learning to perform the music themselves through the purchase and practice of sheet music. Instead, they could purchase a record that they could play over and over again at home at any time of the day or night. It wasn't long before the same entrepreneurs who had thought to market ethnic sheet music were producing and selling foreign-language music records—later known as ethnic records—most often produced at recording studios in an American city like New York or Chicago[4]. As small-scale ethnic record labels flourished, major companies like Columbia and Victor took note.

In 1907, the Victor Talking Machine Company made the first Finnish American recording with John M. Ericson[5]. By the early 1910s, Victor and Columbia offered more ethnic records than English-language records, and Columbia sold records produced by thirty-three different ethnic groups[6]. Labels recognized that customers were more likely to buy a phonograph if they could listen to records in their mother tongue, so producing records in ethnic languages served not only record sales but also helped boost purchases of phonographic equipment[7]. Despite the rampant anti-immigrant sentiment of the World War I era, large record labels continued to produce ethnic recordings, and the trend continued unabated after the war. Finnish-music recording in the United States reached its peak in the 1920s—in 1929, ninety Finnish-language records were produced[8]. It was during this decade that Victor and Columbia each launched a Finnish-language series—Columbia's 3000-F and Victor's V-4000. The production of ethnic records continued well into the 1950s, so that between 1900 and 1960, nearly 30,000 ethnic recordings were produced, approximately 800 of which featured Finnish-language performances[9].

Many of the songs below, recorded by both Finnish and Finnish American musicians, were released by Columbia and Victor and demonstrate the transnational elements of the ethnic recording industry. Following the creation of both the 3000-F and V-4000 series, the two companies collectively produced about 500 Finnish-language records between 1925 and 1935[10]. In

---

1   Niemisto 2013, 22–38
2   Greene 1992, 29–30
3   Gronow 1982, 23
4   Greene 1992, 47–49
5   Gronow 1982, 23
6   Greene 1992, 77
7   Gronow 1982, 3
8   Gronow 1982, 20
9   Gronow 1982, 12
10 Gronow 1971, 179

addition, competing labels—like Brunswick and Edison—and small independent labels—like Cinemart and Solos, both out of New York, and Rönkä Levyt, out of California—produced over 100 records between them.

The many records showcased the musical talents of performers in Finland, performers from Finland touring the United States, and, of course, Finnish Americans[1]. This trans-Atlantic approach sometimes brought Finnish musicians like J. Alfred Tanner to the United States where they would tour for their Finnish American fans and record on their way through New York. In the 1920s, music by Finnish Americans for Finnish Americans became increasingly popular[2]. Musicians like Viola Turpeinen, Hiski Salomaa, and Arthur Kylander traveled the United States, performing at Finn Halls in Finnish American communities and reaching a wider audience by recording songs and dance tunes to be played on phonographs at home.

Viola Turpeinen, the legendary Finnish American accordion player, was born in Champion, Michigan, in 1909. Turpeinen cut her teeth in the Finnish Labor Hall and the Italians' Bruno Hall of Iron River, Michigan, where her family moved shortly after Viola's birth. By the age of sixteen, she was touring the Upper Midwest, playing in dance halls across the region. In 1927, Turpeinen moved to New York City, from which she not only continued periodic performance tours through the Midwest, but also traveled and performed in Sweden and Finland. Just one year after moving to New York, Turpeinen began recording for Victor. In the years to come, Turpeinen recorded over 100 tunes, including solos, duets, and ensemble numbers with her band. She recorded for Victor, Columbia, and eventually Standard as well. After moving to Florida in the late 1950s, Turpeinen continued to perform in the Lake Worth area, where she found a receptive audience at the Finnish Worker's Educational Club. Just six years after moving to Florida, Viola Turpeinen died of cancer in 1958[3].

Despite Viola Turpeinen's outsized importance to Finnish American music, Westerholm's anthology includes only one song by Turpeinen and one about her, the popular "Viola Turpeinen tanssit Kiipillä/Viola Turpeinen at the Dance in Cape Ann." This may simply be because Westerholm's anthology is a Finnish songbook presenting lyrics to popular tunes and Turpeinen was primarily an instrumentalist, not a vocalist. Instead, Westerholm saw fit to feature many songs by songwriters Hiski Salomaa and Arthur Kylander.

Hiski Salomaa was born Hiskias Möttö in Kangasniemi, Finland, on May 17, 1891. After the death of his mother, Hiski moved to the United States in 1909, settling in the Upper Midwest and working as a tailor. Living in Michigan and Minnesota, Salomaa got his start, like Turpeinen, playing the Finnish dance halls of the Upper Midwest and, again just like Turpeinen, he would go on to become one of the best-known Finnish American performers. By 1929, Columbia had taken note and he recorded his first song for the label. Over his lifetime, he would release nearly twenty different records. His songs focused on life as a Finnish immigrant in the New World. Writing about the good, the bad, and the funny, Salomaa's work spoke to the expectations and realities of life in the United States for immigrant men and women. Salomaa's well-known "Tiskarin polka/Dishwasher's Polka" is interesting precisely because it tells of the working conditions that many Finnish women faced in the New World. While his political leanings are still debated, many of his songs appealed to the working class and Finnish members of the Industrial Workers of the World (IWW), an industrial labor union founded in 1905. Indeed, the IWW commissioned two songs from Salomaa.

Hiski's unique musical talents reached back across the Atlantic as his "Lännen Lokari/Logger of the West" became a hit in 1940s Finland and then was used as the theme song for the Metsäradio ("Forest Radio") program in the mid-1950s. Salomaa died in New York around that

---

1   Gronow 1971, 180
2   Gronow 1982, 24
3   Leary 1990, Greene 1992

same time, on July 7, 1957. After his death, Salomaa's music became better and better known in Finland and in 1970, Love Records re-released twelve songs by Salomaa. The years that followed saw further re-releases, and in 1979, a TV show was made about Salomaa in conjunction with a rising interest in comedic musical performance. Today, his music lives on in many recordings and re-releases, including in the work of Simo Westerholm[1].

Arthur Kylander, like Hiski Salomaa and many other Finns, emigrated from Finland just prior to World War I. Born on February 16, 1892, in Lieto, Finland, Kylander moved to the United States around 1914. Kylander worked as a logger and carpenter for some time, crossing the country from Maine to New York, Pennsylvania, Ohio, and Minnesota. By 1925, he had come to Portland, Oregon, where he met Julia Varila, an American-born Finn and composer, pianist, and accordion player. Together, the two went on tour and eventually married in Hibbing, Minnesota. They headed east, where they would live for several years. As a musician, Kylander was especially active in the 1920s and early 1930s writing, performing around the country, and recording several songs including with Victor between 1927 and 1929.

During the height of his musical career, Kylander published two songbooks featuring his jocular songs, titled *Humoristisia lauluja I* and *Humoristisia lauluja II* ("Humorous Songs I and II"). His songs speak to the immigrant experience, revealing a strong affinity for the working class and nods to the IWW. While not performing in the same vein as the peasant comedian on stage, Kylander's humorous lyrics revealed truths about life as a Finnish immigrant in the United States with a comedic touch and appealed to Finns around the country.

In the midst of the Great Depression, Kylander moved to Hollywood, California, to work as a butler. Having made it through the Depression, he and Julia purchased a 240-acre tree farm near Placerville, California, in 1943. His home, which of course included a sauna, became a small resort destination for Finns. He continued to work the farm and he and Julia continued to perform well into the 1960s. As late as 1952, despite being limited by a slow recovery from an appendectomy, Arthur and Julia embarked on a yearlong tour. When Kylander died in 1968 he had become one of the best-known Finnish American musicians of his generation[2].

Johan Alfred Tanner was a popular Finnish performer known for his humorous couplets. Born in Artjärvi on March 16, 1884, and often performing as J. Alfred Tanner, he never immigrated to the United States, but as Pekka Gronow notes, he was "the best-selling Finnish recording artist of the 1910s" (1998, 26). Tanner gained prominence with his performances of rhymed couplets at the Helikon Theater in Helsinki, where he was hired to perform between reels during motion picture screenings. His act, in which he would dress up, play character roles, and perform a variety of acrobatics, were in line with those of the peasant comedians, or bondkomiker, in the United States like Hjalmar Peterson, who performed as a character named Olle i Skratthult.

Tanner became immensely popular in Finland, with people waiting in long lines to attend his performances and printed copies of his songs selling briskly. Although he wrote and memorized his songs, it is clear that he also improvised during performance, and filled his act with lively and topical banter. His lyrics, like Finnish couplets more generally, often engage in playful innuendos and word play that are difficult, if not impossible, to fully translate. While he never immigrated to the US, Tanner toured the United States in 1922 and 1924 and recorded for Victor as well as the German-Finnish label Homocord. His 1922 tour proved a failure, since Red-leaning Finnish Americans regarded him as a White and boycotted his shows ("Kupletin kuningas J. Alfred Tanner" 2006/2016). Nonetheless, his songs themselves became as popular in North America as they were in Finland (Niemelä 1998–1999, 119). Tanner died of tuberculosis on May 27, 1927 ("Kupletin kuningas J. Alfred Tanner" 2006/2016). Laura Henriksson (2015) has written a dissertation that addresses Tanner among other comedians and musicians of his era.

---

1   Westerholm 1983, Gronow 1971, Gronow 1982, Niemelä 1997a, Niemelä 2007, Greene 1992, Greene 2004
2   Westerholm 1983, Impola and Leino Eldridge 2001, Gronow 1982, Greene 1992, Greene 2004, Maki 2002, Niemelä 1997a

Songs from the Stage and the Recording Studio

Dominated by men, with only a few exceptions like the aforementioned Viola Turpeinen, the twenty-seven songs that Westerholm chose for this section of the anthology include a variety of themes. It's no small task to categorize the different tunes—many overlap and many recur throughout this anthology. Nevertheless, while other organizational schemes could be applied, it is useful to categorize the songs Westerholm chose to include along three vectors: immigration, work, and entertainment.

Immigration (Songs 55, 56, 60, 62, 63, 64, 69, 71, 72, 76, 79, 81)

Predictably, songs of immigration—deciding to leave, saying farewells, experiencing the passage to America, and seeing the sights of the New World—figure prominently in recorded songs as in songs featured in the other sections of this anthology. In **Song 56** "Tuhatjärvien, lumien maa/Land of Thousands of Lakes and Snow," recorded with Victor, J. Alfred Tanner sings of the homesickness so many Finns surely felt and ends his song by describing the ways in which families were faced with a great physical as well emotional disjunction as young men and women left Finland for the New World:

Sa tiedät myös maan, jonne koti, vanhukset
sun jälkees' jäivät, kun aloit länteen viiltää.
He ei vaadi sulta mitään, nuo harmaahapsiset,
mutt' silmänurkass' kaihon kyynel kiiltää.
He tuijottavat lieteen, he toivoo joka ilta,
ettei vaan murtuis' sun toiveittesi silta.

—

You know of a land where your parents still reside
Behind they're left as you westward stride.
Nodding a dear gray head,
Smiling for you, privately tears shed.
They gaze upon the fire as they think of you
And hope you are happy as this life you pass through.

Ernest Paananen, who recorded **Song 60**—"Muistatko vielä illan sen/Do You Still Remember That Night?"—for Columbia in 1930, also sings about homesickness and separation, recalling having left a beloved behind:

Pois kuljin kotirannalta
jäi sinne mun ystäväin.
Vaan joskus muistot entiset
ne lämmittää sydäntäin.

—

I left old Finland's shores behind,
So started our time apart.
But sometimes those lingering memories,
They warm my lonely heart.

Hiski Salomaa brings us yet another song of love and loss due to emigration on a Columbia record from 1928. In **Song 62**, "Taattoni maja/My Father's Cottage," Salomaa sings of the cottage that the young immigrant grew up in, the cottage that he left behind, and the family that he misses[1]. This song, while partially autobiographical, is based on a traditional song[2]. Just as Tanner

---

1   Pitkänen and Sutinen 2011, 27–30
2   Niemelä 1998–1999, 124

sings of the mother who remains in Finland, Salomaa reminds us of the distance that remains and the very real possibility of never seeing loved ones again:

> Kun kuusi oli lastansa kuolema vienyt
> ja tuoni kai turvana heille
> ja muisteli sortuuko poikansa tumma
> näille maailman markkinateille.

> Sitten minä kuulin sen kuiskaavan äänen
> noitten Atlannin aaltojen yli
> että kotona on kylmennyt kulkuripojalla
> tuo hyljätyn äitin syli.
> —
> Death had taken from her six of her children,
> To a peaceful strand.
> And she wondered if the son who had left,
> Would perish in that foreign land.

> I heard a voice that was a'whisp'ring to me, it came
> Over the waves and sea.
> Mother's lonely heart it beat no more,
> She had waited for me faithfully.

Salomaa's own mother had died before her only son's departure for America, yet Salomaa captures the regrets and anxieties of many of his countrymen in this image of a lonely woman, seemingly abandoned by her adventurous son and the mysical or telepathic links that let the son know when his mother has finally passed away[1].

For many Finnish immigrants, life in the United States presented a variety of challenges, including language difficulties, unmet expectations, homesickness, and lost love. Tanner's **Song 55** "Niin Amerikassa/So in America," re-released by Matti Jurva for Columbia in 1932, is a biting critique of the expectations versus the reality of immigration:

> Ei Ameriikas' tarvitse kuin painaa nappulaa,
> Niin kaikki pyörät pyörii taikka seisahtaa.
> —
> Life in America is one of luxury and ease,
> Just push a button that's all, life is quite a breeze.

> ...

> Jos taloa siell' rakentamaan tänään aletaan,
> niin huomenna jo vuokralaiset ulos ajetaan.
> Ja sattunut on myöskin niin, että kaksi miestä siell'
> on kuollut kerran häkään, mutta elävät nyt viel'.
> —
> If a house it gets built today, starting at nine o'clock
> Evicted tenants will be thrown out on the block.
> And just the other day, two men they almost up and died,
> It was from breathing wretched air full of carbon monoxide.

---

1   Pitkänen and Sutinen 2011, 30

Song 63, "Savon poian Amerikkaan tulo/A Savo Guy Arrives in America," recorded for Columbia in 1928 by Hiski Salomaa, follows an immigrant from the province of Savo, Finland, to the New World[1]. In this semi-autobiographical song, Salomaa takes us from the sad parting between mother and son to seasickness on the Baltic Sea to the long Atlantic passage before finally arriving in New York[2]. Once in the United States he finds work in the mines, but feels out of place. Not before finding a community of other Finns in the lumber camps does this young immigrant begin to feel at home:

> Amerikkoi meitä tänne tuotihin
> ja mainissa multoo myö luotihin
> piällysmiestä siellä ei tarvittu
> mua ennen oli toisia jo otettu.
> Mutta sitte ku mäntii mehtäkämpille
> savonkielikin kuulosti jo jänkille
>
> —
>
> Now to America we came to stay.
> In dark, dirty mines we worked all day.
> No boss was ever needed, was plain to see,
> They never had much use for a guy like me.
> Now we work the lumber camps where trees abound,
> Here my Savo words they quite normal sound.

Salomaa undercuts this poignant story of an immigrant's life by performing in a broad and comical Savo dialect that mimics the stereotype of the Finnish immigrant rube. Of course, Salomaa was known for his humorous lyrics—and performance style—that sometimes revealed darker truths about the challenges of immigration. In **Song 64** "Talvella maa oli valkoinen/The Ground Was White During Winter," recorded for Columbia sometime around 1930, Salomaa sings a humorous song of lost love and emigration[3]. While still in Finland, the young man finds himself with two girlfriends, one of whom finally tires of him and leaves him. In response, knowing that he'll never find another woman like her again, he leaves for the New World. Once there, he is confronted with the reality of the United States:

> Eikä nuo Atlannin laineetkaan
> kasvanu ruusuja punasia
> vaanhan ne tuutii New Yorkin rantaan
> poikia tuhansia.
>
> —
>
> Roads that lead to America
> They are not all paved with gold
> Still these Finnish men they are lured there
> On the promise of New York they're sold.

Much like Salomaa, Arthur Kylander was known for his comedic songs. In **Song 71** "Siirtolaisen ensi vastuksia/The Immigrant's First Difficulties," produced by Victor in 1928, Kylander describes the language difficulties that immigrants sometimes faced.

> Vieras kieli kuin se kaikui, sitä kuuntelemaan jäin
> ensi sanat mieleen painui, joita muistuttelin näin:

---

1   Pitkänen and Sutinen 2011, 63–69
2   Niemelä 1998–1999, 124
3   Pitkänen and Sutinen 2011, 79–82

"no sir, no sir, no sir, no-o-o-o, no sir,
no sir, no sir, no sir, no!"

—

And I listened to the language that they spoke all around me
And the word I first encountered lingered in my memory:
"No sir, no sir, no sir, no-o-o-o, no sir,
No sir, no sir, no sir, no!"

That phrase, a memorable one, comes back to cause problems for the newly arrived immigrant, who repeats it to a boss and, eventually, has the same phrase repeated back at him when he asks a woman to marry him. This bilingual humor, sung by a man who was himself bilingual, appealed directly to the immigrants who knew what it was like to misunderstand, or be misunderstood, while learning a new language. The song, and others like it, allowed Finnish immigrants to laugh at their own experiences.

In another humorous song, "Selkäranka Tohtori/Spine Doctor" (**Song 76**), from a 1927 Victor record, Kylander tells of a newly arrived immigrant who seems to have discovered the secret to success in the United States: become a chiropractor and claim to be able to cure anything and everything from toe pain, to failing lungs, to baldness. Of course, it is the heavy workload upon arrival that leads him down this newfound career path:

Minä olin tässä maassa alkujaan
vain niinkuin muutkin iikat vanhan maan.
Että harteitani painoi raskas työ
ja kireällä piti pitää suolivyö.

—

I was newly come into this country here,
Like other bumpkins from our homeland dear.
On my shoulders heavy loads they took their toll,
And I got sick of tightening my darn belt hole.

Song 72 "Ennen ja nyt/Before and Now," also by Kylander, appears on the B-side of the same 1928 Victor recording that features **Song 71**. In "Ennen ja nyt," however, Kylander describes the differences he sees between Finland and the United States:

Ennen kun siellä Suomessa puhutella saatiin herroja,
lakki ol poies päästä ja räästä nenä puhtaana.
Poies on sekin kaunistus, mikä viel ompi seuraus,
ehkäpä herroill' itsellä on aavistus!
Näin muuttuu kaikki vallan ympäri maan,
muuttuu kuin ajais autolla vaan, kyllä tosiaan!
Tää nykyaika, se on koneellinen,
ihmeellinen ja kiireellinen koko ihminen.

—

Back home in Finland we felt fright, to the boss we'd be so polite.
Hat in hand stood meekly by, faces clean and noses dry.
This custom's up and gone away, where we are headed from this day?
Maybe the bosses will be able to say.
But now all's changed in places both near and far
No time for that now that we're driving in a car.
And now our lives they are all mechanized,
Wonderized, commercialized, and dehumanized.

In *Humoristisia lauluja I*, Kylander's own publication of his song lyrics, there are two additional verses, one of which describes the oppression of the working class and the rising anxiety of the rich who seem to know that they are responsible for the class inequalities.

While most recorded songs depict the experiences and perceptions of a young man early-on in the immigration process, a few take up the feelings of Finns after years of residence and work in the new land. Kylander reminds listeners of the long-term separation that so many immigrants faced in **Song 81**, "Muistojen valssi/Waltz of Memories," recorded for Victor in 1928. Here, it is a waltz that brings memories of home flooding back. But rather than becoming mired in the past and on regrets for things now passed, Kylander encourages the immigrant, man or woman, to find joy in the fond memories of home:

Sa siirtolais tyttö jos muistelemaan
käyt muistoja mennehiä
ja rakkaimmat muistot jos tulvailemaan,
saa silmäsi kyyneliä,
Pois kyyneleet kuivaa ja nähdä mun suo
taas katseesi hymyilevän.
Käy kanssani valssiin se viihtyä tuo,
käy tunteesi tyynnyttämään.
Kuin elo nuoruuden
—

Oh, immigrant maiden, you dwell on the past,
And ponder a long ago day.
Those memories lingering in your heart do last,
Your tears let me wipe them away.
Those dear recollections should bring you no tears,
Or cloud your sweet smiling face.
Come dance with me now and we'll turn back the years,
Those cares and sad pinings erase.

Song 79 "American suomalainen iso-äiti ja tyttären tytär/Finnish American Grandmother and Granddaughter" comes from Arthur Kylander's unpublished papers and was most likely written sometime in the 1950s. The song describes an English-speaking granddaughter with her Finnish American grandmother, who seems to be bilingual. It's a reminder of the changes that immigrant communities experience as generations began to separate immigrants from their homelands, but also of the opportunity to build a family and a home in the New World. In this song, Kylander plays with the Finnish language, interspersing several lines of dialogue in English:

"But tell me grandma, tell me,
When grandpa says: 'I love you'
How you say in Finnish
'I love you, too!'"

Work (Songs 65, 66, 67, 69, 70, 73, 74, 75, 77)
Work is a common theme in immigrant songs. Whether highlighting low wages and poor working conditions or celebrating the opportunity to earn a living, the songs below give a fuller picture of what work meant to the Finnish immigrant community.

Hiski Salomaa's well-known **Song 65** "Tiskarin polka/Dishwasher's Polka," recorded for Columbia in 1927, describes the labor required of an overworked young woman working in the kitchen of a wealthy American family[1]. Somewhat unique in that it is a song sung by a man that

---

1   Pitkänen and Sutinen 2011, 157–163

focuses on the difficult working conditions experienced by women, we follow the dishwasher as she completes chore after chore at the behest of the woman of the household, all the while looking forward to Thursday, traditionally a day off for domestic servants:

Siellä kun istut sa puoleen yöhön
kotia tultua alottaa työhön
mutta ei kerkii ku dressan vaihtaa
ja hellun kotia laittaa
Minä vaan tiskaan astioita
ja luutalla lakasen lattioita
tilitilitilitilitittattaa
kyllä torstai meitä nyt lohduttaa.
—
We spend the night like that a'chumming,
Then rush home a polka a'humming.
Time to change clothes for work is a'lacking,
Got to send your boyfriend packing.
In the back room I wash and scrub up and
Sweep off the floor boards and then wipe up
Tee-lee tee-lee tee-lee tee-lee tee-tat tee yes and
Thursdays we take it easy.

In contrast, **Song 67**, Salomaa's "Lännen lokari/Logger of the West," which he recorded for Columbia in 1930, describes the freedom of a logger[1]. Of course, that freedom resulted in traveling around the United States in search of work. With travel came one benefit though: women in every town, something this particular logger is happy to brag about:

Täss on lokari ny lännen risukosta
olen kulkenu vaikka missä
olen käynynnä Piuttissa, Lousissa,
Retulaatsissa, Miamissa.
Olen kulkenu merta ja mantereita
ja Alaskan tuntureita
ja kaikkialla hulivilityttäret muistaa
lännen lokareita.
—
I'm a logger from the timber camps of the West,
And I've rambled nigh all over!
I have been out to Butte and L.A. to boot,
Red Lodge and Miami, sir.
I have been on the sea and the continents,
And the peaks up in Alaska!
And just ev'ry place I go the wild girls all know
The loggers of the West.

Salomaa's jaunty song possesses little of the sorrow or critical edge of some of the singer's other works and presents the logger's life as happy-go-lucky and adventurous. Arthur Kylander offers his own take on life as a lumberjack in **Song 77** "Lumber-Jäkki/Lumber-Jack." This song is also comedic but manages to capture more of the harsh realities of life as a lumberjack, deftly dismissing any romanticized notion of life in the woods[2]:

---

1 Pitkänen and Sutinen 2011, 137–142
2 Frandy 2010, 38–40

Siellä ilta myöhällä,
Pojat kuin on petillä,
Silloin tällöin kajahtaapi kumma sävelmä.
Äänen sen jos kuulisi
Herrat, varmaan luulisi,
Että pojill' kämpässä on iltakonsertti.
Mutta unen helmoissa jo pojat uinahtaa
Ja iltaseksi syödyt "binssit" ne ne soinahtaa.
Hongat säestää huminallaan, paistaa täysi kuu.
Runollista, tottamaar se onkin, eikös juu?
—

In the evening late at night,
When the men have gone to sleep,
Here and there, all out of sight,
A melody does seep.
Gentlemen who heard that sound,
Would believe a band they'd found,
Or a hidden orchestra, performing somewhere round.
It's the beans they ate you see, now tooting musically.
And the concert goes all night, it's absolutely free.
Aspens sigh with gas fumes nigh, the moon shines bright and full,
It's poetic yes indeed on evenings warm or cool.

Kylander sang about what he knew, having worked as a lumberjack; Salomaa did the same when he turned his wit upon the music profession in **Song 70** "Laulu taiteilijoista/Song about Artists" (Pitkänen and Sutinen 2011, 232–233). This song pokes fun at the overabundance of artists, but comes with a bite. Salomaa criticizes the boring, derivative nature of some musical genres, noting specifically how some musicians were trying to ride the coattails of Taavetti "Tatu" Pekkarinen, a Finnish comedian and performer who, along with Matti Jurva, recorded extensively for Victor in the 1920s[1]. While Salomaa goes on to attack whiny, arrogant musicians, he also notes the difficulty of life as a musician and reminds everyone of what he loves—polka:

Toiset istuu jo kunnian paikalla
Toiset Pekkarisen Tatunkin paidalla
siinä se on mies joka lauluja laittaa
toiset vain tuloksista maljoja maistaa
himputa himputa himpumpaa
tämä poika polkat aina rallattaa.
—

Some artists are sitting in seats so high.
Others want to find coattails to ride.
Some of them work to create their own song.
While some others are profiting by riding along.
Himputa, himputa, himpumpaa
This boy always wants to hum a polka.

Song 66, "Kemppaisen avioelämä/Kemppainen's Marriage," recorded for Columbia around 1930 by Salomaa, takes a darker approach to work, or the lack thereof[2]. Kemppainen finds himself unemployed while his wife Tiltu heads to work:

---

1   Spottswood 1990, 2591–2592
2   Pitkänen and Sutinen 2011, 101–104

Se lemmenliekki, joka rinnoissamme ennen salamoi
nyt se meidän välillemme synkän pilven löi
Vaik minä olen päivät kotonamme
ja Tiltu töissä käy
silti meidän liitossamme paljon hauskaa näy.
—
That flaming love that burned within our hearts both night and day
It's behind a sullen cloud that hides the light away
Oh, I sit at home, I am moping all day, in misery I lurk
While Tiltu gets her duds on
and then heads off to her work.

The song thematizes some of the surprises or reversals that life in America could bring: Tiltu has proved more successful at adjusting to life in the New World and finding a job than her moping, frustrated husband. Similar to "Kemppaisen avioelämä," **Song 69** "Värssyjä sieltä ja täältä/Verses from Here and There" describes an unemployed Finnish immigrant struggling to get by and the challenges that the working class face with regards to alcohol[1]. Recorded for Columbia around 1931 in the midst of the Great Depression, Salomaa uses the experiences of one Finnish American looking for work to describe the larger societal issues facing the nation:

Wall Striitti se nauraa partaansa
kun kaikki se on saanu alle valtansa.
Paavikin huutaa ny herrassaan
että kirkotkin postaa jo kerrassaan.
Bolseviikit museoita niistä nyt laittaa
se pappien unta hieman kai haittaa
kun niiltäkin alkaa jo loppua työ
kait synkältä näyttää ku syksyinen yö.
—
Oh Wall Street is laughing under its breath,
As we all are working ourselves to death.
The Pope keeps saying the banks are corrupt,
Even the churches they are going bankrupt.
The Bolsheviks buy them as monuments.
Priestly ideals they are long since spent.
The bishop he sits, no one talks to him.
His future is looking gray and grim.

Song 73 also speaks to the transient lifestyle that many new immigrants faced. Recorded by Arthur Kylander for Victor in 1929, "Kulkuri/Wanderer" describes the life of a hobo, the life he leads, the life he wants, and the unfairness of it all:

Me rautatiet laitamme ympäri maan,
itse varkain vaan niillä ajetaan.
Ja vaikkapa preerillä kylvän ja puin
olla saanut olen tyhjin suin.
Alaskan, Montanan,
kaivoksissa myöskin väliin aherran,
Utahin, Teksasin
metsissäkin heilunut on kirveeni.

---

1   Frandy 2010, 41–42; Pitkänen and Sutinen 2011, 214–220

Oh, railroads we built in this great big country.
Now those trains they pass me efficiently.
And though on the prairie I plow and I sow,
Still my belly's empty even so.
I have mined Montana,
And even the hills of great Alaska.
I have cut Texas trees,
Likewise I have felt Utah's mountain breeze.

Kylander, known for his union-friendly songs, sings of a burgeoning labor activist in **Song 74**, "Paitaressu Vihtori/Shirttail Victor," recorded for Victor in 1928. Accustomed to always getting his way, Victor whines, begs, and even demands to get what he wants. As a child it is endearing, as a lover it is annoying, as a worker it is dangerous, because when Victor asks, his brothers follow suit:

Työhönkin jo Vihtori, veljinensä aloitti,
Palkka-orjan raskas taival eteen aukeni.
Alkoi myöskin valjeta Vihtoorille asia
että, työnsä tuloista hän sai vaan muruja.
Niinpä, kuin poosu taaskin ohi asteli:
"Palkka on liian pieni," lausui Vihtori.
Ja kuin hän tahtoi, poosua tahtoi, palkkaansa nostamaan
niin, poosu ylimielin hälle lausui vaan:
Et saa, et saa, et saa, et saa Vihtori.
Et saa, et saa, et saa Vihtori.
—
Victor worked with his brothers,
His labor enriched others.
Slowly he began to see, his work was slavery.
Working in the blazing sun,
Victor never thought was fun.
Earning little pay, Victor knew he would soon be done.
He began to think about what he had to do.
He always worked hard, but his dollars were so few.
"What you are paying ain't nearly enough," to his boss he said one day.
Then the boss glowered at him and finally did say:
"No-no, no-no, mustn't do that Victor!
No-no, no-no, no, you can't Victor!"

Similar to **Song 74**, **Song 75** "Työttömän valssi eli 'Come around again'/Waltz of the Unemployed; 'Come around again'" shows support for the workingman in a song that folklorist Tim Frandy notes has a comic twist that lightens the message, but still argues that, "the song is as overtly political as any other song of the era" [1]. Published by Kylander in *Humoristisia lauluja I*, the version that Westerholm includes is from Kosti Tamminen's record from 1927 for Victor. In it, a drifter looks for work, only to be told to "come 'round again.'" He hears the same refrain in the breadline and again from his former lover. He takes solace, even joy, though that it isn't just him; even the rich find themselves in the breadline:

---

1   Frandy 2010, 36

Vaikk' nälissäin kuljen niin kuitenkin
Siit lohtua rintaani saa,
Kun tiedän ett' vuorostaan herratkin
Leipälainissa viell' jonottaa,
Ja silloin saan sanoa minäkin näin:
Come around again, yes, come around again.
Hyödyllist' työtä kuin ensin teet,
Niin sitte sä come around again.

—

Though traipsing around ever hungry,
It does my heart good just to see,
That sometimes the rich men are lined up,
In the same bread-and-soup line as me.
And then it is my turn to say this to them:
"Come 'round again, yes come 'round again.
When you get the idea to do real work,
Well then, won't you come 'round again?"

Entertainment (Songs 57, 58, 59, 61, 68, 78, 80)

Despite the challenges of immigration, there was plenty of entertainment to be found for Finns in the New World. Entertainment could range from humorous skits—like those of J. Alfred Tanner, which were part of a larger trend of immigrant comic performers who mixed humor and stereotype to appeal to an immigrant audience—to songs and dance—like Viola Turpeinen's performances that brought nearly everyone onto the dance floor.

In fact, Antti Syrjäniemi recorded **Song 58**, "Viola Turpeinen tanssit Kiipillä/Viola Turpeinen at the Dance in Cape Ann," for Victor in 1929, recounting just how much fun the dance was when Viola Turpeinen came to Cape Ann, Massachusetts, to perform:

Harvoin on polkattu sellaista kyytii
harvoin on sakeammin astuttu.
Mummotkin ukkoja jäähylle pyyti
ne sano että tässä on jo kastuttu.
Ja tyttö se soitti kun taivaan kellolla
hittantilatula hittantaa.
Ja farmarit niitti kun heinää pellolla
hittantilatula hittantaa.

—

Seldom before has a polka gone so fast,
And seldom have dance floors been packed so tight.
Grandmas said a breather they needed at last, for
Dripping from sweat they felt so soaked that night.
And the girl she played like on heavenly bells, she went
Hittan tilatula hittantaa
Farmers like haying on slopes and on dells, they went
Hittan tilatula hittantaa.

Syrjäniemi's lively song gives us a glimpse of how raucous and exuberant a Finn Hall dance could be. Cape Ann and other communities near it outside of Gloucester, Massachusetts, had sizeable populations of Finnish immigrant men, who worked as stone cutters and haulers in local granite quarries that supplied materials essential for urban buildings and roads throughout the Eastern seaboard in the era before the advent of industrial concrete. Living in boarding houses and working long days full of back-breaking labor, men could look forward to dances at the Finn Hall as a welcome respite and ideal occasion for socializing and courtship. In Syrjäniemi's song, the dance floor is packed with enthusiastic dancers, young and old, sweating profusely and making the most of the opportunity to enjoy great music.

While **Song 58** sings of Viola Turpeinen's music, **Song 59** is Viola Turpeinen's music, though the lyrics are sung by her husband, William Syrjälä. Turpeinen's "Unelma-valssi/Dream Waltz," from her 1938 solo-album with Victor, tells simply of a boy falling in love with a girl as they dance:

> Kun vieno soitto hiljainen unelmat aukaisee,
> kun nuorukainen neidolleen kätensä tarjoilee.
> Hiljallensa katsein näin unelman saavuttaa,
> on onnellista ylkä näin, näin neidon omistaa.
> —
> A gentle note comes drifting by, the music of the band.
> A dapper young man greets his girl, and offers her his hand.
> Dreams of love they so fill his heart, as dancing she does twirl,
> And happiness it fills his mind, to think that she's his girl.

Similar to Turpeinen's "Unelma-valssi" is **Song 61**, "Tuletko tyttö tanssiin/Will You Come and Dance Girl?," by Kuuno Sevander. Here, an older Finn looks back on life, remembering just how much fun the dances could be:

> Nuoruuden päivät on viel
> muistossani,
> kun kuljin ja kuhertelin
> ja tanssin laulaen.
> Pirtissä viulut ne soi
> kun nuoret karkeloi:
> Tule vaan, tule vaan,
> tule tyttöni tanssimaan.
> —
> Those days of my youth gone by,
> How time does fly.
> I danced with the maidens so free,
> And flirted shamelessly.
> Violins inside they played,
> Young folks they danced and swayed.
> Come with me, come with me,
> My dear come and dance with me.

Song 78, "Mikon ja Mantan Floridan matka/Mikko's and Mantta's Trip to Florida," comes from Arthur Kylander's unpublished papers (like **Song 79**, "American suomalainen iso-äiti ja tyttären tytär") and describes life for the Finnish American in the United States long after immigration. Mikko and Mantta, a rather crotchety married couple, have taken a vacation to Florida and find themselves in a Finn Hall, reliving memories of dances from their younger days, and perhaps hoping to relive more than just memories:

> Tanssi vain kiihtyy ja kaikk' hyvin viihtyy,
> joku sitten huutaa et "vaihtakaa!"
> Mantakin luuli kun äänen sen kuuli
> että hän uuden nyt miehen saa.

Vaan kaikki ei nyt mennytkään niin jetsulleensa.
Juuri kun taas vaihto oli viimeinen
Manta silloin huomasikin harmiksensa:
Kainalossa olikin se entinen!

—

Everyone's dancing and good cheer's advancing,
Then comes the call "Change your partner now!"
Mantta she figures she'll get a new fella,'
She gets excited and but how.
Oh life is never as one might think it would be,
Or as it should be, right or wrong.
When all is done and she now looks at her partner,
She's back with Mikko as all along.

While these songs about entertainment are entertaining in their own right, they also carry with them cultural details that demonstrate the continuation of Finnish traditions in the New World and their fusion with American customs. Such is the case, for instance, with **Song 68**, "Dahlmannin paartit/Party at the Dahlmans'" [1]. The song was recorded by Salomaa in 1929 for Columbia and describes the tradition of celebrating a person's name day, including by lifting the person into the air:

Ja se aamuyö oli vasta reilua
Koska minäkin jo aloin siellä heilua.
Missis Dahlmanni ylös vielä nostettiin
Ja se pöytälamppu lahjaks sille ostettii.

—

Oh the party lasted to the break of day.
From that drinking and dancing my poor legs did sway.
There's Mrs. Dahlmann on their shoulders lifted high.
And a fancy table lamp for her they did buy.

"Missis Dahlmann" referred to Kate Dahlmann of Hancock, Michigan, the wife of Salomaa's friend Matti Dahlmann [2]. In addition to lifting the guest of honor, the song recounts another traditional Finnish feature, the abundant drink available at the party, despite the fact that the song was released during the Prohibition. The Dahlmanns and their friends were not to be counted among the Temperance Finns. They also appear notably wealthy, providing an array of food and beverages to their guests into the wee hours of the morning, including "hot dogsit, ice creamit" ("hotdogs and ice cream").

In 1928, Elmer Lamppa and H. Saarinen recorded **Song 57**, "Pelti-Liisa/Tin Lizzie," for Victor. In it, the young Finnish boy compares his Ford Model T to a woman. Full of sexual innuendo, the song extolls the virtues of having a car instead of a girlfriend:

Eikä se liisani vehnästä syö,
se kasoliinia haukkaa.
Vaikka' en sitä koskaan piiskalla lyö,
niin tyytyväisnä se laukkaa.

Toisinaan hänkin tosin motkottaa,
jurnuaapi joutavasta.

1   Pitkänen and Sutinen 2011, 153–155
2   Pitkänen and Sutinen 2011, 153

Mutt' sukkelaan suunsa kiinni saa
kun painan vain nappulasta.
—

My Lizzie don't go in for sweets,
She only guzzles gas.
She don't need no spurs nor any treats,
She just gallops good and fast.

Sometimes she'll grumble and complain,
About big and little stuff.
But with a little button I can gain
Peace when I have had enough.

Of course, no Finnish American songbook would be complete without mention of the sauna.
Song 80, "Suomalainen ja sauna/A Finn and the Sauna," recorded by Arthur Kylander in 1929
for Victor, is a comedic take on the importance of the sauna to the Finn:

Toisinaan arvellaan, suomalaista heimoa kun tutkitaan,
mikä sen pohjoisen on kansakunnan tunnusmerkki yhteinen?
Myös tutkin sitä minäkin ja siksi voin nyt laulaa,
että se on sauna varmaankin,
koska kerran saunaa kaipaa suomalainen aina
joka lauantaina vielä täälläkin.
—

Yes indeed, it's agreed, when the Finnish nation's studied we concede.
Recognized, and surmised, quantitatively it has been analyzed.
There's one thing that I will sing, yes every Finn will wanna
sit inside a sauna, all night long.
Saturday that is the day when saunas are a'heating,
Sauna stones are steaming and you can't go wrong.

55. Niin Amerikassa
So in America

Couplet by J. Alfred Tanner (1884–1927). Tanner made two tours to America in 1922 and 1924 but proved unpopular due to his politics. Th. Weismann produced a sound recording of the song in 1930 (Homocord 0.4-23085). Matti Jurva recorded it again in 1932 (Columbia DY 24). For details see Pekka Gronow's Studies in Scandinavian-American Discography I and II. Helsinki, 1977.

Ei A-me-rii-kas tar-vit-se kuin pai-naa nap-pu-laa Niin kaik-ki pyö-rät pyö-rii
Life in A-mer-i-ca is one of lu-xu-ry and ease Just push a but-ton that's all

taik-ka sei-sah-taa. Siks A-me-ri-kan ku-nin-kaal-la on-kin help-po työ hän
life is quite a breeze. That's why A-mer-i-can kings have so lit-tle they must do, just

is-tuu vaan sen na-pin vier-ess' ja ap-pel-sii-nii syö, jaa jaa jaa niin ja jaa, jaa
push that but-ton eat-ing or-ang-es the whole day through. Oh yes and yes, and yes oh

se on ih-me-maa ei-pä-hän se muu-ten ois-kaan A-me-rii-kan maa,
yes an awesome place that they call A-mer-i-ca or the U-ni-ted States.

niin-kuin nä-kyy heill' on toi-sen laist' kun meill', mutt' me-nos-sa-han
Life is different there, not like it is 'round here. But some-day we will

me-kin ol-laan ke-hi-tyk-sen teill'.
be just like them, that day's com-ing near.

Ei Ameriikas' tarvitse kuin painaa nappulaa,
Niin kaikki pyörät pyörii taikka seisahtaa.
Siks' Ameriikan kuninkaalla onkin helppo työ,
hän istuu vaan sen napin vieress' ja appelsiinii syö,
Jaa jaa jaa, niin ja jaa, jaa se on ihme maa,
eipähän se muuten oiskaan Ameriikan maa,
Niinkuin näkyy, heill' on toisen laist' kun meill',
mutt' menossahan mekin ollaan kehityksen teill'.

Jos taloa siell' rakentamaan tänään aletaan,
niin huomenna jo vuokralaiset ulos ajetaan.
Ja sattunut on myöskin niin, että kaksi miestä siell'
on kuollut kerran häkään, mutta elävät nyt viel'.
Jaa jaa jaa, niin ja jaa, jaa :,:

Siell' dollareita paljon on, siks' yks' ja toinen täält'
lähtee niitä kahmaisemaan siitä läjän päält'.
Sitt' huomataankin vasta, kun ollaan perillä,
ett' tulos onkin nolla ja kynnet verillä.
Jaa jaa jaa, niin ja jaa, jaa :,:

Sikakin kun esimerkiks' siellä lahdataan,
ei hukkaan jouda mitään, kaikk' talteen otetaan.
Ääni pannaan purkkiin ja postimerkki pääll',
sitä saamme kuulla sitten autoissamme tääll'.
Jaa jaa jaa, niin ja jaa, jaa :,:

Neitoset siell' nuortuu ja miehet laihtuvat
ja suomalaisten kesken usein vaimot vaihtuvat.
Mutt' vaihtuminen sentään käy niin tiuhaan siellä maass',
ett' vuoden päästä jokainen on omillansa taas.
Jaa jaa jaa, niin ja jaa, jaa :,:

Rouvat on niin hienoja, ett' romaanist'kin ain'
piika lukee alun ja rouva lopun vain.
Piika istuu herran kanssa, jos ei rouvaa näy
ja piika siellä rouvan eestä toiletissa käy.
Jaa jaa jaa, niin ja jaa, jaa :,:

Naimisiinkinmeno siell' on hyvin mukavaa,
siinänkin se tahtoo olla "hori-opin" maa.
Siell' lapset käy jo koulua kuin täällä samallaill',
vaikka vanhemmat ne vielä ovat vihkimistä vaill'.
Jaa jaa jaa, niin ja jaa, jaa :,:

Life in America is one of luxury and ease,
Just push a button that's all, life is quite a breeze.
That's why American kings have so little they must do,
Just push that button eating oranges the whole day through.
Oh, yes and yes, and yes, oh yes an awesome place
That they call America or the United States.
Life is different there, not like it is 'round here
But someday we will be just like them, that day's coming near!

If a house it gets built today, starting at nine o'clock
Evicted tenants will be thrown out on the block.
And just the other day, two men they almost up and died,
It was from breathing wretched air full of carbon monoxide.
Oh, yes and yes, and yes :,:

There's money everywhere for us, there's piles there to be had
That's why so many leave here, every gal and lad,
Of course we do not notice 'til we finally get there,
That our pockets stay empty and our cupboards they stay bare.
Oh, yes and yes, and yes :,:

Oh when they kill the pig to eat, well nothing goes to waste
They even save the hooves and make them into paste
They catch the voice and put it in a postmarked, see-through jar
Then we can hear it squealing as we're driving in our car
Oh, yes and yes, and yes :,:

There women stay quite young and men they stay there nice and trim
And Finnish men will trade in wives that don't suit them
The trading gets so common there among the Finnish men
That by year's end, each man has got his old wife back again
Oh, yes and yes, and yes :,:

Oh ladies there, they act so fine that when they read a book
They'll only read the end, the rest is for the cook
The maid sits with the husband, if the wife is out to tea
And she must warm the toilet seat before the wife will pee
Oh, yes and yes, and yes :,:

Oh weddings there are so easy, where everything's a cinch
A marriage can be planned if you are in a pinch
The children go to school there in the land of "hurry up"
Though mom and dad they have not gotten wedding dates locked up
Oh, yes and yes, and yes :,:

56. Tuhatjärvien, lumien maa
Land of Thousands of Lakes and Snow

As with **Song 55**, sung by J. Alfred Tanner (1884–1927). This song was apparently composed for Tanner's American tour. Tanner recorded the song himself in America in 1924 (Victor 77789).

On maa, tuolla Pohjolan partahill' on maa,
miss' huojuu hongat, korpikuuset kuiskaa.
Miss' talven tuulet ja tuiskut tuivertaa
ja vieras harvoin, aniharvoin muistaa.
Mutt' kelle on tuttu sen salopuiden huurre
ja lapsena tallaama metsäpolun uurre,
niin hälle se on muisto ja hän voi huudahtaa:
Se on tuhatjärvien, lumien maa.

On maa, jossa hanget hopein hohtavat
ja Pohjolan taivas räiskii revontulta.
Tääll' vierahan viitat mun tietän' johtavat
ja kulun suuntaa kannustaapi kulta.
Ma orjanruusuna liehittelen liljaa,
petyn — nousen — muistot vierii hiljaa
ain' maahan tuonne, kauas, karuun Pohjolaan,
luokse tuhatjärvien, lumien maan.

Sa tiedät myös maan, jonne koti, vanhukset
sun jälkees' jäivät, kun aloit länteen viiltää.
He ei vaadi sulta mitään, nuo harmaahapsiset,
mutt' silmänurkass' kaihon kyynel kiiltää.
He tuijottavat lieteen, he toivoo joka ilta,
ettei vaan murtuis' sun toiveittesi silta.
Sä muista heitä, muista, ett' isiemme maa,
ompi tuhatjärvien, lumien maa.

Oh, there is a land that is far up in the north,
Where spruce trees whisper, and pine trees sway.
The winds blow so brutally,
Visitors venture there rarely.
But they who recall frost upon the trees
They shout and nod as their memories are freed.
The land of a thousand lakes so clear,
And snows a plenty that are so dear.

Oh, there is a land where the snow banks silver shine
Where Northern Lights they sparkle fine.
Foreign sights flood my mind
Of my lost love they do remind.
A fluttering lily like an orphan rose
Here I stand, the memories press on in throes.
The land of a thousand lakes so dim and drear,
And snows a plenty both far and near.

You know of a land where your parents still reside
Behind they're left as you westward stride.
Nodding a dear gray head,
Smiling for you, privately tears shed.
They gaze upon the fire as they think of you
And hope you are happy as this life you pass through.
The land of a thousand lakes remember there
And snows a plenty lying everywhere.

57. Pelti-Liisa
Tin Lizzie

Recorded by Elmer Lamppa (tenor) and H. Saarinen (accordion) in 1928 (Victor 8047). Lyrics also appeared in the collection Humoristinen laulukirja [Humoristic song book], published in Superior, Wisconsin, during the 1920s.

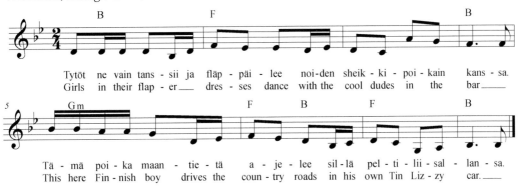

Tytöt ne vain tans - sii ja fläp - päi - lee noi-den sheik - ki - poi - kain kans - sa.
Girls in their flap - er___ dres - ses dance with the cool dudes in the bar___

Tä - mä poi - ka maan - tie - tä a - je - lee sil - lä pel - ti - lii - sal - lan - sa.
This here Fin - nish boy drives the coun - try roads in his own Tin Liz - zy car.___

Finnish American terminology used in this song:
Kasoliini = gasoline
Krinuliini = crinoline, English term for a calf-length skirt popular during WWI
Fläppäilee = dancing as a flapper, a dress and dance common to young women of the 1920s
Sheikkipojat = sheik, dude, a slang term for young men in the 1920s
Peltiliisa = belt lizzie or a Ford "Tin Lizzie"

Tytöt ne vain tanssii ja fläppäilee
noiden sheikkipoikain kanssa.
Tämä poika maantietä ajelee
sillä peltiliisallansa.

Kumista on kengät, raudasta luut,
tuoksunansa kasoliini.
Paksussa maalissa posket ja muut,
nahasta sen krinuliini.

Sylinsä on hytkyvä pehmoinen,
siinä mä istua tykkään.
Vaikkapa kauankin istahtanen,
niin pois ei se luotansa lykkää.

Liisallani loimuaa silmätkin
kuin kirkkain sähköjen valo.
Niilläpä näkee hän pimeelläkin,
vaikk' piiloss' on tähtein palo.

Hiukan vain silittelen liisaani
ja kutitan leuan alle,
silloinpa valmis tuo armaani
on viemään minut maailmalle.

Eikä se liisani vehnästä syö,
se kasoliinia haukkaa.
Vaikka' en sitä koskaan piiskalla lyö,
niin tyytyväisnä se laukkaa.

Girls in their flapper dresses
Dance with the cool dudes in the bar.
This here Finnish boy drives the country roads,
In his own Tin Lizzie car.

Shoes are of rubber, bones of steel
And her perfume gasoline.
She's got makeup that will never peel
Of leather, her crinoline.

I love to bask in her soft embrace,
In her lap I long could sit.
That's a place that I wouldn't want to leave,
We are the perfect fit.

My Lizzie's eyes, they shine so bright
She's got highbeams for my sake.
With them we can see everything at night,
My girl's always awake.

Sometimes I stroke, with love, my car,
And I tickle her sweet chin.
There's no telling how we've gone so far,
Or the places we have been.

My Lizzie don't go in for sweets,
She only guzzles gas.
She don't need no spurs nor any treats,
She just gallops good and fast.

Toisinaan hänkin tosin motkottaa,	Sometimes she'll grumble and complain,
jurnuaapi joutavasta.	About big and little stuff.
Mutt' sukkelaan suunsa kiinni saa	But with a little button I can gain
kun painan vain nappulasta.	Peace when I have had enough.

58. Viola Turpeinen tanssit Kiipillä
Viola Turpeinen at the Dance in Cape Ann

Recorded in 1929 by Antti Syrjäniemi, originally from Haapajärvi (Victor V4040). Performance taken from the only known copy of the record and re-recorded on the album Siirtolaisen muistoja [Memories of the migrant] (RCA PL 48115) in 1978. Syrjäniemi (1892–1962) was a shoemaker and singer of couplets from Cape Ann, Massachusetts. See Pekka Gronow's article on Syrjäniemi Kansanmusiikki 2/79. The song's "Kiipi" refers to Cape Anne. Regarding Viola Turpeinen, see **Song 59**.

Vie - lä - kin seik - ka se mie - lee - ni joh - tuu kun Tur - pei - sen tyt - tö o - li rem - mis-
I see it now like it was yes - ter - day when that Tur - pei - nen's daugh - ter did to town ar -

sä. O - li - pa se sel - lais - ta ren - to - a tou - huu, kum - ma kun kaik - ki py - sy
rive. With a cat - chy tune she start - ed to play, Peo - ple they won - dered how they

hen - gis - sä. Ha - nu - ri kun lau - le - li tyt - tä - ren rin - noil - la hit - tan
would sur - vive. That ac - cor - di - on it rang out from her chest, it went hit - tan -

ti - la - tu - la hit - tan - taa. Nuo - ret ja van - hat hyp - pe - li in - nol - la
ti - la - tu - la hit - tan - taa. Both young and old they were danc - ing their best they went

hit - tan ti - la - tu - la hit - tan - taa.
hit - tan ti - la - tul - la hit - tan - taa.

Vieläkin seikka se mieleeni joutuu
kun Turpeisen tyttö oli remmissä.
Olipa se sellaista rentoa touhuu,
kumma kun kaikki pysy hengissä.
Hanuri kun lauleni tyttären rinnoilla
hittan tilatula hittantaa.
Nuoret ja vanhat ne hyppeli innolla
hittan tilatula hittantaa.

Alku jo näytti ett' passaa se kyllä
niin kaikki oli itsensä reilanneet.
Nuorilla vanhoilla parast oli yllä
oli mummotkin itsensä peilanneet.
Kaikki ne tanssivat papat sekä mammatkin
hittantilatula hittantaa.
Tanssi ne lapset ja tanssi ne ammatkin
hittantilatula hittantaa.

Vaarikin kimposi polkan tahtiin
notkea heti tuli rammasta.
Jäi penkille vain pari mummoa vahtiin
nekin sanoi kutkuttavan varvasta.
Kiihty se vauhti kun tyttö se päästeli
hittantilatula hittantaa.
Ja moni sano mitä tässä turhia säästeli
hittantilatula hittantaa.

Suutarit hakkas kun kenkää lestillä
nikkarit lykki kun höylällä.
Oli siellä vientiä emännill ja leskillä
tytöt oli tuulella nöyrällä.
Ja muurarit laski kuin moskaa tiilelle
hittantilatula hittantaa.
Ja seppäkin astui kun kuumalle hiilelle
hittantilatula hittantaa.

Harvoin on polkattu sellaista kyytii
harvoin on sakeammin astuttu.
Mummotkin ukkoja jäähylle pyyti
ne sano että tässä on jo kastuttu.
Ja tyttö se soitti kun taivaan kellolla
hittantilatula hittantaa.
Ja farmarit niitti kun heinää pellolla
hittantilatula hittantaa.

Meni siellä pitkät ja meni siellä pätkät
eikä heitä tarvinnut yllyttää.
Kiihty se vauhti ett kerran jo mätkähti
ja joitakin pyörikin jo pyllyllään.
Mitä kun tyttö niin koreasti soitteli
hittantilatula hittantaa.
Ei kumma jos neljällä kontilla koitteli
hittantilatula hittanttaa.

Oli siellä paksuu oli siellä hoikkaa
toisilla suukin oli törrössä.
Harvoin on nähty niin komiata roikkaa
akoillakin tukat oli pörrössä.
Ja tyttö se soitteli, nauroi ja rallatti
hittantilatula hittantaa.
Ja kaikki ne sano että kyllä se kannatti
hittantilatula hittantaa.

I see it now like it was yesterday,
When that Turpeinen's daughter did to town arrive.
With a catchy tune she started to play,
People they wondered how they would survive!
That accordion it rang out from her chest, it went
Hittan tilatula hittantaa.
Both young and old they were dancing their best, they went
Hittan tilatula hittantaa.

Right from the start folks were decked out so fine,
They were dressed in their Sunday duds from toe to top.
Young ones and their elders did gleam and shine
At the mirror ladies made a stop.
Mothers, fathers, kids, they were dancing like crazy, oh
Hittan tilatula hittantaa
Children and parents and all in-between they went
Hittan tilatula hittantaa.

Grandpa was dancing to her polka beat, yes,
The music it made him flex from toe to cap.
Only two old ladies did keep to their seat, yes,
Even those grannies with their toes did tap.
As the tempo rose one young girl took to panting, said:
Hittan tilatula hittantaa
"Hold nothing back!" all the others were ranting, said:
Hittan tilatula hittantaa.

Like they were hammering the cobblers did pound,
And the carpenters danced like they were planing wood.
Housewives and widows were too few to go 'round,
While girls who weren't married humbly by them stood.
It seemed like the masons were mortaring lots, they went
Hittan tilatula hittantaa
Blacksmiths they stepped like on coals that were hot, they said
Hittan tilatula hittantaa.

Seldom before has a polka gone so fast,
And seldom have dance floors been packed so tight.
Grandmas said a breather they needed at last, for
Dripping from sweat they felt so soaked that night.
And the girl she played like on heavenly bells, she went
Hittan tilatula hittantaa
Farmers like haying on slopes and on dells, they went
Hittan tilatula hittantaa.

Dancers were tall while some others were small
But no coaxing was needed to enter the fray.
Spinning on their backsides while others they did fall,
To Viola's music every hip did sway.
How that girl did play, it did bring such delight, she went
Hittan tilatula hittantaa
Crawling on the floor by the end of night, they went
Hittan tilatula hittantaa.

Some girls were plump while some were thin and proud,
And then some girls were spouting words that were so crude.
Seldom has one seen such a fine-looking crowd.
Old ladies' hairdos they were all askew,
And that girl she played, as she laughed and she sang, she went
Hittan tilatula hittantaa
And everyone's voices happily rang, they went
Hittan tilatula hittantaa

59. Unelma-valssi
Dream Waltz

From Viola Turpeinen's solo album Victor V4175 of 1928 [corrected in pen to 1938] Accordionist and singer Viola Turpeinen was born in Champion, Michigan, in 1909 and died in Lake Worth, Florida, in 1958. From the late 1920s onwards she was the best known and most popular Finnish American artist. In 1933, she married William Syrjälä of Cloquet, Minnesota. Syrjälä, who had been born in Vesivehmaa, became a professional musician already in 1913 and continued performing in his old age in Lake Worth. In his time, Syrjälä played with some of the best known musicians in the United States, e.g. cornet player Väinö Kauppi and accordionist Antti Kosola. See Kansanmusiikki 2/83. Syrjälä said he wrote this waltz for a play. Viola Turpeinen recorded it half by chance but when the producer met her performance with enthusiasm, she recorded some ten more records. The waltz was published in the liner notes to the album Siirtolaisen muistoja [Memories of a migrant] RCA PL 40115, in 1978.

Kun vie - no soit - to hil - jai - nen u - nel - mat au - kai - see, ____
A gen - tle note comes drift - ing by, the mu - sic of the band, ____

____ kun nuo - ru - kai - nen nei - dol - leen kä - ten - sä tar - joi - lee. ____
____ A dap - per young man greets his girl, and of - fers her his hand. ____

____ Hil - jal - len - sa kat - sein näin u - nel - man saa - vut - taa, ____
____ Dreams of love they so fill his heart, as danc - ing she does twirl, ____

____ on on - nel - lis - ta yl - kä näin, näin nei - don o - mis - taa. ____
____ and hap - pi - ness it fills his mind to think that she's his girl. ____

Kun vieno soitto hiljainen unelmat aukaisee,
kun nuorukainen neidolleen kätensä tarjoilee.
Hiljallensa katsein näin unelman saavuttaa,
on onnellista ylkä näin, näin neidon omistaa.

Kun vieno tuuli humajaa ja rannat loiskuaa,
niin nuoret kirkkain katsehin voi onnen saavuttaa.
Iltarusko rusoittaa ja tähdet vilkuloi,
oi onnea ja autuutta, min rakkaus se toi.

A gentle note comes drifting by, the music of the band.
A dapper young man greets his girl, and offers her his hand.
Dreams of love they so fill his heart, as dancing she does twirl,
And happiness it fills his mind, to think that she's his girl.

The breeze sings to us tenderly, and waves lap silently.
The young they see with eyes so clear, and long for happiness.
Setting sun shines and stars come out, above the sparkling sea.
And speak of joys and sorrows, too, that lovers can possess.

60. Muistatko vielä illan sen
Do You Still Remember that Night?

Singer Ernest Paananen, composed by the Paananen-Kosola orchestra. From the recording Col 3165-F or DI 179, in 1930. Paananen made all in all some five records. Paananen is mentioned as the composer, but the song was also rather well-known in Finland at this time.

Oi armahain, oi ystäväin
älä unhoita minua!
Niin kauan kuin vereni lämmin on
minä muistan sinua.

Muistatkos vielä illan sen
kun vaivuimme unelmiin?
Kun loiste rannan rakkahan
sai meidät suudelmiin.

Pois kuljin kotirannalta
jäi sinne mun ystäväin.
Vaan joskus muistot entiset
ne lämmittää sydäntäin.

Beloved friend you are so dear,
Oh please never forget me.
Oh as long as it's beating strong and true,
My heart will remember thee.

Do you remember that fair night,
When we shared our dreams in bliss?
Oh glimmering waves as they came ashore,
Accompanied our first kiss.

I left old Finland's shores behind,
So started our time apart.
But sometimes those lingering memories,
They warm my lonely heart.

61. Tuletko tyttö tanssiin
Will You Come and Dance Girl?

From the record Col 3134-F or DI 41, from 1929. Heikki Tuominen produced a waltz of the same name in 1929 (Odeon A 228093). Tuominen's record lists Oskar Nyström as the composer. Kuuno Sevander produced six records in the United States. In the 1930s he moved to the Soviet Union and seems to have been a folk artist of note for some years in Petroskoi/Petrozavodsk.

Nuo - ruu - den päi - vät on viel_____ muis - tos - sa - ni,_____ kun
Those days of my youth gone by_____ How time does fly_____ I

kul - jin ja ku - her - te - lin_____ ja tans - sin lau - la - en._____
danced with the mai-dens so free_____ and flirt - ed shame - less - ly._____

Pir - tis - sä viu - lut ne soi_____ kun nuo - ret kar - ke - loi:_____
Vi - o - lins in - side they played_____ Young folks they danced and swayed___

___ Tu - le vaan,_____ tu - le vaan,_____ tu - le tyttö - ni tan - si maan___
___ Come with me,_____ come with me_____ My dear come and dance with me.____

Nuoruuden päivät on viel
muistossani,
kun kuljin ja kuhertelin
ja tanssin laulaen.
Pirtissä viulut ne soi
kun nuoret karkeloi:
Tule vaan, tule vaan,
tule tyttöni tanssimaan.

Soitto se valssia soi
ja poijat tyttöjä toi.
Mäkelän Mandi tuli kans
ja mukana renki Frans.
Toisiinsa vilkuili niin
ja Franssi kävi Mandiin kiin:
Tule vaan, tule vaan,
tule Mandini tanssimaan.

Tanssittiin valssia niin,
aivan pyörryksiin,
perään ei annettu ei,
vaan poijat tyttöjä vei.
Isäntä nurkassa myös
otti emäntää kiinni vyöst:
Tule nyt, tules nyt,
ennenkuin sä myöhästyt.

Those days of my youth gone by,
How time does fly.
I danced with the maidens so free,
And flirted shamelessly.
Violins inside they played,
Young folks they danced and swayed.
Come with me, come with me,
My dear come and dance with me.

Boys took their sweethearts along,
Heeding the song.
And Mäkelä's Mandi was fair,
As farmhand Franz stood there.
All it took was but a glance,
Then Franz asked her to dance.
Come with me, come with me,
Mandi, come and dance with me.

We danced that old waltz just right,
All through the night.
We sang and we danced without stop,
Us boys and girls we hopped.
The old man there in the wings,
He grabs his wife and sings,
Come with me, come with me,
Or too late it soon will be.

62. Taattoni maja
My Father's Cottage

Col. 3202-F, from 1932. Re-released in 1982, CBS 25197. Composed and performed by Hiski Sa-lomaa. Lyrics for this and the following song published in the same album.

Ei tä - män po - jan ko - ti suu rem pi ol lu ku kar ta non koi ran kop pi
The young man's cot - tage it was na - ry so big as a dog's house at the man - or

vaan se o li mu le niin hel - lä ja nät - ti ja ai - no - a rau - han sop - pi.
but it was for me so___ nice and free it was peace-ful with-out an - y clam - or.

Ei tämän pojan koti suurempi ollu
ku kartanon koiran koppi
vaan se oli mulle niin hellä ja nätti
ja ainoa rauhan soppi.

Taattoni maja oli matala ja pieni
ja porrasta siin oli kaksi
kun läksin mä taattoni porraspuulta
tään maailman kulkijaksi

Taattoni majan raitilla kasvoi
kaksi pihlajapuuta
niiden juurilla istuin illat pitkät
ja katselin kaunista kuuta.

Kun annansilmä ja auringonkukka
se ikkunalaudalla kukki
hämyhetkin hiljaa se hyrähteli
tuo äitini vanha rukki.

Ku hyljätty äitini rukkinsa ääressä
kehräili pitkät illat
ja kyyneleet ne poskilta vierähteli
jotta kasteli vierahat villat.

Kun kuusi oli lastansa kuolema vienyt
ja tuoni kai turvana heille
ja muisteli sortuuko poikansa tumma
näille maailman markkinateille.

Sitten minä kuulin sen kuiskaavan äänen
noitten Atlannin aaltojen yli
:,: että kotona on kylmennyt kulkuripojalla
tuo hyljätyn äitin syli. :,:

The young man's cottage it was nary so big
As a dog's house at the manor.
But it was for me so nice and free,
It was peaceful without any clamor.

My father's cottage it was lowly and small
It had two stairs made of stone.
When I took my leave from my father's doorstep,
Out into the world alone.

Out on the road beside my father's cottage
Grew two rowan trees.
And I would sit there alone in the evening,
Comforted by moon and breeze.

When in the spring all of the flowers did bloom,
In pots on the windowsill.
My mother she would sit at her old spinning wheel,
And I'd listen to the hum and trill.

My lonely mother she would sit at her wheel,
A'spinning by moonlight.
Tears were streaming down her care-worn cheeks, they were
Dampening the wool all night.

Death had taken from her six of her children,
To a peaceful strand.
And she wondered if the son who had left,
Would perish in that foreign land.

I heard a voice that was a'whisp'ring to me, it came
Over the waves and sea.
:,: Mother's lonely heart it beat no more,
She had waited for me faithfully. :,:

63. Savon poian Amerikkaan tulo
A Savo Guy Arrives in America

Col 3081-F, 1928. Although the label mentions a "piika," ("girl"), the song is clearly about a male migrant, as he works in a mine. The song evinces Hiski's tendency to use slang, dialect, and Finnish American terminology sometimes called "Finnglish." The representation of Savo dialect here is not entirely accurate in terms of diphthongs and final consonants but words are typical.

Myö tän - ne mua - han kot - to kun läh - het - tii, ja äi' - il - le hy - väs - ti
When lea - ving for this land that's so far a - way, fare - well dear old mo - ther,

jä - tet - tii ni vet - tä si - tä tul sil - lon sil - mis - tä.___ mel - keen ku uk - ko - sen
we did say. She whim - pered and she cried and her tears did fall like rain co - ming down in a

pil - vis - tä. Huo - men - ua - mul - la ol - tiin Hang - on nie - mel - lä
thun - der squall. On the morn - ing there - af - ter we came to Han - ko.

hu - as - tet - ti myö sa - von kie - lel - lä vaik - ka en - kel - is - koo o - li - si jo
There we chat - ted lots like back in Sa - vo. Though by speak - ing there in Eng - lish we could

o - san - nut niin ei - pä tuo - hon kuk - kaa vaan vas - tan - nut.
sure get by, our talk ing like in Sa - vo got no re ply.

Myö tänne muahan kottoo kun lähettii
ja äi'ille hyvästi jätettii
niin vettä sitä tul sillon silmistä
melkeen ku ukkosen pilvistä.
Huomenuamulla oltiin Hangonniemellä
huastettiin myö savonkielellä
vaikka enkeliskoo olisi jo osannut
niin eipä tuohon kukkaa vaan vastannut.

Itämer ku se ylpeesti lainehti
ja Arcturus meitä jo tuuvitti
kotrantoo myö laivassa katottii
kun majakasta valkeeta näytettii.
Merikippeitä alko jo olemaan
ja minnäi ku ruppee jo tuulemaan
eväsputelista otin vuan tuikkuja
ja piälle söin suolasia muikkuja.

Sitte ku oltiin myö Hullissa
ja lävitte piästii myö tullista
niin masinalla mua yl myö ajettii
ja Liverpollii myö suavuttii.
Tuas laivoo ku mäntii myö kahtomaa
entistä pitempöö ja äikempöö
niin oikeen se silloin hirvitti
kun viimosen kerran se huuatti.

Tähet kun ne tuikkii taivaalla
oltiin tuas Atlannin uavalla
Allan-linjalaivalla
myrsky se käy ja muata ei näy
Mutku New Yorkin ranta alko lähetä
kot'eväs minun pussistani vähetä
ol ihan niinku uuvesti syntynä oes
kun piäs sieltä Atlannin myrskyistä pois.

Amerikkoi meitä tänne tuotihin
ja mainissa multoo myö luotihin
piällysmiestä siellä ei tarvittu
mua ennen oli toisia jo otettu.
Mutta sitte ku mäntii mehtäkämpille
savonkielikin kuulosti jo jänkille
kun porilainen alko siellä soveltaa
ja savolainen piältä vua komentaa.

When leaving for this land that's so far away,
"Farewell dear old mother," we did say.
She whimpered and she cried and her tears did fall,
Like rain coming down in a thunder squall.
On the morning thereafter we came to Hanko.
There we chatted lots like back in Savo.
Though by speaking there in English we could sure get by,
Our talking like in Savo got no reply.

We looked out at the breathtaking Baltic Sea,
The steamliner Arcturus welcomely.
From deckside we watched our native shore,
It slid out of sight and was seen no more.
Oh the waves of the ocean they went to my head,
Seasick down in steerage I felt half dead.
From my travel picnic basket I got rations few,
A couple salted fish I began to chew.

Then after all that sailing to Hull we came,
And passed there through customs and made our claims.
Then by a locomotive we made our way,
In Liverpool, we had a stay.
Then we went to the harbor to behold our ship.
It was big and long, from stern to tip.
And it gave us all the willies when at once it blew,
Its great big horn shook us through and through.

The twinkling of stars in the night time sky,
The Atlantic passage made time go by.
A Mr. Allan owned that steamer there,
And storms they were raging and land nowhere.
When at last in the distance we saw New York bay,
My rations were low, nearly gone away.
And we felt at that moment we were born again,
Saved from the ocean by shore right then.

Now to America we came to stay.
In dark, dirty mines we worked all day.
No boss was ever needed, was plain to see,
They never had much use for a guy like me.
Now we work the lumber camps where trees abound,
Here my Savo words they quite normal sound.
And if some old man from Pori tries to have his say,
This Savo man will take his command away.

64. Talvella maa oli valkoinen
The Ground Was White During Winter

Col. 3169-F circa 1930. Composer listed as Wäinö Kauppi & Co. Kauppi was a well-known cornet player. The words of this song appear in several Finnish ring dances.

Tal - vel - la maa o - li val - koi - nen ja__ ke - säl - lä kel - las - ta - va
Win - ter__ ground it is cold and white, while sum - mer turns all green.

kak - si o - li hei - li - ä täl - lä - kin po - jal - la ja toi - nen o - li her - ras - ta - va.
This here lad has got two girl__ friends and the one thinks that she's a queen.

Talvella maa oli valkoinen
ja kesällä kellastava,
kaksi oli heiliä tälläkin pojalla
ja toinen oli herrastava.

Ja se parempi kun erokirjan kirjoitti
sille kotimökin akkunalle,
sano nyt minä lähden jo toisen kanssa
papin pakinoille.

Jos se ois ollu se huonompi heili
en surisi sen perään,
mut sitä minen sure etten uutta mä saa
mutta sellasta en saa enää.

Kun helluni jätti niin tämä poika läksi
näille Amerikan kultamaille,
mut kun köyhästä torpasta kotosin mä olen
niin rikkautta jäin minä vaille.

Eikä nuo Atlannin laineetkaan
kasvanu ruusuja punasia,
vaanhan ne tuutii New Yorkin rantaan
poikia tuhansia.

Kun laivamme lippua liehutteli
toi ankara pohjantuuli,
täällä New Yorkin rannassa neekerityttö
mua helluksensa se luuli.
Niin New Yorkin rannassa neekerityttö
mua helluksensa se luuli.

Winter ground it is cold and white,
While summer turns all green.
This here lad has got two girlfriends
And the one thinks that she's a queen.

She wrote a letter jilting me
At my cottage dropped it by
She went to the priest with another man
And in her letter she told me why.

If I had lost the other girl
It wouldn't bother me
I'll find another, but not one like her,
One of her quality.

When she finally turned me away
I went across the sea
But as just a poor boy coming to America
That doesn't make life easy.

Roads that lead to America
They are not all paved with gold
Still these Finnish men they are lured there
On the promise of New York they're sold.

Flags of our ship they were fluttering
As a northern wind did blow
That was when a black New Yorker girl pegged me
As a guy she would like to know,
On the shores of New York harbor.
As a guy she would like to know,

65. Tiskarin polkka
The Dishwasher's Polka

Col. 3045-F, 1927.

Finnish American terminology used in this song:
Dressa = dress, outfit
Iistiläistä = Easterner
Kitsi = kitchen
Milkman = milkman

Äm - mät ne huu - taa juo ja mäs - sää mi - nä vaan as - ti - oi - ta
Fan - cy boss la - dies eat - ing, shout - ing, while I got dish - es to be

tis - kaan täs - sä kah - vi pan - us - ta tah - toi maa - han men - nä
scrub - bing, and there's plen - ty "Hey girl - ie look out, cof fee's spilled out!"

e - hän mi - nä kaik - ki - hin len - nä. Milk man se var - hain mai - to - a kan - taa ei
They just keep me flat out__ run - ning. Milk man he brings the milk way too ear - ly and

rau - has - sa tah - to nuk - ku - a an - taa koi - ra - kin tar - teis ul - ko - na käyt - tää
I'd rath - er have some shut eye sure - ly. Dog needs to pee and get out__ quick - ly.

kis - sal - le kup - pi täyt - tää. Mi - nä vaan tis - kaan as - ti - oi - ta ja
Cat needs her milk poured strict - ly. In the back room I wash and scrub up__

luu - tal - la la - ka - sen lat - ti - oi - ta ti - li - ti - li ti - li - ti - li - tit - tat taa kyl - lä
sweep off the floor __ boards and then wipe up. Tee-lee tee-lee tee-lee tee-lee tee-tat tee yes and

tors - tai mei - tä nyt loh - dut - taa.
Thurs-days we take it ea - sy.

Ämmät ne huutaa juo ja mässää
minä vaan astioita tiskaan tässä
kahvi pannusta tahtoi maahan mennä
ehän minä kaikkihin lennä.
Milkman se varhain maitoa kantaa
ei rauhassa tahto nukkua antaa
koirakin tartteis ulkona käyttää
kissalle kuppi täyttää.
Minä vaan tiskaan astioita
ja luutalla lakasen lattioita
tilitilitilitilitittattaa
kyllä torstai meitä nyt lohduttaa.

Joskus kun ämmä on kitsiin tullu
niin siellä se huutaa kun puolihullu
ootko sä laittanu ukolle ruokaa
hälle nyt kahvia tuokaa.
Munkkinen pitäisi tenavalle taittaa
lapselle tarttis resuaki vaihtaa
papukaija huutaa piikaa piikaa
ovikello rinkaa
Minä vaan tiskaan astioita
ja luutalla lakasen lattioita
tilitilitilitilitittattaa
kyllä torstai meitä nyt lohduttaa.

Sitte ku on tullunna torstai-ilta
niin polkasta notkuu se haalin silta
kun Janne se vie sitä lännen mallia
Puavo Iistiläistä.
Toiset ne puhkii sieltä ja täältä
aivan dressakin tahtoi puota päältä
nuoret ne hyppää ympäri haalia
vanhat ne nurkassa mäiskää
Orkesteri soittaa hiitula hiitaa...
tilitili...
kyllä torstai meitä nyt lohduttaa.

Sieltä hellun ku lähtee kotia tuomaan
kahvilaan mennään otetaan juomaa
kupit siellä kalisee ryskää ja räiskää
on tunne kun Härmän häissä.
Siellä kun istut sa puoleen yöhön
kotia tultua alotta työhön
mutta ei kerkii ku dressan vaihtaa
ja hellun kotia laittaa
Minä vaan tiskaan astioita
ja luutalla lakasen lattioita
tilitilitilitilitittattaa
kyllä torstai meitä nyt lohduttaa.

Fancy boss ladies eating, shouting,
While I got dishes to be scrubbing and there's plenty
"Hey, girlie, look out, coffee's spilled out!"
They just keep me flat out running.
Milkman he brings the milk way too early and
I'd rather have some shut eye surely.
Dog needs to pee and get out quickly.
Cat needs her milk poured strictly.
In the back room I wash and scrub up,
Sweep off the floor boards and then wipe up.
Tee-lee tee-lee tee-lee tee-lee tee-tat-tee
Yes, and Thursdays we take it easy.

Sometimes the lady comes out blazing
She just lays it on—boy she is crazy!—
"Get my husband something to eat
He needs coffee now, I repeat."
Sonny needs doughnuts for a treat and the
Baby needs diaper changed to smell sweet and
Parrot calls out "come here you darn girlie"
Doorbell rings too early.
In the back room I wash and scrub up and
Sweep off the floor boards and then wipe up
Tee-lee tee-lee tee-lee tee-lee tee-tat-tee yes, and
Thursdays we take it easy.

Then when it's Thursday night at Finn hall
There's a polka shaking the ceilings, floors, and walls!
Janne he plays like he's from Austin,
Puavo plays like he's from Boston.
Others they sashay this way and that way and
Girls want to drop their dress on the mat and
Young guys jumping 'round the dance hall
Old folks don't heed the call.
The band plays out hee-tu-la hee-taa-taa
pr-pr-pr-pr-pr-pr-hee-taa
Hee-lu hee-lu hee-lu hee-lu lee yes, and
Thursdays we take it easy.

Fellas they take their gals to café
For a drink after dancing the night away.
Coffee cups clinking this way, that way,
It's like Härmä's wedding day.
We spend the night like that a'chumming,
Then rush home a polka a'humming.
Time to change clothes for work is a'lacking,
Got to send your boyfriend packing.
In the back room I wash and scrub up and
Sweep off the floor boards and then wipe up
Tee-lee tee-lee tee-lee tee-lee tee-tat tee yes and
Thursdays we take it easy.

66. Kemppaisen avioelämä
Kemppainen's Marriage

Col. 3169-F circa 1930. See **Song 64**.

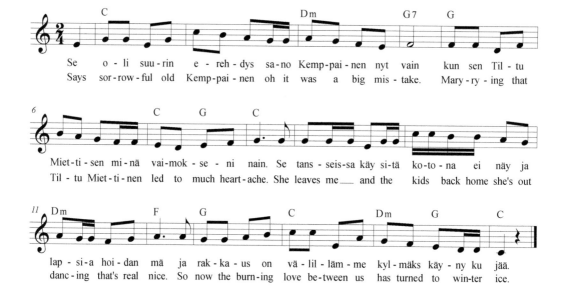

Se o-li suu-rin e-reh-dys sa-no Kemp-pai-nen nyt vain kun sen Til-tu
Says sor-row-ful old Kemp-pai-nen oh it was a big mis-take. Mar-ry-ing that

Miet-ti-sen mi-nä vai-mok-se-ni nain. Se tans-seis-sa käy si-tä ko-to-na ei näy ja
Til-tu Miet-ti-nen led to much heart-ache. She leaves me___ and the kids back home she's out

lap-si-a hoi-dan mä ja rak-ka-us on vä-lil-läm-me kyl-mäks käy-ny ku jää.
danc-ing that's real nice. So now the burn-ing love be-tween us has turned to win-ter ice.

Se oli suurin erehdys sano Kemppainen nyt vain
kun sen Tiltu Miettisen minä vaimokseni nain.
Se tansseissa käy, sitä kotona ei näy
ja lapsia hoidan mä.
Rakkaus on välillämme kylmäks käyny ku jää.

Se lemmenliekki, joka rinnoissamme ennen salamoi
nyt se meidän välillemme synkän pilven löi
Vaik minä olen päivät kotonamme
ja Tiltu töissä käy
silti meidän liitossamme paljon hauskaa näy.

Minä ennen kävin päivät työss
olin miesten parhaita
sill aikaa Tiltun luona
myös alkoi käydä varkaita
ja sehän meidän kotimme nyt pirstaleiksi löi
ja kun Tiltu eilen tavaramme kaikki halvennuksell möi.

Nyt lapsemme hän hoidettavaks laittoi vieraille
ja minut hän nyt laittoi aivan puillen paljaille
näin Kemppainen nyt lauleli
ja murtunut oli miel
ja pulloansa suuteli et vertyi hieman kiel
Näin Kemppainen...

Says sorrowful old Kemppainen "Oh it was a big mistake.
Marrying that Tiltu Miettinen led to much heartache.
She leaves me and the kids back home,
She's out dancing, that's real nice.
So now the burning love between us has turned to winter ice."

"That flaming love that burned within our hearts both night and day
It's behind a sullen cloud that hides the light away
Oh, I sit at home, I am moping all day, in misery I lurk
While Tiltu gets her duds on
and then heads off to her work."

"I used to be a working man, I was among the best
Till Tiltu with her antics started marriage vows to test.
Our wedded life it was shattered as thieves in the night did creep,
And now my Tiltu's selling off our furnishings for cheap."

"Now into others' caring, she has sent our kids away.
There's no place for me there, she's given me the boot, they say.
I'll sing about my misery," said Kemppainen mournfully
And he can kiss the bottle now that keeps him company.

67. Lännen lokari
Logger of the West

Col. 3158-F published in 1930. Composer Wäinö Kauppi, Larsen & Co. While some scholars and audience members have interpreted Salomaa's "Lousissa" as St. Louis (e.g., Pitkänen and Sutinen 2011, 153), others have noted that it was a common name for Los Angeles, an interpretation that adds a further dimension to the singer's assertion that a "tähti" (star) awaits him there. The line "mut onkos ollu Iistin Iikka?" (literally, "has Iistin Iikka been here?") refers to a well-known hobo Iikka Niemi, whom Hiski Salomaa met shortly before composing this song. Reportedly the two men argued about which of them had visited more places (Pitkänen and Sutinen 2011, 141–142). The translation below substitutes "city slicker" to capture the assumed caché of being from the East, as opposed to the singer's presumed Upper Midwestern background. Salomaa composed the song in Chicago. Niemi eventually returned to Finland, bringing home with him abundant stories of his time in America as well as a transcription of Salomaa's song.

Täss on lo-ka-ri ny län-nen ri-su-kos-ta o-len kul-ke-nu vaik-ka-mis-sä. O-len
I'm a log-ger from the tim-ber camps of the west, and I've ram-bled__ nigh all o-ver. I've been

käy-nyn-nä Piut-tis-sa, Lou-sis-sa, Re-tu-laats-is-sa, Mi-a-mis-sa. O-len
out to__ Butte and L A to boot, Red-Lodge and__ Mi-am-i, sir. I have

kul-ke-nu mer-ta ja man-te-rei-ta ja A-las-kan tun-tu-rei-ta ja
been on the sea and the con-ti__ nents and the peaks up in A-las-ka! And just

kaik-ki-al-la hu-li-vi-li tyt-tär-et muis-taa län-nen lo-ka-rei-ta.
ev'ry place I go - the wild__ girls all__ know the log-gers of the West.

Täss on lokari ny lännen risukosta
olen kulkenu vaikka missä
olen käynynnä Piuttissa, Lousissa,
Retulaatsissa, Miamissa.
Olen kulkenu merta ja mantereita
ja Alaskan tuntureita
ja kaikkialla hulivilityttäret muistaa
lännen lokareita.

Ja lokari on lokari ja hellunkin ottaa
vaikka toisen emännästä
ja vesi ei tuu silmiin vaikka ne taukoo
Iistin flikat näkymästä.
Sillä Piuttiss on ruusu ja Lousis on tähti
ja Alaskassa pulmusia,
ja kaikki ne kuiskii; oletkos sä nähnynnä
lännen kulkuria?

Miss on Meksikon Lempi ja Honolulun Impi
ja Filippiinin keltanen flikka,
siellä lokari on ollut heidän keskellänsä
mut onkos ollu Iistin Iikka?
Miss on kulkurin kulta, sydän iskeepi tulta,
niin kaunis on heillä jo tukka,
sä kun laulun kun kuulet, niin linnuksi luulet
taasen rakastuupi lännen jukka.

On Friskossa käyty, on Orengoni nähty,
miss on kesä sekä lumiset vuoret.
Takotass on puitu, Palm Piitsilla uitu,
ja hellutettu vanhat ja nuoret.
Mutta punapuun kantoon kun torppansa laittaa,
niin sinne se ilon päivä koittaa.
Vaikka maailman myrskyt meitä tuudittaa
niin vapaus se varmasti voittaa.

I'm a logger from the timber camps of the West,
And I've rambled nigh all over!
I have been out to Butte and L.A. to boot,
Red Lodge and Miami, sir.
I have been on the sea and the continents,
And the peaks up in Alaska!
And just ev'ry place I go the wild girls all know
The loggers of the West.

Now a logger is a guy who'll take him a gal,
Even if she is somebody else's.
Never fear, not a tear will he shed at all,
When he leaves those Eastern lasses.
'Cause a Butte gal is fine, L.A. stars they shine,
what a snow bird in Alaska!
and they whisper one and all, "Have you seen this fall,
that rambler of the West?"

Where's a Mexicali gal, Honolulu pearl,
Or a pretty Filipina,
There this logger has been with them one and all,
Better than any city slicker.
Where I cast my eye, my heart beats high,
What beauties head to toe!
If their singing you heard, you would think it a bird,
This logger's heart does know.

Now Frisco I've seen, Oregon I have been,
Where there's summer and mountains cold.
To Dakota I've come, at Palm Beach I've swum,
Greeting friends both young and old.
When you build your house, settle 'neath the pine,
That day for joy you'll shout.
Though the storms of life can cause us strife,
Freedom finally does win out.

Finnish American terminology used in this song:
Frisko = San Francisco
Lokari = logger
Lousi = St. Louis or Los Angeles
Orengoni = Oregon
Palm Piitsi = Palm Beach
Piutti = Butte, Montana
Retulaatsi = Red Lodge, Montana
Takota = Dakota
Friskossa = in San Francisco
Orengoni = Oregon

68. Dahlmannin paartit
Party at the Dahlmans'

Col. 3111-F, 1929. Composed by Härninen's orchestra. William Syrjälä had joined the orchestra to replace Wäinö Kauppi in 1928.

Mi - nä kut-sun sain ker - ran kes-tei-hin mis-is Dahl-man-nin ni-mi-päi-vä-paar-tei-hin ei
Got an in-vite to a fine fes-ti vi-ty, Mrs. Dahl-mann's name day___ par-ty. No

i - lot siel-lä si - nä yö-na puut-tu-neet sil-lä su-rut o-li kai-kil-le suut-tu-neet. Siellä
shor - tage of mer-ri-ment o-ver there. They had let___ go of ev-er-y sin-gle care. They

juo - mi-a o-li mon-ta sort-ti-a pe-lat-tiin-pa hie-man myös___
sat play-ing cards with___ such de-light, sip-ping on their drinks all_____ through

kort - ti-a. Ei-hän ih-me o-le ol-lut jos koh-me-lo on tul-lut tuol-la
the___ night. Oh it comes as no sur-prise if the day-light hurts your eyes, that's a_____

Dahl-man-nin___ yl-lä-tys-paar-teis-sa.
hang ov-er from Dahl-mann's par-ty.

Finnish American terminology used in this song:
Biiri = beer
Hot dogsit = hot dogs
Ice creamit = ice cream
Paartit = party

Minä kutsun sain kerran kesteihin,
Missis Dahlmannin nimipäiväpaarteihin.
Ei ilot siellä sinä yönä puuttuneet
Sillä surut oli kaikille suuttuneet.
Siellä juomia oli monta sorttia,
Pelattiinpa hieman myös korttia.
Eihän ihme ole ollu jos kohmelo on tullu
Tuolla Dahlmannin yllätyspaarteissa.

Paartivieraat ne Dahlmannin yllätti,
Lapset nurkkihin nukku että pyllähti.
Koira vieraita alkoi myös haukkua
Itse Dahlmanni tarjosi naukkuja.
Pikku tuikun anto koirankin huulelle,
tuli Bobikin jo paremmalle tuulelle.
Eihän ihme ole ollu jos kohmelo on tullu
Sille Dahlmannin yllätyspaarteissa.

Juhlapöytä oli kauniiksi laitettu
Ja viinit oli lasihin jo kaadettu.
Siellä gramofoni soitteli valssia
Ja nuoremmat alkoi myös tanssia.
Minä tanssihin pyysin missis Hiiliä.
Toiset joivat ja söivät Norjan silliä.
Eihän ihme ole ollu jos kohmelo on tullu
Tuolla Dahlmannin yllätyspaarteissa.

Ja se aamuyö oli vasta reilua
Koska minäkin jo aloin siellä heilua.
Missis Dahlmanni ylös vielä nostettiin
Ja se pöytälamppu lahjaks sille ostettii.
Hot dogsit, ice creamit syötiin viel
Ka biirillä kostutettiin kiel.
Eihän ihme ole ollu jos kohmelo on tullu
Tuolla Dahlmannin yllätyspaarteissa.

Got an invite to a fine festivity,
Mrs. Dahlmann's name-day party.
No shortage of merriment over there,
They had let go of every single care.
They sat playing cards with such delight,
Sipping on their drinks all through the night.
Oh it comes as no surprise if the daylight hurts your eyes,
That's a hangover from Dahlmann's party.

The guests all surprised Mrs. Dahlmann,
In bed slept all of her children.
The Dahlmann's noisy dog was always barking lots,
While that Dahlmann offered us all some shots.
They dribbled some booze on the puppy's lips,
He was so happy after those few sips.
Oh it comes as no surprise if the daylight hurts your eyes,
That's a hangover from Dahlmann's party.

Oh the table it was laid out rich and fine,
Every seat had a glass that was filled up with wine.
The gramophone all wound up started then to play,
And the young folks started waltzing the night away.
I offered to dance with old Mrs. Hill.
Fancy plates of herring people ate their fill.
Oh it comes as no surprise if the daylight hurts your eyes,
That's a hangover from Dahlmann's party.

Oh the party lasted to the break of day.
From that drinking and dancing my poor legs did sway.
There's Mrs. Dahlmann on their shoulders lifted high.
And a fancy table lamp for her they did buy.
There were hot dogs and ice cream for us all to eat.
Mugs full of cold beer were a further treat.
Oh it comes as no surprise if the daylight hurts your eyes,
That's a hangover from Dahlmann's party.

69. Värssyjä sieltä ja täältä
Verses from Here and There

Col. 3189-F circa 1931. Composed by the Kosola orchestra. Antti Kosola and his orchestra are often mentioned on record labels of the time.

Nyt työ-tä mi-nä o-len taas kat-sel-lut piek-sun-poh-jat-ki ha-jal-le
Oh it is pret-ty tough to find work to-day. And the soles on my shoes they're nigh

as-tel-lut ja kan-nat-ki men-ny on lin-tal-le. Kä-ret
torn a-way. My heels they are a-ching from walk-ing 'bout, and I

sil-mi-hin kat-soo ja tar-kal-leen et-tä mis-sä-hän mah-taa
look at my hands and they're all worn out. I__ stare and ask "What is

vi-ka taas ol-la kun uu-si-a ei a-la jal-koi-hin tul la. Kur-jal-ta näyt-tää
wrong with me? I'm just not as__ young as I used to be." And I look like a beg-gar

ai-ka jo tää ja har-maak-si käy taas monen pojan pää
with bills to pay. The hair on my head keeps turn-ing gray.

Finnish American terminology used in this song:
Postata, postuun partaalla, postottaa = to exhaust, starve, die, go bankrupt, "huppis"
Horsi = horse
Republiikki = Republican
Demokraatti = Democrat
Wall Striitti = Wall Street

Nyt työtä minä olen taas katsellut
pieksun pohjatki hajalle astellut
ja kannatki menny on lintalle.
Käret silmihin katsoo jo tarkalleen
ett missähän mahtaa vika taas olla
kun uusia ei ala jalkoihin tulla.
Kurjalta näyttää aika jo tää
ja harmaaksi käy taas monen pojan pää.

Wall Striitti se nauraa partaansa
kun kaikki se on saanu alle valtansa.
Paavikin huutaa ny herrassaan
että kirkotkin postaa jo kerrassaan.
Bolseviikit museoita niistä nyt laittaa
se pappien unta hieman kai haittaa
kun niiltäkin alkaa jo loppua työ
kait synkältä näyttää ku syksyinen yö.

Jos enklannin työläiset lakkoontuu
Yrjö yskähän aina silloin sairastuu
ja prinssin horssikin kompastuu
ja nenä hältä joka kerta loukkaantuu.
Sotakorvaukset Saksalla purree jo vatsaa
Espanja kuninkaansa laittoi nyt matkaan.
Ei Ranskassa työttömyys kai haittanne tuo
kun maailman rikkaat siellä mässää ja juo

Setä Sami se on myös viisas mies
se bisneksen kyllä hyvin tarkoin ties.
Meillä puhuvat kuvatkin on vallassa
moni taiteilija on ollu pannassa
masina se heidänkin paikkansa otti
ja työttömäks kadulle ne tuhansia johti.
Moni soittaja halvalla pillinsä möi
ja lunssina viimeiset tinansai söi.

Meitä finnoja on täällä setä Samin maas
noin viitisensataa tuhatta
täällä me elämme kuin taivahas
vaikk moni on tullu tänne luvatta.
Meillä puoluehommat on suuria
on haalit kun baabelin muuria
mones paikassa niitä on meillä jo kuus
ja riita kun syntyy niin tehdään uus.

Vaikka republiikki meitä nyt hallitsee
silti demokraatti aika se vallitsee
ja kaikki on postuun partaalla
yhä odotamme mielillä hartaalla.
Moni poika lyöny on jo rukkaset tiskiin
ja juonunna nykyajan huonoa viskii
että töppöset ylös aina keikahtaa
jo viimeisen kerran veisataa.

Oh, it is pretty tough to find work today,
And the soles on my shoes they're nigh torn away.
My heels they are aching from walking 'bout,
And I look at my hands and they're all worn out.
I stare and ask "What is wrong with me?
I'm just not as young as I used to be."
And I look like a beggar with bills to pay.
The hairs on my head keep turning gray.

Oh Wall Street is laughing under its breath,
As we all are working ourselves to death.
The Pope keeps saying the banks are corrupt,
Even the churches they are going bankrupt.
The Bolsheviks buy them as monuments.
Priestly ideals they are long since spent.
The bishop he sits, no one talks to him.
His future is looking gray and grim.

In England striking is what workers do.
And that makes King Georgy catch the flu.
The royal horse will stumble down.
And the king will bump his nose on the ground.
War reparations are hurting the Germans.
Spain sent their king on a trip to be certain.
French unemployment? Never fret,
The rich will guzzle everything they get.

Yes, Uncle Sam is a smart old man.
He's got himself a good business plan.
Here talking pictures stole the role,
Real artists are stuck living on the dole.
Mechanization took their work away,
And thousands are jobless on the street today.
The musicians sold their work for cheap,
And spent their last money so they could eat.

We live in this country of Uncle Sam's.
Five hundred thousand do we stand.
They tell us life here it is heavenly,
Though many of us came illegally.
Party politics they are a big thing here,
We've built us halls both far and near.
In some places we've built more than six.
We build new halls our squabbling to fix.

Although a Republican now has clout,
A Democrat is going to win out.
So everyone marches up the stairs,
Taking on their shoulders what's rightfully theirs.
Many a man stops at a bar to drink,
Like bad whiskey this life sure does stink.
Flat on the ground and boots in the air,
He sings about how it's all unfair.

70. Laulu taiteilijoista
Song about Artists

Tä - mä lau - lu on ny - ky - a - jan tai - tel - i - joist o - let - te - kos kuul - lu te
Here's a lit - le___ dit - ty a - bout art - ists to - day. Have you ever heard a - ny of

en - nen moist___ nii - tä nyt syn - tyy kun sat - teel - la sie - ni - ä
them___ play? They sprout up like mush - rooms in sum - mer rain. There are

ja jou - kos on suu - ria jou - kos on pie - niä him - pu - ta him - pu - ta him - pum - paa
big ones and small ones on stage they are play - in' Him - pu - ta him - pu - ta him - pum - paa

tä - mä poi - ka pol - kat ai - na ral - lat - taa.
This boy al - ways wants to hum a po - ol - ka.

Finnish American terminology used in this song:
Djässi = Jazz

Tämä laulu on nykyajan taiteilijoist
olettekos kuullut te ennen moist?
Niitä nyt syntyy kun satteella sieniä
ja joukos on suuria joukos on pieniä.
Himputa himputa himpumpaa
tämä poika polkat aina rallattaa.

Toiset istuu jo kunnian paikalla
Toiset Pekkarisen Tatunkin paidalla
siinä se on mies joka lauluja laittaa
toiset vain tuloksista maljoja maistaa
Himputa himputa himpumpaa
tämä poika polkat aina rallattaa.

Vaikka musiikki on taiteista suurempaa
nii soittajat sen on yhä kurjempaa
torvee ne puhaltaa ja viuluva nyhtää
taskut on empty se meinaa jo tyhjää
Himputa himputa himpumpaa
tämä poika polkat aina rallattaa.

Kaikki taiteilijat ovat itserakkaita
ovat toinen toistansa parhaita
mutta turneematkoja kaikki nyt laittaa
jo Virsulan Maijakin konsertin antaa
Himputa himputa himpumpaa
tämä poika polkat aina rallattaa.

Sama ohjelma heillä on kaikilla
niin Maijalla myöskin kuin Maikilla
eipä heiltä löyty yhtään uutta
vaikka heitä kuuntelis sataa kuutta
Himputa himputa himpumpaa
tämä poika polkat aina rallattaa.

Mutta parempata ei meillä taiteesta näy
nyt vanhaki roska se täytestä käy
musiikista aakkosia meillä ei oo kellään
mut gramofonilevyihinkin laulamahan mennään
Himputa himputa himpumpaa
Täällä tämä poika polkat aina rallattaa.

Meistä raskaalta tuntuu tuo arkinen työ
siks turneekimatkoille lähetään myö
joka nyt vaan lauluja viisikin ossaa
ja konsertin antoon lähtee jo hoksaa
nii ääni saa olla ku pässillä
kerran ohjelmaa jatketaan djässillä
kerran ohjelmaa jatketaan djässillä.

Here's a little ditty about artists today.
Have you ever heard any of them play?
They sprout up like mushrooms in summer rain.
There are big ones and small ones, on stage they are playin'
Himputa, himputa, himpumpaa
This boy always wants to hum a polka.

Some artists are sitting in seats so high.
Others want to find coattails to ride.
Some of them work to create their own song.
While some others are profiting by riding along.
Himputa, himputa, himpumpaa
This boy always wants to hum a polka.

Even though good music is the finest art,
Players get for pay an empty cart.
They blow on their horns and pluck their violins,
Pockets are empty – always have been.
Himputa, himputa, himpumpaa
This boy always wants to hum a polka.

All artists are cocky, so arrogant,
Each one thinks that they are heaven sent.
Each Mike and Maija is out on tour,
But truth to be told, their talent is poor.
Himputa, himputa, himpumpaa
This boy always wants to hum a polka.

Mike and Maija play the same old songs,
Thinking that everyone will sing along.
Everything they do's been done before,
It's a lineup guaranteed to bore.
Himputa, himputa, himpumpaa
This boy always wants to hum a polka.

But there is nothing better to be found.
Everywhere I look, there's just trash around.
No one knows music's ABC's,
But record deals they're making with ease.
Himputa, himputa, himpumpaa
Here this boy always wants to hum a polka.

Our daily labor it has made us sore.
That's why we're heading out on tour.
Knowing a few songs is all it will take,
To go and play and pretend to be great.
Your voice can sound like an old jackass,
'Cause that's good enough for singing jazz
'Cause that's good enough for singing jazz.

71. Siirtolaisen ensi vastuksia
The Immigrant's First Difficulties

From Arthur Kylander record Victor 81507 from 1928. All songs by Kylander in this volume are used by permission of composer Erik Lindström, owner of the rights.

Taak - se jäi jo Suo - mennie - mi häi - pyi tai - vaan - kan - nen taa
Vie - ras kie - li kuin se kai - kui, si - tä kuun - te - le - maan jäin
Oh the love - ly shores of Fin - land, dis - ap - peared be - hind me,
And I lis - tened to the lan - guage that they spoke all a - round me,

Mui - den lail - la joh - ti tie - ni tän - ne län - nen kul - ta - laan. "no sir,
en - si sa - nat mie - leen pai - nui, joi - ta muis - tut - te - lin näin: "no sir,
to the gol - den land I head - ed with its op - por - tu - ni - ty.
and the words I first en - coun - tered lin - gered in my me - mo - ry:

no sir, no sir, no - o - o - o, no sir, no sir, no sir, no sir,
no sir, no sir, no - o - o - o, no sir, no sir, no sir, no sir,

no!"
no!"

Finnish American terminology used in this song:
Horiop = hurry up
Teik joor taim = take your time

Taakse jäi jo Suomenniemi, häipyi taivaankannen taa,
muiden lailla johti tieni tänne lännen kultalaan.
Vieras kieli kuin se kaikui, sitä kuuntelemaan jäin
ensi sanat mieleen painui, joita muistuttelin näin:
"no sir, no sir, no sir, no-o-o-o, no sir,
no sir, no sir, no sir, no!"

Rautatielle kuin mä kuulin, että miestä tarvitaan
työhön pääsin, sekä luulin: työssä myöskin olla saan.
Huudettiinpa mulle siellä: "horiop" ja muutakin
mä kuin en ymmärtänyt vielä, siksipä vain vastasin:
"no sir, no sir, no sir, no-o-o-o, no sir,
no sir, no sir, no sir, no!"

Kerran taas kuin määrää vailla Missourissa astelin,
rakastuin ma aika lailla, nuoreen neitoon tietenkin.
Vannoin hälle: "rakkahani, sua yksin lemmin vain,"
pyysin: "tullos omakseni," mutta vastauksen sain:
"no sir, no sir, no sir, no-o-o-o, no sir,
no sir, no sir, no sir, no!"

Lentoansa aika lentää, sitä ei voi vastustaa,
mutta myöskin aina sentään aika jotain opettaa.
Ymmärrän jo mainiosti, sanotaan jos: "teik joor taim,"
vaan "horiop" ken huudon nosti, siihen yhä tuumin vain:
"no sir, no sir, no sir, no-o-o-o, no sir,
no sir, no sir, no sir, no!"

Oh the lovely shores of Finland disappeared behind me,
To the golden land I headed with its opportunity.
And I listened to the language that they spoke all around me
And the words I first encountered lingered in my memory:
"No sir, no sir, no sir, no-o-o-o, no sir,
No sir, no sir, no sir, no!"

To the railroad station I went, when I heard they needed men,
I was lucky, got the job, and started working right then.
And they hollered, hot and bothered "Hurry up, get it in gear!"
But I did not understand them, so I answered loud and clear:
"No sir, no sir, no sir, no-o-o-o, no sir,
No sir, no sir, no sir, no!"

And I wandered, nowhere to go, 'til I came to Missouri.
There I fell hard for a maiden whom I wanted to marry.
So I told her "dear I'll love you, all my days and forever,"
And I asked: "will you be mine?" But all I got was this answer:
"No sir, no sir, no sir, no-o-o-o, no sir,
No sir, no sir, no sir, no!"

Time it flies as we get older, that's a fact we can't resist.
But we learn a little something the longer we exist.
When folks tell me: "take your time," well, I understand them of course,
But "hurry up?" to that I just respond without remorse:
"No sir, no sir, no sir, no-o-o-o, no sir,
No sir, no sir, no sir, no!"

72. Ennen ja nyt
Before and Now

From the B side of Arthur Kylander's record Victor 81507 from 1928. Kylander's pamphlet Humoristisia lauluja I lists the song as "Paatuva kansa" [Hardening people]. The song has two additional verses and a refrain that runs "Nyt paatuu kansa vallan ympäri maan, herrat alkaa hermostumaan, syytä tosiaan. He tuskin rauhas' voivat nukkuakaan, surra saavat kohtaloaan, syytä tosiaan." [Now people harden under oppression throughout the land, and gentlemen begin to get nervous for sure. They can hardly sleep in peace at night, and can mourn their fates for sure].

Päi - vät ja vuo - det vaih - tu - vat, en - ti - set ta - vat muut - tu - vat,
Time it just keeps on fly - ing by. Cus - toms and ha - bits up and die.

ih - mi - nen tä - mä ny - kyi - nen var - sin on kii - rei - nen. Muu - ta - ma vuo - si
Peo - ple to - day are bu - sy, so bu - sy they are diz - zy. It was not ve - ry

ta - kai - sin rau - has - sa vie - lä e - let - tiin, hil - jal - leen he - vos - kyy - dil - lä
long a - go that things were dif - fer - ent you know. Folks hitched up horse and bug - gy when

hyr - ry - tel - tiin. Vaan nyt on tois - ta kaik - ki au - tol - la vaan
out they would go. But now all's changed, we drive in cars with big tires.

las - kee kuin tulta sam-mut - ta-maan kyl - lä to-si-naan! Tää ny - ky - ai - ka, se on
Rac - ing a - boutlike we're put - ing out fires. And now our lives they are all

ko - neel-li-nen, ih - meel - li - nenja kii - ree-li-nen ko - ko ih - mi - nen.
me - chan - ized won - der - ized com - mer - ci - al-ized and de - hu-man - ized.

Päivät ja vuodet vaihtuvat, entiset tavat muuttuvat,
ihminen tämä nykyinen varsin on kiireinen.
Muutama vuosi takaisin rauhassa vielä elettiin,
hiljalleen hevoskyydillä hyrryteltiin.
Vaan nyt on toista, kaikki autolla vaan
laskee kuin tulta sammuttamaan, kyllä tosiaan!
Tää nykyaika, se on koneellinen,
ihmeellinen ja kiireellinen koko ihminen.

Kansa se ennen kuunteli, pappi kuin heitä nuhteli,
syntejä anteeks juotti, niin tuotti se kolehdin.
Maailmanloppu lähenee, kirkossakäyvät vähenee,
pastoriparan tulotkin vain pienenee.
Näin muuttuu kaikki vallan ympäri maan,
muuttuu kuin ajais autolla vaan, kyllä tosiaan!
Tää nykyaika, se on koneellinen,
ihmeellinen ja kiireellinen koko ihminen.

Ennen kun siellä Suomessa puhutella saatiin herroja,
lakki ol poies päästä ja räästä nenä puhtaana.
Poies on sekin kaunistus, mikä viel ompi seuraus,
ehkäpä herroill' itsellä on aavistus!
Näin muuttuu kaikki vallan ympäri maan,
muuttuu kuin ajais autolla vaan, kyllä tosiaan!
Tää nykyaika, se on koneellinen,
ihmeellinen ja kiireellinen koko ihminen.

Time it just keeps flying by, customs and habits up and die.
People today are busy, so busy they are dizzy.
It was not very long ago, that things were different then, you know.
Folks hitched up horse and buggy when out they would go.
But now all's changed, we drive in cars with big tires,
Racing about like we're putting out fires.
And now our lives they are all mechanized,
Wonderized, commercialized, and dehumanized.

People they'd go on Sabbath day, listening to what the preacher'd say.
They'd repent their every sin, while the church raked money in.
Though Judgment Day is coming fast, church attendance it has long passed.
The preacher's comfy income, it just will not last.
For now all's changed in places both near and far.
No time for that now that we're driving in a car.
And now our lives they are all mechanized,
Wonderized, commercialized, and dehumanized.

Back home in Finland we felt fright, to the boss we'd be so polite.
Hat in hand stood meekly by, faces clean and noses dry.
This custom's up and gone away, where we are headed from this day?
Maybe the bosses will be able to say.
But now all's changed in places both near and far
No time for that now that we're driving in a car.
And now our lives they are all mechanized,
Wonderized, commercialized, and dehumanized.

73. Kulkuri

Wanderer

From Kylander's record Victor V4037, 1929. Record also produced by Kosti Tamminen, Victor 79404, 1927. On Tamminen's record the song is entitled "Hoobo valssi" [Hobo waltz]. Kylander uses the same name Hoobo in his pamphlet Humoristisia lauluja I. The song is also performed by Kai Lind on the album Lännen lokarin lauluja [Songs of the logger of the west] YFLP 1-857, 1967.

Mä jou-tu-nut maa-il-malla oon kul-ke-maan, se-kä hoo-boks vaan mu-a
I've had to wan-der a-round this wide, wide world "Look, a ho-bo!" taunts that are

sa-no-taan. Ja vaik-ka-pa kul-ku-ni kat-ke-ra on, o-len
free-ly hurled. But though tram-ping a-round so bit-ter can be, still I

sit-ten-kin vaan su-ru-ton._____ E-lo tää pi-an jää,
have to say that I'm hap-py._____ Life will soon pass a-way

siks en su-rul' tah-do si-tä him-men-tää. Hau-dan taa jää-dä
so I won't let sor-rows cloud my day. Sor-row's o'er af-ter

saa kaik-ki mi-kä i-lo-an-ni var-jos-taa.
life, that's when I'll be tram-ping at last free from strife.

Finnish American terminology used in this song:

Com' on boy = c'mon boy
Hoobo = hobo
Paksikaara = boxcar
Preeri = prairie

Mä joutunut maailmalla oon kulkemaan,
sekä hooboks vaan mua sanotaan.
Ja vaikkapa kulkuni katkera on,
olen sittenkin vaan suruton.
Elo tää pian jää,
siks en surull tahdo sitä himmentää.
Haudan taa, jäädä saa
kaikki mikä iloani varjostaa.

Me rautatiet laitamme ympäri maan,
itse varkain vaan niillä ajetaan.
Ja vaikkapa preerillä kylvän ja puin
olla saanut olen tyhjin suin.
Alaskan, Montanan,
kaivoksissa myöskin väliin aherran,
Utahin, Teksasin
metsissäkin heilunut on kirveeni.

Ja aina kun tulee tuo talvinen sää,
kohti etelää menee poika tää.
Etelän neidotkin oottavat siel,
jos he viime reissun muistaa viel.
Ääni soi: com'on boy!
enpäs toki kutsuansa kieltää voi.
Musta suu, I love you,
siimeksensä meille suopi palmupuu.

Oi tyttö sua mukaani ootan mä ain,
sua ootan ain, lähde matkaan vain.
Sun kanssasi leipäni, paistini jaan,
aina kun vain kanan kiine saan.
Illalla, polvella,
nuotiolla tuudittelen sinua.
Sitten taas piittaillaan,
ja paksikaaras poies surut tanssitaan.

I've had to wander around this wide, wide world.
"Look, a hobo!" taunts that are freely hurled.
But though tramping around so bitter can be,
Still I have to say that I'm happy.
Life will soon pass away.
So I won't let sorrows cloud my day.
Sorrows o'er after life.
That's when I'll be tramping, at last free from strife.

Oh, railroads we built in this great big country.
Now those trains they pass me efficiently.
And though on the prairie I plow and I sow,
Still my belly's empty even so.
I have mined Montana,
And even the hills of great Alaska.
I have cut Texas trees,
Likewise I have felt Utah's mountain breeze.

And when that winter weather comes blowing cold,
This boy heads south for some girls to hold.
The southern girls waiting there are so pretty,
Do you think they'll remember me?
Then one calls, "come on boy,"
And I just can't pretend to hide my joy.
Pretty girl, I love you,
Underneath the palm tree, all night through.

"My darling I promise to cherish you so,
Take my hand in yours and away we'll go.
My bread and my roast with you I will sure share,
Yes, for you I'll always care.
Ev'ry night by the fire
I'll sing my songs, until you tire,
With no cares, near or far,
We will be a-dancing in a fine boxcar."

74. Paitaressu Vihtori
Shirttail Victor

From Kylander's Humoristisia lauluja II, published in New York. Kylander also recorded the song in 1928 on the record Victor 80520.

Finnish American terminology used in this song:
Poosu = boss

_38_ F C G7 · · · · · · · C · F · G7 · Dm · G7 · · · C

et saa, et saa Vih - to - ri! Tu - le poi - es äi - din pie - ni lem - mik - ki ei saa,
no - no no you can't Vic - tor! But be - cause he was' - nt used to hear-ing no He ig -

_46_ F C G7 · · C · C · · · · F · G · C

et saa, et saa Vih - to - ri! Vaan Vih - to - ri kun kiel - toon ain' ol' tot - tu - nut
nored it when she said__ so. He want-ed more and more and more and ev - en more!

_53_ · F · · G7 · · · · C · C · Am

ei äi - din kiel - to - a hän to - deks' us - ko - nut, hän tah - toi ja tah - toi
So he__ begged and plead - ed, asked and cried and swore. And all that whin - ing

_58_ · C · · · · G · C · F · · ·

vaan sik - si kun sai ja äi - ti - ä har - mit - ti kuin myös-kin tah - to - maan hän
it was an-noy - ing__ that is__ ver - y true Be - cause his broth - ers al - ways

_63_ G7 · · C

vel - jet yl - lyt - ti!
want - ed some then too!

195

Paitaressu Vihtori,
oli äidin lemmikki,
veljeksistä kaikkein nuorin pikku vekkuli.
Teki äiti mitä vaan,
alkoi vaikka leipomaan,
Vihtori myös heti kohta alkoi vaatimaan:

Taikinaa maistaa tahtoo tahtoo Vihtori
anna jo äiti, anna pikku suukkooni
ja kun jo pöydältä astian laidasta
Vihtori kiinni saa
näin äiti muori silloin aina varoittaa:
ei saa, ei saa, ei saa, ei saa, Vihtori
ei saa, et saa et saa Vihtori!
Tule poies äidin pieni lemmikki
ei saa, et saa, et saa Vihtori!
Vaan Vihtori kun kieltoon ain' ol' tottunut
ei äidin kieltoa hän todeks' uskonut,
hän tahtoi ja tahtoi vaan, siksi kuin sai
ja äitiä harmitti
kuin myöskin tahtomaan hän veljet yllytti.

Aika riensi, Vihtori
kasvoi, varttui, vanheni.
Nuorukaisna tanhuvilla kylän kisaili.
Myöskin Liisa Maria,
juuri kukkaan puhkeeva,
lemmen leikkiin Vihtoria alkoi kietoa.
Kaunis ol' kesäilta sirkat sirisi,
nurmella Liisan kanssa istuvi Vihtori.
Ja kuin hän tahtoi, Liisalta tahtoi,
suutelon pikkasen,
niin Liisa vastustella koetti, lausuen:
Ei saa, et saa, ei saa, et saa, Vihtori!
Ei saa, et saa, et saa Vihtori!
Katsos nyt kuin rypistit mun "dressin."
Ei saa, et saa, et saa Vihtori!
Vaan Vihtori kuin kieltoon ain' ol' tottunut,
ei Liisan kieltoakaan todeks' ottanut.
Hän tahtoi ja tahtoi vaan siksi kuin sai
ja Liisaa se harmitti
kuin myöskin tahtomaan hän veljet yllytti.

Työhönkin jo Vihtori, veljinensä aloitti,
Palkka-orjan raskas taival eteen aukeni.
Alkoi myöskin valjeta Vihtoorille asia
että, työnsä tuloista hän sai vaan muruja.
Niinpä, kuin poosu taaskin ohi asteli:
"Palkka on liian pieni" lausui Vihtori.
Ja kuin hän tahtoi, poosua tahtoi, palkkaansa nostamaan
niin, poosu ylimielin hälle lausui vaan:
Et saa, et saa, et saa, et saa Vihtori.
Et saa, et saa, et saa Vihtori.
Kyllin suuri sulla on jo palkkasi.
Et saa, et saa, et saa Vihtori.
Vaan Vihtori kuin kieltoon ain' ol' tottunut,
ei poosun kieltoakaan todeks' uskonut
hän tahtoi ja tahtoi vaan, siksi kuin sai
ja poosua harmitti, kuin myöskin tahtomaan hän veljet yllytti.

Mama's favorite was Victor,
A rascal he was for sure.
Never mattered what she'd do, he'd always follow her.
If she ever went to bake,
He would follow, beg for cake:
"Mommy, mommy, gimme, gimme just a little taste
Please mommy let me have a little taste of dough."
And mommy said "You had some just a bit ago."
Then that boy, he reached for the pan and grabbed the cake away,
Then mother looked at him and finally did say:
"No-no, no-no, mustn't do that Victor!
No-no, no-no, no, you can't Victor!"
But because he wasn't used to hearing no,
He ignored it when she said so.
He wanted more and more and more and even more,
So he begged and pleaded, asked and cried and swore.
And all that whining it was annoying, that is very true,
Because his brothers always wanted some then too!

Time flew by and Victor grew,
Older and more handsome too.
In the village dancing was what he liked to do.
Lisa liked to dance also.
Victor tried his love to show.
Crickets chirped that cool summer night when the wind did blow.
Lisa sat next to him, staring at the sky.
Victor smiled and thought he'd give a kiss a try.
"Just a kiss, just one little kiss, just one little kiss today."
But Lisa turned her head, and then all she did say:
"No-no, no-no, mustn't do that Victor!
No-no, no-no, no, you can't Victor!"
But because he wasn't used to hearing no,
He ignored it when she said so.
He wanted more and more and more and even more,
So he begged and pleaded, asked and cried and swore.
And all that whining it was annoying, that is very true,
Because his brothers always wanted some then too!

Victor worked with his brothers,
His labor enriched others.
Slowly he began to see, his work was slavery.
Working in the blazing sun,
Victor never thought was fun.
Earning little pay, Victor knew he would soon be done.
He began to think about what he had to do.
He always worked hard, but his dollars were so few.
"What you are paying ain't nearly enough," to his boss he said one day.
Then the boss glowered at him and finally did say:
"No-no, no-no, mustn't do that Victor!
No-no, no-no, no, you can't Victor!"
But because he wasn't used to hearing no,
He ignored it when he said so.
He wanted more and more and more and even more,
So he begged and pleaded, asked and cried and swore.
And all that whining it was annoying, that is very true,
Because his brothers always wanted some then too!

75. Työttömän valssi eli "Come around again"
Waltz of the Unemployed; "Come around again"

From Kosti Tamminen's record, Victor 79357, 1927. Composed by William Larsen. The recording includes guitar, although the performer is not mentioned on the label. In Kylander's Humoristisia lauluja I, two further verses are included, in which the unemployed person searches for a place to live and thinks about heaven and life's hard knocks.

Kun kul - jin ma kul - ku - rin lail - la o li mul - le - kin käy - nyt
When drift - ing a round as a ho - bo, it would hap - pen to me ev - ery

niin,_____ ett' työ - tä mä o - lin myös vail - la, me - nin teh - tai - siin
day._____ I ne - ver could find me em - ploy - ment, though at fac - t'ries and

ja kai - vok - siin._____ Vaan kaik - ki all' sil - loin sain kuul - la vain sen "Come
mines I would stay._____ But each time the fore - man he'd say to me plain, "Come

'round a - gain yes come 'round a - gain Me eh - kä jos jos - kus viel' tar - vi -
round a - gain, yes come 'round a - gain. May - be there will be some - thing here for

taan ei tie - dä vaan, come 'round a - gain."_____
you. Who knows, won't you come 'round a - gain?"_____

Finnish American terminology used in this song:
Leipälaini = breadline (leipä is Finnish for bread)

Kun kuljin ma kulkurin lailla,
Oli mullekin käynyt niin,
Ett' työtä mä olin myös vailla,
Menin tehtaisiin ja kaivoksiin.
Vaan kaikkiall' silloin sain kuulla vain sen
Come around again, yes, come around again,
Me ehkä jos joskus viell' tarvitaan,
Ei tiedä vaan, come around again.

Kun nälkääkin aloin jo tuntemaan,
Leipälainista lohtua hain
Vaan kaikk' oli ehditty jakamaan.
Minä tyhjänä palata sain.
Ja jakaja mulle vain taas sanoi sen
Come around again, yes, come around again.
Taas huomenna jos sulla nälkä on,
Niin sitte sa come around again.

Myös entisen lemmityn tapasin
Ma kerran näin matkallani.
Jo naimisiss' oli siks' arvelin:
Hän kotiinsa mun kutsuvi.
Taas erehdyin, sillä sain kuulla taas sen,
Come around again, yes, come around again.
Taas joskus kun ukkokin työssä on,
Niin sitte sä come around again.

Vaikk' nälissäin kuljen niin kuitenkin
Siit lohtua rintaani saa,
Kun tiedän ett' vuorostaan herratkin
Leipälainissa viell' jonottaa,
Ja silloin saan sanoa minäkin näin:
Come around again, yes, come around again.
Hyödyllist' työtä kuin ensin teet,
Niin sitte sä come around again.

When drifting around as a hobo,
It would happen to me every day,
I never could find me employment,
Though at factories and mines I would stay.
But each time the foreman, he'd say to me plain,
"Come 'round again, yes, come 'round again.
Maybe there will be something here for you.
Who knows, won't you come 'round again?"

When feeling the deep pangs of hunger,
I did stop by the bread and soup line.
When everyone had got their portion,
Still I stood there a'waiting to dine.
But the lady, she smiled, and just said to me plain,
"Come 'round again, yes come 'round again.
If tomorrow your hunger still irks you,
Well then, won't you come 'round again?"

I ran into my former true love,
As I wandered through town one fine day.
I saw from her ring she was married,
But I thought she might ask me to stay.
But I was mistaken, and she said to me:
"Come 'round again, yes come 'round again.
And when my old man is away at work,
Just then, won't you come 'round again?"

Though traipsing around ever hungry,
It does my heart good just to see,
That sometimes the rich men are lined up,
In the same bread-and-soup line as me.
And then it is my turn to say this to them:
"Come 'round again, yes come 'round again.
When you get the idea to do real work,
Well then, won't you come 'round again?"

76. Selkäranka Tohtori
Spine Doctor

From Kylander's record Victor 80185, 1927. The song also appears in Kylander's pamphlet Humoristisia lauluja II. Song also performed by Kai Lind in the album Lännen kokarin lauluja [Songs from the logger of the west] YFLP 1-857, 1967.

Mi - nä o - lin täs - sä maas - sa al - ku - jaan vain niin - kuin muut - kin ii - kat
I was new - ly come in - to this coun - try here like o ther bump - kins from our

van - han maan et - tä har - tei - ta - ni pai - noi ras - kas työ ja
home - land dear. On my shoul - ders hea - vy loads they took their toll, and

ki - re - äl - lä pi - ti pi - tää suo - li - vyö. Mut - ta si - ten kuin hiu - kan mi - nä
I got sick of tight - en - ing my dern belt hole. But when once I___ be - came A - mer -

jän - kis - tyin ja muu - ten - kin ma sil - loin e - dis - tyin se - kä luo - ta - ni hei - tin poi - es
i - can - ized well then a new game I___ soon sur - mised. that is when I___ up and threw a -

sho - ve - lin ja uu - den u - ran it - sel - le - ni val - it - sin. Nyt ma
way my spade and smart - ly I a new ca - reer de - ci - sion made. Now I

ar - vol ta ni o - len her - ra toh - tor - ri yes sir! D. C. Kai - ro - präk - to - ri
am the em - in - ent and no - ted doc - tor, yes sir! doc tor chi - ro - pra - ctor

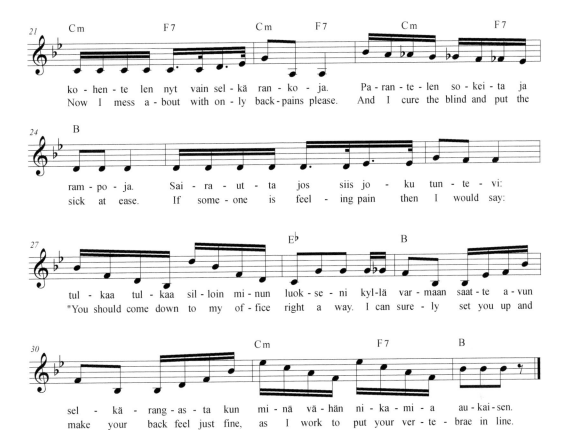

ko - hen - te len nyt vain sel - kä ran - ko - ja.   Pa - ran - te - len so - kei - ta ja
Now I mess a - bout with on - ly back - pains please.   And I cure the blind and put the

ram - po - ja.   Sai - ra - ut - ta jos siis jo - ku tun - te - vi:
sick at ease.   If some - one is feel - ing pain then I would say:

tul - kaa tul - kaa sil - loin mi - nun luok - se - ni kyl - lä var - maan saat - te a - vun
"You should come down to my of - fice right a way. I can sure - ly set you up and

sel - kä - rang - as - ta kun mi - nä vä - hän ni - ka - mi - a au - kai - sen.
make your back feel just fine, as I work to put your ver - te - brae in line.

Minä olin tässä maassa alkujaan
vain niinkuin muutkin iikat vanhan maan.
Että harteitani painoi raskas työ
ja kireällä piti pitää suolivyö.
Mutta sitten kuin hiukan minä jänkistyin
niin muutenkin ma silloin edistyin,
sekä luotani heitin poies shovelin
ja uuden uran itselleni valitsin.
Nyt ma arvoltani olen herra tohtori
yes sir! D. C. Kairopräktori
kohentelen nyt vain selkärankoja.
Parantelen sokeita ja rampoja.
Sairautta jos siis joku tuntevi:
tulkaa; tulkaa silloin minun luokseni
kyllä varmaan saatte avun
selkärangasta kun
minä vähän nikamia aukaisen.

Sattuisi jos maksannekin halkeamaan
Ja keuhkot toimisi ei ollenkaan;
Taikka kipu tuntuis pikkuvarpaassa.
Niin syy se johtuu kaikki selkärangasta.
Myöskin niillä kuin ovat mustasukkaiset.
Ja päästä keltä lähtee hivukset.
Heillä varmaan on, sen ma tiedän kuitenkin.
Selkärangas' vika, niinpä tietenkin!
Mutta luokseni jos aikoinaan vaan saavutte
Parannetuks' myöskin tulette,
Ihmisruumis se on niinkuin masina,
Silloin tällöin pitää "over haulata."
Läpi ken on käynyt minun kuurini
Runnaa taas kuin Fordin-Heikin träktori.
Kaikki varmaan saavat avun
Selkärangasta, kun
Minä vähän nikamia aukaisen.

Minun luokseni on tullut sairaita
Kuin selkärangat oli vinossa,
Mutta paikoilleen vaan nekin asetin
Ja taisi ehkä mennä vähän liikaakin.
Yksi paikka mun täytyy vielä tutkia
Tuo pieni nuppi takaraivolla,
Sitte alan mä ihmisiä yllättää
Ja kuolleitakin haudoistansa herättää.
Täss' on tohtori kuin käyttää luonnon oppia
Eikä anna yhtään troppia,
Luokseni ken kerran vaan on saapunut,
Muualle ei enää ole kulkenut,
Sairautta jos siis joku tuntevi
Tulkaa, tulkaa, tulkaa vaan mun luokseni
Kyllä varmaan saatte avun
Selkärangasta kun
Minä vähän nikamia aukaisen.

I was newly come into this country here,
Like other bumpkins from our homeland dear.
On my shoulders heavy loads they took their toll,
And I got sick of tightening my darn belt hole.
But when once I became Americanized,
Well, then a new game I soon surmised.
That is when I up and threw away my spade,
And smartly I a new career decision made.
Now I am the eminent and noted doctor,
Yes, sir, doctor chiropractor.
Now I mess about with only back pains please.
And I cure the blind and put the sick at ease.
If someone is feeling pain then I would say:
"You should come down to my office right away.
I can surely set you up and make your back feel just fine,
As I work to put your vertebrae in line."

"If it happened that your liver split in two,
Or your lungs quite completely failed on you,
Or if you feel pain within your little toe,
Oh, the cause is in your spinal column, don't you know?
And it's also the cause of any jealousy,
A source of baldness it's just got to be.
Oh no matter what ails you it is due to the spine.
And that is what we know in this great field of mine.
So if you just come to see me while there is still time,
I can fix you up so you are prime.
Like a fine machine the human body is,
Offering an overhaul that is my biz.
Those who make a point to see chiropractors,
They perform their functions like good Ford tractors.
I can surely set you up and make your back feel just fine,
As I work to put your vertebrae in line."

There have come to consultations people sick,
Whose spinal columns look like crooked sticks.
I can restore backbones with my special touch,
Though sometimes I'll admit I fix them up too much.
I just must take a gander at one further place,
A nub that is behind your skull and face.
If I do what I'm able, I can sure surprise,
For I can cure a person even after he dies.
Here's a doctor using all of nature's wizardry,
And does not need any pharmacy.
Those who come to me to get my expert care,
After consultation they won't go elsewhere.
If someone is feeling pain, then I would say:
"You should come down to my office right away.
I can surely set you up and make your back feel just fine,
As I work to put your vertebrae in line."

77. Lumber-Jäkki
Lumber-Jack

Appears on Side B of **Song 78**. Kylander's Humoristisia lauluja II includes an additional verse omitted from the record but included below. The song is also performed by Arttu Suuntala on the album Lännen lokarin lauluja [Songs of the Logger of the West] YFLP 1-897, 1967.

Ter-vei-si-ä kor-ves-ta, sy-dän-maal-ta sa-lol-ta, vil-lin luon-non
Deep in-side the wil-der-ness, snug-gled in the for-est dale, that's the land of

lai-tu-mil-ta met-sän po-ves-ta. Mis-sä rie-mut kau-pun-gin
na-ture's bliss from where this song does hale. Ci-ty ways are no-where found,

pois-sa on ja muu-ten-kin po-jat siel-lä e-lää saa kuin min-kit luos-ta-rin.
in that rus-tic field and fell. Men who live there all are bound there like a monk to dwell.

Niin-pä kär-si-väl-li-syys se y-li kuo-hah-ti. Lum-ber-Jäk-ki
Pa-tience starts to wear real thin and life can prove a bore, lum-ber jacks in-

käm-pän jät-ti se-kä päät-te-li: Yk-si e-lo e-let-tä-vä meil-lä om-pi
side their camps are han-ker-ing for more. "Life is short and now's the time the ev'-ning's just be-

vaan, siis nyt po-jat kau-pun-gis-sa hiu-kan juh-li-taan.
gun. Let's set off and hit the town where we can have some fun.".

Finnish American terminology used in this song:
Binssi = bean

Terveisiä korvesta,
sydän maalta, salolta,
villin luonnon laitumilta, metsän povesta.
Missä riemut kaupungin
poissa on ja muutenkin
pojat siellä elää saa kuin munkit luostarin.
Niinpä kärsivällisyys se yli kuohahti.
Lumber-Jäkki kämpän jätti sekä päätteli:
Yksi elo elettävä meillä ompi vaan,
siis nyt pojat kaupungissa hiukan juhlitaan.

Tunnelmasta korpien,
Herrat laulaa ihaillen,
Kuinka kaikk' on runollista alla honkien.
"Lumber-Jäkki" eikös vaan,
Onnen poika tosiaan,
Kuin saa siellä honkain alla elää eloaan.
Ruokana, — no tietysti, on tuore liha ain',
Säilytetty Chicago'ssa vuosikymmenen vain.
Siellä marjat makiat on eessä mansikat;
"Binssiksi" tok' kaupungissa niitä haukkuvat.

Siellä ilta myöhällä,
Pojat kuin on petillä,
Silloin tällöin kajahtaapi kumma sävelmä.
Äänen sen jos kuulisi
Herrat, varmaan luulisi,
Että pojill' kämpässä on iltakonsertti.
Mutta unen helmoissa jo pojat uinahtaa
Ja iltaseksi syödyt "binssit" ne ne soinahtaa.
Hongat säestää huminallaan, paistaa täysi kuu.
Runollista, tottamaar se onkin, eikös juu?

Kyllä on siell' korvessa
Niin runollinen tunnelma,
Että kaupunkiinkin vielä sieltä tultua,
Silmissä on neitonen,
Herran jee, niin suloinen!
Olkoon ijältänsä vaikka kuudenkymmenen.
Oikeimpa se mieli oisi suukko suikata,
Halata ja kiikutella hiukan polvella.
Kuin on täynnä runollista korven tunnelmaa,
Voihan siinä muutenkin viel' hiukan hairahtaa.

Meillä metsän pojilla
Ei oo toki hienoja
Vaatteita ja muitakaan ei herras tapoja.
Myös ei sanahelinää
Käytä metsän pojat nää,
"No perkele" on tervehdys kuin tuttu yllättää.
Kumarrukset, hienot vaatteet, helske sanojen,
Peittona vain voipi olla häijyn sydämmen.
Ne, ne sopii ruhtinaalle, diplomaatille.
Vaan ei meille, lokareille, korven pojille.

Deep inside the wilderness,
Snuggled in the forest dale,
That's the land of nature's bliss
From where this song does hale.
City ways are nowhere found,
In that rustic field and fell.
Men who live there all are bound,
There like a monk to dwell.
Patience starts to wear real thin and life can prove a bore.
Lumberjacks inside their camps are hankering for more.
"Life is short and now's the time, the evening's just begun.
Let's set off and hit the town where we can have some fun."

Of the forest's atmosphere,
Poets write with sheer delight,
How it is so fine and dear
When aspens are in sight.
Lumberjacks, poets opine,
Count among the blessed fine
Since they get to spend their days,
In forests so sublime.
Poets say the lumberjacks eat fresh meat every day.
Truth be told, it's mighty old (and) comes from Chicago way.
Strawberries the poets think are from the forest got,
Fruit we eat is no such treat, it's beans we have a lot.

In the evening late at night,
When the men have gone to sleep,
Here and there, all out of sight,
A melody does seep.
Gentlemen who heard that sound,
Would believe a band they'd found,
Or a hidden orchestra, performing somewhere round.
It's the beans they ate you see, now tooting musically.
And the concert goes all night, it's absolutely free.
Aspens sigh with gas fumes nigh, the moon shines bright and full,
It's poetic yes indeed on evenings warm or cool.

In the rugged wilderness,
Wrapped in mystic forest bliss,
Women folk, they are no joke,
And sorely, sorely missed.
Coming to the town at last,
There's a maiden walking past.
"My oh my, now that's a pie,"
Though nearly sixty-five.
"I would gladly steal a kiss and yes, some necking do,
Hug a bit and rocking sit, and such the whole night through."
When one's full of mystic bliss from living in the woods,
It's perhaps quite natural to want to sample goods.

We the forest denizens,
Aren't the finest dressing men.
No, our duds are no great shakes,
We're ragged at the ends.
So it is with what we say,
We're no fancy popinjays.
"No perkele" we do say when greeting a good friend.
Manners fine, and words divine, are things we do not use.
Such, we think, may well conceal a cheating heart or ruse.
Diplomats and lumber barons may such words employ,
But to us good lumberjacks, such things they just annoy.

An additional verse exists[1], although it is unclear if it was included in the original.
Westerholm did not include the following verse in *Reisaavaisen Laulu Ameriikkaan*:

Viime värsyss laulussa
Lauletaan nyt ajasta
Kuin Lumber-Jäkki astuvat taas kohti korpea.
Ei Jäkki niinkuin nykyinen
Se ero näät on sellainen
Että, joka mihen taskussa on kortti punainen.
He silloin työnsä tuloista saa osan suuremman
Ja herroille he antavat sen korven tunnelman.
Kämpän seinät tutisee ja korpi kumajaa,
Kuin kimoukselliset laulut illoin kajahtaa.

In our ditty's final lines,
We sing of the sighing pines,
That will greet us once again when to the woods we march.
But those men won't be like now,
There's a difference, yes and how:
In each pocket there will sit a bright red union card.
Lumberjacks will get themselves a better working deal.
Gentlemen in city streets can keep their forest feel,
Music makes the camp walls shake and forest loudly ring,
As the loggers proudly now, their union songs do sing.

---

1   Leary and March 1993: 269–271

78. Mikon ja Mantan Floridan matka
Mikko's and Mantta's Trip to Florida

From Arthur Kylander's unpublished papers. This song, as well as **Song 79** were apparently composed some twenty or thirty years later than Kylander's other songs, dating perhaps from the 1950s.

On ke - sä men - nyt ja syk - sy on tul - lut, Mik - ko on työ - stän - sä vä - sy -
Au - tumn has come, sum-mer is now___ ex - pired. Mik - ko is fed up, he's just plain

nyt. Man - ta kun haas - taa,___ Mik - ko vain vas - taa "En mi - nä jak - sa___ ei, ei,
tired. Mant - ta's com - plain - ing "It's just not sus - tain - ing!" Mik - ko just ans - wers "No not

nyt." Man - ta se sa - noi et - tä homeh - tuu - han täs - sä, läh - de - tään nyt vaikka
now." Man - ta says "Why are we just sit - ting here rot - ting? Let's take a trip to

Flor - i - daan. Aivan si - nä o - let niin - kuin ole - ma-ton äs - sä! Mik - ko jo
"Flor - i - da! Get off your duff and get your tail in___ gear now! Mik - ko says:

myön - tää___ "Men - nään vaan."
"Sure, I'll go pack the car!"

On kesä mennyt ja syksy on tullut,
Mikko on työstänsä väsynyt.
Manta kun haastaa, Mikko vain vastaa
"En minä jaksa, ei, ei, nyt."
Manta se sanoi että "homehtuuhan tässä,
lähdetään nyt vaikka Floridaan.
Aivan sinä olet niinkuin olematon ässä!"
Mikko jo myöntää: "No mennään vaan."

Pakkanen paukkuu ja koiratkin haukkuu,
vaan auto on valmiiksi rasvattu.
Ilmojen laatu on tiedoksi saatu
ja tiekin on kartasta katsottu.
Eikä se ota kuin vaan päiviä kaksi
kun taakse on jäänyt se talven sää.
Ilma se käy yhä lauhkeammaksi
ja kohta on kuumana nenän pää.

Pyörät kun pyörii niin päässäkin hyörii,
katsoppas, katsoppas mittariin.
Suorat ja väärät kuin on monet määrät,
niin karttuu jo maileja tuhansiin.
"Tuolla jo kasvavat appelsiinit!"
Mikko se Mantalle huudahtaa.
Missähän lienee ne krokotiilit,
aatoskin Mantaa jo puistattaa.

On haalille tultu ja terveiset tuotu,
uutiset kuultu ja kerrottu.
Lyöty on kättä kun on näkemättä
vuosia oltu, on muisteltu.
Ja kohta kun kuuluu se tanssin tahti
nuoruuden aikoja muistuttaa.
Oiskohan polvissa vielä se mahti?
Kohtahan siitäkin tiedon saa.

Tanssi vain kiihtyy ja kaikk' hyvin viihtyy,
joku sitten huutaa et "vaihtakaa!"
Mantakin luuli kun äänen sen kuuli
että hän uuden nyt miehen saa.
Vaan kaikki ei nyt mennytkään niin jetsulleensa.
Juuri kun taas vaihto oli viimeinen
Manta silloin huomasikin harmiksensa:
Kainalossa olikin se entinen!

Mikko ja Manta ja Atlantin santa
ne tuttuja myös ovat toisilleen.
Sinne he riensi ja kaikki sen tiesi
ettei he olleet siellä yksikseen.
Siellä on väkeä kuin Hentusen häissä,
sannalla kellii ja paistattaa.
Toisilla läskiäkin on läjäpäissä,
toiset vaan luitansa kuumentaa.

Pohjolan tuulet jos sinä luulet
ett' kylmästi sulle ne ärjyilee,
mieleesi paina: Niin lämmin on aina
kun Golfin virta se syleilee.
Viel' rannalla Mantakin ihmetteli että:
"Enpäs ois itsekään uskonut,
noin paljon on suolaista ja lämmintä vettä
aivan kuin Mikko ois sen laskenut."

Ilo on nyt loppu ja kotia on hoppu,
yksi suru Mantalla on kuitenkin.
Hän sanoo: "Voi nyt sentään on santaa jäänyt kenkään
ja taisi sitä jäädä vielä sinnekin."
Mikko se Mantallensa lohdutuksen antaa:
"Turhia älä käy suremaan,
muistoksi se Floridasta siellä täytyy kantaa
ja syksyllä tulemme taas uudestaan."

Autumn has come, summer is now expired.
Mikko is fed up, he's just plain tired.
Mantta's complaining "It's just not sustaining!"
Mikko just answers "No, not now."
Mantta says "Why are we just sitting here rotting?
Let's take a trip to Florida!
Get off your duff and get your tail in gear now!"
Mikko says: "Sure, I'll go pack the car!"

Winter it's freezing, and dogs they are wheezing
Everything's ready to take off now.
Weather reports have been carefully scanned,
And routes for the journey are now all planned.
"Just two days' driving and in summer we're thriving
we'll bid farewell to cold and snows.
Temperatures rising with each mile that we're driving,
We'll start to thaw out from toes to nose!"

Wheels are a'rolling, the driver's extolling,
"Look at the temperature climbing high!"
Crooked and straight, roadways pass small and great.
as thousands of miles they go speeding by.
"Look, over there I can see oranges growing,"
Mikko is crowing joyfully.
Happily thinking of the fruit he's all smiles,
while Mantta frets about crocodiles.

Now to the Finn hall they've come, and they greet all.
There is much news to be told and heard.
Hands must be shaken as memories awaken—
"It's been so long since we've had some word.
Soon there's the rhythm of the dance
That will shake us and it will take us to the past.
I wonder if I can still cut up the rug so?
Now we will find that out pretty fast!"

Everyone's dancing and good cheer's advancing,
Then comes the call "Change your partner now!"
Mantta she figures she'll get a new fella,'
She gets excited and but how.
Oh life is never as one might think it would be,
Or as it should be, right or wrong.
When all is done and she now looks at her partner,
She's back with Mikko as all along.

Beaches of Florida, Mikko and Mantta
Now get acquainted very well.
There by the ocean a mighty commotion,
Packed like sardines the beaches swell.
Folks they are sprawled out on the sand as they're tanning,
Faces they're fanning in the heat.
They're jammed together like at Hentunen's wedding,
And they are sweating from head to feet.

If winter chills you let Florida fill you
With all the joys of the warm Gulf stream.
Breezes will play in the warm sunny day,
As Mantta she lounges in the summer steam.
Salty the water that she sees does abound there,
Waves all around her, rise and fall.
"Well, this is something that I never imagined,
It's as if Mikko had planned it all!"

Joy is subsiding as home they are riding,
Mantta says she has but one regret.
"I've got some sand that is stuck in my sandal,
Can't get it out, whether dry or wet."
Mikko looks over, and he says so to soothe her:
"It's just a little souvenir.
Keep it beside you so the memories don't leave you,
We're heading back there this coming year!"

79. American suomalainen iso-äiti ja tyttären tytär
Finnish American Grandmother and Granddaughter

See note for **Song 78**.

Is - tuu i - so-äi - ti kei - nu tuo-lis - saan_____ ja
There sits dear old grand - ma in her rock - ing chair,_____ her

tyt - tä - ren - sä tyt - tö is - tu - vi pol - vel - laan._____ Niin
daugh - ter's love - ly daugh - ter per - ches be - side her there._____ So

mo - net ky - sy - myk - set lap - si ky - se - lee_____ ja i - so-
ma - ny come the ques - tions from that lit - le child._____ and pa - tient-

äi - ti vas - taa, vas - taa ja hy - myi - lee._____ I - so - äi - ti hän
ly old grand - ma an - swers with a smile._____ Dear old grand-ma she

it - se - kin var - maan o - li lap - se - na is - tu - nut kai_____ myös-kin
must have once al - so sat be - side her own grand-mo - ther so._____ At the

pol - vel - la mum-mon-sa ar - maan se - kä tie - to - ja ky - sel - len sai._____
foot of her own Na - na's rock - er she once al - so got ans-wers to all._____

—— Ty - tär ty - tä - ren kie - li on toi - nen sa - nat toi - set kuin
—— Yes, her grand-daugh-ter's lan-guage is differ - ent, and her ques-tions are

hän ky - se - lee_____ Mut - ta tun - ne se on sa - man-lai - nen i - so-
not quite the same,_____ but the feel-ing is just as it was then, back be-

Finnish American terminology used in this song:

Höpsis = nonsense

äi - dil - le näin pu - he - lee:_____ Once u - pon a time long, long a - go mine
fore she to this coun - try came._____ Once u - pon a time long, long a - go mine

grand - pa was hand - some and gay_____ and grand - ma was love - ly and beau - ti -
grand - pa was hand - some and gay_____ and grand - ma was love - ly and beau - ti -

ful my mo - ther said one day_____ but tell me grand - ma, tell
ful my mo - ther said one day._____ but tell me gand - ma, tell

me, when grand - pa says: "I love you"_____ How you say in Fin -
me, when grand - pa says: "I love you"_____ How you say in Fin -

nish I love you, too!_____ "Kuin you!"_____
nish 'I love you, too'!"_____ "Like you!"_____

Istuu isoäiti keinutuolissaan
ja tyttärensä tytär istuvi polvellaan.
Niin monet kysymykset lapsi kyselee
ja isoäiti vastaa, vastaa ja hymyilee.
Isoäiti hän itsekin varmaan
oli lapsena istunut kai
myöskin polvella mummonsa armaan
sekä tietoja kysellen sai.
Tytär tyttären kieli toinen
sanat toiset kuin hän kyselee
mutta tunne on samanlainen
isoäidille näin puhelee:
Once upon a time, long long ago
mine granpa was handsome and gay
and grandma was lovely and beautiful
my mother said one day
but tell me grandma, tell me
when grandpa says: "I love you"
How you sai in Finnish
"I love you, too!"

Kuin aurinko jo laski ja päivä hämärtyi
niin väsyi myöskin lapsi hän kyselyyn kyllästyi.
Tuo lännen iltarusko, ne viime säteet toi
jos kerron, ehk' et usko, se kuvan niin kauniin loi.
Isoäiti hän aivan kuin loisti
niinkuin aikoina nuoruudessaan,
kasvoiltansa se uurteetkin poisti,
vanhat muistot myös toi tullessaan.
Isoisä hän myös oli siellä
oli torkkunut kai unissaan
unen helmassa ehk' oli vielä
kuin hän hyräili näin lauluaan.
Once upon a time, long long ago
yes, granpa was handsome and gay
and grandma was lovley and beautiful
as granddaughter is today
but tell me grandma, tell me
when grandpa says: "I love you"
And grandma said in Finnish
"Höpsis to you!"

There sits dear old grandma, in her rocking chair,
Her daughter's lovely daughter, perches beside her there.
So many come the questions from that little child,
And patiently old grandma answers with a smile.
Dear old grandma she must have once also
Sat beside her own grandmother so.
At the foot of her own Nana's rocker,
She once also got answers to all.
Yes, her granddaughter's language is different,
And her questions are not quite the same,
But the feeling is just as it was then,
Back before she to this country came:
"Once upon a time, long, long ago
Mine grandpa was handsome and gay
And grandma was lovely and beautiful,"
My mother said one day.
"But tell me grandma, tell me,
When grandpa says: 'I love you'
How you say in Finnish
'I love you, too!'"

As the sun is setting, comes the end of day,
And now the small girl's interest gradually ebbs away.
The final rays of daylight streak the western sky,
"If now I were to tell you, you might well think I lie,"
Dear old grandma her face is now beaming
And her wrinkles they all disappear
As of memories pleasant she's dreaming
That come teeming back from yesteryear
Dear old grandpa is peacefully slumb'ring,
And he murmurs as if still asleep,
Some lines of an old song he's mumbling
From his lips they do quietly creep:
"Once upon a time, long, long ago,
yes, grandpa was handsome and gay
And grandma was lovely and beautiful
As granddaughter is today."
"But tell me grandma, tell me
When grandpa says: 'I love you'
And grandma said in Finnish
'Höpsis to you!'"

80. Suomalainen ja sauna
A Finn and the Sauna

Originally on Kylander's record Victor V4021, 1929.

Toi - si - naan   ar - vel - laan,   suo - ma - lais - ta hei - mo - a kun tut - ki - taan,
Yes in - deed   it's a - greed,   when the Fin - nish na - tion's stu - died we con - cede.

mi - kä sen   poh - joi - sen___ kan - sa - kun - nan tun - nus - merk - ki   yh - teinen, Myös
Rec - og - nized, and sur - mised, quan - ti - ta - tive - ly it has been an - al - yzed.

tut - kin si - tä mi - nä - kin ja   sik - si voin nyt lau - laa   et - tä se on sau - na
There's one thing that I   will sing yes ev - ry Finn will wan - na   sit in - side a sau - na

var - maan - kin   Kos - ka ker - ran sau - naa kai - paa   suo - ma - lai - nen ai - na
all   night long.   Sa - tur - day that is   the day when sau - nas are a' heat - ing

jo - ka lau - an - tai - na vie - lä   tääl - lä - kin.
sau - na stones are steam - ing and you can't go wrong.

Toisinaan arvellaan, suomalaista heimoa kun tutkitaan,
mikä sen pohjoisen on kansakunnan tunnusmerkki yhteinen?
Myös tutkin sitä minäkin ja siksi voin nyt laulaa,
että se on sauna varmaankin,
koska kerran saunaa kaipaa suomalainen aina
joka lauantaina vielä täälläkin.

Myös kerrotaan: kulkemaan kun Suomen poika läksi kerran Afrikkaan,
miss' ei jää, talven sää, eikä lumimyrskyt taida myllertää,
siellä pienet neekeritytöt taatelia tarjoi
palmupuiden varjoon kehoitti.
Vaikka hiukan lämmitti se Suomen pojan mieltä,
saunaan hetken päästä hän jo kaipaili.

Saunassa lauteilla, siellä kun saa rapsutella vastalla,
ikävää se vähentää, myöskin ikää saunassa voi pidentää.
Rakkauskin, jos se alkaa liian paljon vaivaa,
sydämestä kaivaa, pakoittaa,
silloin paras kiireesti on saunan parveen rientää,
ettei tauti liian suurta valtaa saa.

Suomen mies, jos siis ties sinne johtaa miss' ei loista kotilies,
kuusikko, kannikko kotikunnan poissa on ja koivikko.
Koivulehdon puutteessa on hyvä silloin muistaa,
että pippurpuista myös vastan saa.
menee vaikka suomalainen päiväntasaajalle,
saunan sinne kumminkin hän rakentaa.

Ja vihdoin sen vaelluksen, kun teemme täältä maailmasta viimeisen
ja aukaistaan joskin vaan meille ovi sinne vaikka kuumimpaan,
niin se kuumuus suomalaista sielläkään ei haittaa,
varmaan kiukaan laittaa, kuumentaa
ja löylyn ottaa, tottamaar, niin tulisen ja tuiman,
että Pelsepuupiakin naurattaa.

Yes indeed, it's agreed, when the Finnish nation's studied we concede.
Recognized, and surmised, quantitatively it has been analyzed.
There's one thing that I will sing, yes every Finn will wanna
sit inside a sauna, all night long.
Saturday that is the day when saunas are a'heating,
Sauna stones are steaming and you can't go wrong.

A Finn one day, sailed away, came to Africa where he then long did stay.
Black girls there, everywhere, served him fruit and drinks to boot the whole long day.
Winter chill and northern ills and snow fall in a flurry,
Were not there a worry, life was good.
Resting there without a care it might have been an option,
But he craved his sauna like a real Finn would.

Sauna time, we recline, there upon the benches so to warm our spines.
Free from strife, stress of life, head inside the sauna when your heart does pine.
Sweat away your cares today, in the sauna so steamy,
Feeling oh so dreamy, that's the spot.
Take a seat, and rest your feet, and whisk your back so briskly.
You will find a rested mind when piping hot.

Finnish man, if he can, cuts up birch tree branches in his native land.
But it's clear, when he's here, other trees can furnish him with whisks so dear.
Spruce and pine can work just fine for aiding circulation,
In exotic nations, try some spice.
Even if he finds himself a'living on th'equator,
He won't rest until he builds a sauna nice.

When at last, living fast, Judgment day arrives, with our sentence passed.
Even if, verdict stiff, we get sent to that place where the heat don't lift,
Finnish man, he'll stop and plan a brand new Finnish sauna.
He will always wanna heat stones well.
Beezelbub will watch him scrub and take his nice hot sauna.
He will laugh to see the Finn enjoying hell.

81. Muistojen valssi
Waltz of Memories

From Kylander's Humoristisia lauluja II. Also recorded on Victor 68901, 1928.

Kun kuuntelen sointuja sävelien
kuin valssi se vienosti soi,
niin muistoja ajoista mennehien
tää valssi taas mieleeni toi.
On muistoja paljon, on katkeria,
vaan niitä nyt muistele en.
Ma valssissa pyörien suloisia
vaan muistoja muistuttelen:

Kuin elo nuoruuden
viel' oli kukassaan
sen ajan menneisen
taas elän uudestaan.
Pois huomis huolet jää
ja tunne arkinen,
kuin rinnan tyynnyttää
Tää valssi muistojen.

Kuin nuoruus se ilosta uhkueli,
ei huolia muistanutkaan,
käsvarrelle lemmitty uinueli
Oi! kuinka se hurmasikaan.
Ja valssi kuin aalloilla temmeltäen
niin hauskasti heilahteli.
Ja sydänkin kuohuissa sävelien
niin viihtyen sykähteli.

Kuin elo nuoruuden...

Sa siirtolais tyttö jos muistelemaan
käyt muistoja mennehiä
ja rakkaimmat muistot jos tulvailemaan,
saa silmäsi kyyneliä,
Pois kyyneleet kuivaa ja nähdä mun suo
taas katseesi hymyilevän.
Käy kanssani valssiin se viihtyä tuo,
käy tunteesi tyynnyttämään.

Kuin elo nuoruuden...

Whenever comes drifting a waltz tune so fine,
Whenever it reaches my ear,
Then memories aplenty come flooding to mind,
Of times in my past oh so dear.
Some memories are lovely and others are hard,
Though these I do not dwell upon.
While spinning about in the beat of a waltz,
The beautiful times linger on:

Those flowering days of old,
Have long since passed me by,
But memories gleaming gold,
Return to my mind's eye.
Away the cares of life,
When now a waltz does start,
And all my daily strife,
Is lifted from my heart.

When youthful and happy and brimming with glee,
No worries to darken my door.
For she in my arms snuggled up peacefully,
I could not want anything more.
The waltz was like sailing on smooth gentle seas,
My spirit was lifted so high.
My heart was aquiver in those melodies,
And beat its own fervent reply.

Those flowering days of old...

Oh, immigrant maiden, you dwell on the past,
And ponder a long ago day.
Those memories lingering in your heart do last,
Your tears let me wipe them away.
Those dear recollections should bring you no tears,
Or cloud your sweet smiling face.
Come dance with me now and we'll turn back the years,
Those cares and sad pinings erase.

Those flowering days of old...

V. Jälkisanat. Lost Treasures Found.
James P. Leary

In 1983 Simo Westerholm's *Reisaavaisen laulu Ameriikkaan* was published solely in Finnish despite unarguable appeal to North American descendants of the Finnish diaspora. Twenty-five years later it was held by only three American libraries among thousands contributing to the WorldCat online catalog of itemized collections. A relentless advocate for the worth of folk traditions, Westerholm would have wished a wider audience for his historical anthology of songs expressing the actual and imagined experiences of Finnish immigrants. *Songs of the Finnish Migration* assures that audience through a significantly expanded bilingual edition of Westerholm's landmark work.

Tom DuBois and Marcus Cederström, assisted by translators Sara Tikkanen and Hilary Virtanen, have not only produced English translations for each of eighty-one songs, but also admirably, painstakingly, elegantly offered *singable* translations matching the originals' ineffable sense and spirit. DuBois and Cederström commendably shift Westerholm's appendices so that notes and sources are conjoined with each song, as are glossaries for "Finnglish" transformations of English loan words and esoteric occupational terms. And they add extensive new section introductions drawing upon pertinent research situating songs in relation to historical and cultural conditions in Finland and Finnish America.

Simo Westerholm would have appreciated such savvy collaborators, as productive teamwork exemplified his professional career. Born in 1945 in Kiukainen, within the Satakunta region of southwestern Finland, he earned a degree in English philology at the University of Turku in 1967. His direction shifted in 1970, thanks to inspirational lectures by Erkki Ala-Könni (1911–1996), director of the University of Tampere's Department of Folk Tradition from 1965–1976 and a co-founder of the Kaustinen Folk Music Festival. Westerholm commenced folk music field research throughout Finland in summer 1971, by 1973 he had founded the folk music band Kyläpelimannit [The Village Fiddlers], contributing clarinet and vocals, and in 1974 he became Deputy Director of the Folk Music Institute at Kaustinen, eventually serving as Director. Although Finnish folk music was his abiding concern, Westerholm made significant contributions to our understanding of Finnish American music beyond his 1983 anthology, especially in partnership with Pekka Gronow and Toivo Tamminen.

Long associated with the University of Helsinki, Gronow began his internationally revered explorations of historic commercial recordings in the late 1960s with a series of discographies chronicling 78 rpm records made in the early 20th century by Finnish Americans for Columbia and Victor labels (Gronow 1969a, 1969b, 1973, 1977–1978). In 1978, he also produced an influential LP and accompanying booklet, *Siirtolaisen Muistoja/The Immigrant's Memories*, reissuing and illuminating 78 rpm recordings made by such stellar Finnish American performers as Arthur Kylander, Hiski Salomaa, and Viola Turpeinen (1978). Toivo Tamminen, an independent scholar and accordionist from Riihimäki, undertook research on Finnish American musicians in the 1980s, notably resulting in a series of eighteen essays featuring performers on historic 78 rpm records, published initially in Kaustinen's folk music journal, *Kansanmusiikki*, and later, thanks to translations by Roy Helander, in the Finnish American newspaper *Raivaaja* (The Pioneer). Among them: profiles of Juho Koskelo (1996), Antti Kosola (1997), Lyyli & Aili Vainakainen (1998), Hannes Laine (1999a), and The Maki Trio (1999b).

In 1992 Gronow, Tamminen, and Westerholm combined forces, with assistance from Juha Niemela, a Turku folklore graduate student and Fulbright scholar at the University of Wisconsin, to produce *Lauluja lännen kultalasta* [Songs of the Golden West]: *Finnish American Recordings, 1907–1938* under the auspices of the Folk Music Institute in Kaustinen. The first of three CDs in a "Finnish American Recordings" series featuring illustrated booklets with Finnish notes and English summaries, it was succeeded by *Arthur Kylander: Oi, Kuinka Engeliksi Mielin* (Arthur Kylander: Oh, How Like an Angel) in 1994, and by *Ernest Paananen: Naimahommia* (Ernest Paananen: Wedding Affairs) in 1995. Cooperating similarly from 2002–2004, the trio produced four CDs and booklets for Turku's Artie Music label reissuing recordings made from 1928–1951 by Viola Turpeinen, the renowned American *hanuri-prinsessa* [accordion princess].

The respective research of Gronow and Tamminen relied at the outset on trips to America, particularly the Upper Midwest. In the early 1970s, for example, Gronow sought out Rudy Kemppa (1909–1992) of Hancock, Michigan. Born in nearby Toivola, Kemppa began buying Finnish American records in the early 1920s, commenced promoting touring performers in the 1930s, and hosted a Finnish music program from 1947–1970 on Hancock's WMPL and Calumet's WDHF radio stations[1]. His massive collection, acquired and shipped by Gronow, formed the basis of pre-WWII Finnish American 78s held by the Suomen äänitearkisto/Finnish Institute of Recorded Sound. In the 1980s, Tamminen likewise visited elderly recording artists and their descendants throughout Finnish America, acquiring reminiscences, images, and documentary evidence.

In the early 1990s, as part of a "Roots in Finland" initiative commemorating seventy-five years of Finnish independence, Simo Westerholm and Kaustinen colleagues made several treks through Finnish America seeking not only descendants of bygone recording artists, but also currently active musicians and researchers. Struck by encounters in the Upper Peninsula of Michigan, Minnesota, and Wisconsin, Westerholm reported in the *Finnish Music Quarterly* that "Finnish identity has survived most intact in the northern regions of the Mid-West, where Finnish polkas and waltzes sound out through the dance-halls at the hands of second and third-generation Finns"[2].

In Hancock, Michigan, he met with kantele player and music professor Melvin Kangas of Suomi College (now Finlandia University), and in Calumet with Oren Tikkanen who in 1990 "produced a cassette called *Children of the Finnish Immigrant*, Finnish American music from Upper Michigan, which received the award of Outstanding Folk Recording from the American Folklife Center" at the Library of Congress. Minnesota visits included Joyce Hakala, leader of the kantele group *Koivun Kaiku* [Echo of the Birch], who was "in the process of writing a full exposé of the kantele's history in America," as well as Diane Jarvi, brothers Eric and Kip Peltoniemi, and Paul Niemisto–all of whose music Westerholm found to be "American in spirit, but strongly flavoured by Finnish influences"[3]. Westerholm and Kolehmainen likewise ventured to Mount Horeb, Wisconsin, where I was working at the Wisconsin Folk Museum. Familiar with a double LP and booklet I'd produced featuring first and second generation Finns from Michigan and

---

1   Kemppa 1979 and 1980
2   Westerholm 1992: 35
3   Westerholm 1992: 35–36

Wisconsin–*Accordions in the Cutover: Field Recordings from Lake Superior's South Shore* (1986)–and an essay on accordionist Art Moilanen (1988), Westerholm borrowed selectively from my photographs, field recordings, and notes for copying by Kaustinen's archives.

Our last get-together was in Milwaukee, October 1994, when the American Folklore Society and the Society for Ethnomusicology met jointly. We hoped to rendezvous again on November 14, 2009, for the 100th anniversary of the birth of Viola Turpeinen, the Finnish American "accordion princess." Toivo and Heikki Tamminen had organized a commemorative event at a farmer's hall near Riihimäki, and Pekka Gronow and I were to be on the program with Simo. Sadly, Simo Westerholm had a heart attack a few days before, and by 2010 he was dead.

Through his final years and beyond, Simo's generosity, inspiration, and memory persist in Finnish America, particularly among those he visited in the early 1990s. Joyce Hakala completed her book regarding North American kantele-players, with Simo's assistance and back cover endorsement: "*Memento of Finland* stands as a thorough and excellent treatise on the kantele and its role among the Finns from the distant past to the present day"[1]. A decade later Hakala produced a superb study of Marjorie Edgar, an early researcher on Finnish American folksongs, that included Edgar's unpublished collection of songs from Minnesota Finns (2007). Her Acknowledgments salute Simo for sharing "musical expertise," reviewing drafts of the manuscript, and providing "encouragement, words of good cheer, and tolerant understanding"[2].

Paul Niemisto similarly offered heartfelt thanks in the Dedication of his book chronicling brass bands of Finnish workers on the Minnesota Iron Range: "this book honors Simo 'Holmi' Westerholm, Kaustinen ethnomusicologist and tenor horn player in the *Kaustinen Seitsikko* [Kaustinen Septet], who took great interest in this research and was my Finnish 'guru' until the very end. I really wish I could put a copy of the book in his hands"[3].

Kip Peltoniemi counted Simo among "Finnish pals" in the booklet for his *Minnesota Tango* CD (2001), while waggishly riffing on Westerholm's 1992 observation on the "Finnish-flavoured" American music of New World kin:

In the early eighties, I fell under the sway of the "middle pre-post-modernist school" of button accordionists (a.k.a. "the Fargo School"). Influenced by their bold repertoires, I began feverishly and indiscriminately infusing Finnish undercurrents into cowboy songs, roots rock, fifties and sixties country, doo wop, tango, parodies, labor songs, wedding songs, Beat rants, supernatural ballads, and so on.

Eric Peltoniemi carried on likewise, notably penning and performing a powerful mixed Finnish-English song in 2015, "*Punainen*" [The Red] illuminating the disparagement of left-wing Finnish immigrant union miners as drunken back-stabbing savages[4]. The first verse resonates with many songs in Westerholm's anthology.

Toivo Mäki, you goddamn Finn,
Puna, puna, puna, puna, punainen!
Curse his name! Blacklist him!
Puna, puna, puna, puna, punainen!

Subsequently recorded by Topi Saha, a young Finnish musician whose father, Hannu, was a Kaustinen colleague of Westerholm, the song figures prominently in the acclaimed 2017 Finnish film *Ikitie* [The Eternal Road], in which a blacklisted union activist leaves America for his homeland, only to find "Whites" tormenting "Reds" in the aftermath of Finland's civil war, while

---

1   Hakala 1997
2   Hakala 2007: ix
3   Niemisto 2013: v
4   Peltoniemi and Kaartinen 2017

across the border in Soviet Karelia, the mythic land of the Finnish *Kalevala*, idealistic Finnish American settlers find their dreams of a worker's paradise dashed brutally by Stalin's purges.

Diane Jarvi too has steadily produced stellar recordings like *bittersweet* (2014) involving Finnish and Finnish American musicians, new settings for older traditional and 78 rpm era songs and tunes, and her own bi-cultural compositions. And Oren Tikkanen remains a tireless performer and producer whose many accomplishments include *Lumber Jäkki: Old Finnish-American Songs & Harmonica* (2014), featuring twenty-one songs and tunes from Les Ross, Sr. (1923–1914). Born in Eben Junction, Michigan, to immigrant parents and steeped in a repertoire exemplary of Upper Peninsula Finns, Ross knew rare local songs that would have fit well with Westerholm's anthology, especially *"Työmiehen Matkat Michiganissa"* [The Workman's Travels in Michigan], learned from the Tuisku brothers, Yooper economic migrants to Detroit in the 1940s.

On July 2, 2002, during an interview with Les at his son's home in Negaunee, he told me he learned the song in a bar frequented by Finns on Woodrow Wilson Street in Detroit in 1941: "They were singing and I was bending my ear, listening and listening. Finally I got the whole song." When coaxed, Les spontaneously offered this witty verse-by-verse, albeit not singable, translation.

I was born in Finland on a road where birch trees were growing.
I was born in the sauna.

Then I started to America. I spoke the Finnish tongue,
But when I hoboed around the country my tongue changed and my mind changed.

I went to work at CCI mines, pushed a tram car there and
Learned how to use a pick and to watch for danger.

Then I got another job by Calumet and Hecla. They upped with a timber man.
I thought I was a good miner, but they called me a greenhorn.

I stopped in Palomaki's Tavern and I ordered many, many times.
I was astonished at all the brands they had on the shelf there.

I found a sweetheart. We used to go to the park in the evenings.
She was a nice, nice girl and we had a lot of fun.

Always modest, Les concluded with the qualification that "It sounds a lot better when you sing it in Finn."

In 1937 folklorist Alan Lomax made field recordings for the Library of Congress featuring similar set-in-America songs from UP Finns in Newbury and Amasa especially. Although none figured in Westerholm's 1983 anthology, he mentioned in his subsequent report on Finnish America that "a certain amount of field research was accomplished in the USA already from Alan Lomax's time onwards"[1]. Eventually I was able to work with Susanna Linna Moliski, Tom DuBois, and others to publish lyrics, translations, and background regarding several kindred Lomax-collected songs in *Folksongs of Another America: Field Recordings from the Upper Midwest, 1937–1946* (2015). And Tim Frandy, Hilary Virtanen, and I each embedded additional lyrics and translations from Lomax's field recordings within essays for a special issue of *Journal of Finnish Studies* devoted to "Finnish-American Songs and Tunes, from Mines, Lumber Camps, and

---

1   Westerholm 1992: 33

Workers' Halls"[1]. One of the songs, "Varoitus Duluthin Pojille," Amasa lumberjack Frank Maki's rollicking account of misadventures in a Duluth whorehouse, was recorded by J. Karjalainen, "the Finnish Bruce Springsteen," on his 2008 CD *Paratiisin Pojat* [Paradise Boys].

Elsewhere Juha Niemela's bilingual "Finnish American Songs" (2003), available as an online PDF through the Finnish Immigration Institute in Turku, includes otherwise overlooked yet illuminating songs resonating with those in Westerholm's anthology. And "*Teräksen Soitto*"/Song of Steel, composed around 1930 by a union militant Axel Simonen in Pittsburgh, is nestled amidst other English and transcribed/translated "foreign" songs in Jacob A. Evanson's neglected essay, "Folk Songs of an Industrial City" (1949: 451–453). Beyond these few instances, scarcely any translated immigrant songs concerning the Finnish American experience have been published previously.

We are indebted, consequently, to Simo Westerholm and to translators Tom DuBois, Marcus Cederström, Sara Tikkanen, and Hilary Virtanen for their revelatory and restorative efforts. On December 14, 2017, just as the manuscript for this revised publication was completed, Oren Tikkanen, in anticipation of an imminent event, emailed asking if I knew of a good translation for Arthur Kylander's "Savon pojan Amerikkaan tulo." Fortuitously I did. Marcus and Tom—committed to repatriation and revived performances–immediately sent him the entire manuscript. Oren's response evokes Simo's dreams, addresses fellow descendants of the Finnish diaspora, and is the last word for this Afterword.

Marcus, et al.

THANK YOU! This so generous of you.

I told Simo Westerholm many years ago that he had given us Finnish-Americans our lost heritage back, and now you fellows have enhanced that treasure chest by giving us the keys to open it.

(If my gratitude is so effusive that I embarrass the Finns in the crowd, I humbly say *anteeksi* [sorry]).

But seriously, this is wonderful!

Oren

---

1   Frandy 2010; Leary 2010; Virtanen 2010

Works Cited:

Asplund, Anneli. 1994. *Balladeja ja arkkiveisuja. Suomalaisia kertomalauluja.* Helsinki: Suomalaisen Kirjallisuuden Seura/Finnish Literature Society.

Chronwall, J. H. 1893. Axel och Hilda. Ny visbok av B.C.

DuBois, Thomas A. 1995. *Finnish Folk Poetry and the Kalevala.* New York: Garland Publishing.

_____. 2004. "The Little Song-Smith: A Printed Folksong Anthology and Its Reception among Ingrian Peasants, 1849–1900" In *Folk Song: Tradition, Revival, and Re-Creation.* Ed. Ian Russell and David Atkinson. Aberdeen: The Elphinstone Institute, University of Aberdeen, 2004, 41–52.

_____. 2005. "'I'm a Lumberjack and I'm Okay...': Popular Film as Collective Therapy in Markku Pölönen's Kuningasjätkä (1998)" in *Transnational Cinema in a Global North: Nordic Cinema in Transition,* ed. A. Nestingen and T. G. Elkington. Detroit, Wayne State University Press, 243–260.

_____. 2006. *Lyric, Meaning and Audience in the Oral Tradition of Northern Europe.* Notre Dame: University of Notre Dame Press.

Evanson, Jacob A. 1949. "Songs of an Industrial City," in *Pennsylvania Songs and Legends,* ed. George Korson. Baltimore: The Johns Hopkins Press, 423–466.

Fitchburg Daily Sentinel. June 14, 1916. "Concert by Young Finnish Soprano." *Fitchburg [MA] Daily Sentinel.* 2.

Fitchburg Sentinel. November 26, 1937. "Hukari Recital Creates Interest." *Fitchburg [MA] Sentinel.* 7.

Frandy, Tim. 2010. "Lust, Labor, and Lawlessness: The Bad Finn in Finnish American Folksong." *Journal of Finnish Studies,* 14.1: 29–45.

Greene, Victor. 1992. *A Passion for Polka: Old-Time Ethnic Music in America.* Berkeley: University of California Press.

_____. 2004. *A Singing Ambivalence: American Immigrants between Old World and New, 1830–1930.* Kent, Ohio: The Kent State University Press.

Gronow, Pekka. 1969a. "American Columbia Finnish Language 3000 Series," part 1, *Record Research,* issue 101 (October), 8–9.

_____. 1969b. "American Columbia Finnish Language 3000 Series," part 2, *Record Research,* issue 102 (November), 10.

_____. 1971. "Finnish-American Records." *JEMF Quarterly,* 7.24: 176–185.

_____. 1973. *American Columbia Scandinavian "E" and "F" series/Amerikkalaisen Columbian pohjoismaiset sarjat.* Helsinki: Suomen äänitearkisto/Finnish Sound Archives.

_____. 1977–1978. *Studies in Scandinavian-American discography,* 2 volumes. Helsinki: Suomen äänitearkisto/Finnish Sound Archives.

_____. 1978. *Siirtolaisen Muistoja/The Immigrant's Memories.* LP record & booklet. Helsinki: Finnish RCA PL 40155.

_____. 1982. "Ethnic Recordings: An Introduction." *Ethnic Recordings in America: A Neglected Heritage.* Washington D.C.: American Folklife Center, Library of Congress.

_____. n.d. "Työväenlauluja levytettiin Yhdysvalloissa." *Tiellä Sananvapauteen.* https:—sananvapauteen.fi/artikkeli/259 Accessed March 13, 2018.

Gronow, Pekka and Saunio, I. 1998. *An International History of the Recording Industry.* Trans. C. Moseley. London: Cassell.

Hakala, Joyce. 1997. *Memento of Finland: A Musical Legacy.* St. Paul, Minnesota: Pike Bone Music.

_____. 2007. *The Rowan Tree: The Lifework of Marjorie Edgar, Girl Scout Pioneer and Folklorist, With Her Finnish Folk Song Collection, Songs from Metsola.* St. Paul, Minnesota: Pike Bone Music.

Henriksson, L. 2015. *Laulettu huumori ja kritiikki J. Alfred Tannerin, Matti Jurvan, Reino Helismaan, Juha Vainion ja Veikko Lavin kuplettiäänitteillä.* Ph.D. Dissertation, University of Helsinki. Permalink: http:—urn.fi/URN:ISBN:978-952-68347-0-2.

Immigration and Naturalization Service. 1915. *Passenger and Crew Lists of Vessels Arriving at New York, New York, 1897–1957.* Microfilm Publication T715, 1897–1957, roll 2443, line 13, page 127. Retrieved from National Archives at Washington, D.C. via Provo, UT: Ancestry.com Operations, Inc., 2010. Accessed March 15, 2018.

_____. 1930. *Passenger and Crew Lists of Vessels Arriving at New York, New York, 1897–1957.* Microfilm Publication T715, 1897–1957, roll 4763, line 13, page 109. Retrieved from National Archives at Washington, D.C. via Provo, UT: Ancestry.com Operations, Inc., 2010. Accessed March 13, 2018.

Impola, H. and M. Leino Eldridge. 2001. "The Life and Songs of Arthur Kylander." *New World Finn* October–November 2001:14–18.

Ironwood Daily Globe. February 4, 1927. "Music Lovers Will Hear Noted Singer." *Ironwood [MI] Daily Globe.* 4.

IWW (1995). *Songs to Fan the Flames of Discontent: The Little Red Songbook, International Edition.* Ypsilanti, Michigan: Industrial Workers of the World.

Jarvi, Diane. 2001. *bittersweet.* Minneapolis: Lupine Records, CD LR-1008.

Karjalainen, J., and Veli-Matti Järvenpää. 2008. *Paratiisin Pojat: Amerikansuomalaisia lauluja/ Finnish-American Folksongs.* Tampere, Finland: Poko Records, CD 167.

Kemppa, Rudy. 1979. Tape recorded interview by Matt Gallman and Sarah Poynter. Hancock, Michigan, July 23. Ethnic Music in Northern Wisconsin and Michigan, Mills Music Library, University of Wisconsin.

_____. 1980. Field notes by James P. Leary. Hancock, Michigan, November 19. Ethnic Music in Northern Wisconsin and Michigan, Mills Music Library, University of Wisconsin.

Kirby, David. 1989. "The Labour Movement," in *Finland. People, Nation, State*, ed. M. Engman and D. Kirby. London: Hurst & Company, 193–211.

Knipping, M. 2008. *Finns in Wisconsin. Revised and expanded edition*. Madison: Wisconsin Historical Society.

"Kupletin kuningas J. Alfred Tanner." (2006/2016). *Yle*. (2006/2016). Retrieved from https:— yle.fi/aihe/artikkeli/2006/12/08/kupletin-kuningas-j-alfred-tanner

Leary, James P. 1986. *Accordions in the Cutover: Field Recordings from Lake Superior's South Shore*. Ashland and Mount Horeb, Wisconsin: Northland College and Wisconsin Folk Museum, double LP and booklet.

_____. 1988. "Reading the 'Newspaper Dress': An Expose of Art Moilanen's Musical Traditions,' in Michigan *Folklife Reader*, ed. C. Kurt Dewhurst and Yvonne Lockwood. East Lansing: Michigan State University Press, 205–223.

_____. 1990. "The Legacy of Viola Turpeinen." *Finnish Americana*, 8: 6–11.

_____. 2010. "Yksi Suuri Union: Field Recordings of Finnish IWW Songs," *Journal of Finnish Studies* 14:1, 6–17.

_____. 2015. *Folksongs of Another America: Field Recordings from the Upper Midwest, 1937 1946*. Madison: University of Wisconsin Press and Dust-to-Digital.

Leary, James P. and Richard March 1993. "Farm, Forest, Factory: Songs of Midwestern Labor," in *Songs About Work: Essays in Occupational Culture for Richard A. Reuss*, ed. A. Green. Bloomington: Folklore Institute Special Publications, no. 3, 253–286.

Lindström, Varppu. 2003. *Defiant Sisters—A Social History of Finnish Immigrant Women in Canada*. Toronto: Aspasia Books.

Luoma, Ellen. 1979. "Courtship in Finland and America: Yöjuoksu versus the Dance Hall" *Finnish Americana* 22: 66–76.

Maki, D. 2002. "Arthur Kylander: More than a Musician." *The Finnish American Reporter* August 1, 2002, 4.

Mhic Grianna, R. B. 1953. *Songs of a Donegal Woman*. RTÉ 178: Dublin, RTÉ.

Michigan Department of Community Health, Division for Vital Records and Health Statistics. 1931. *Death Records*, 1867–1950. Retrieved via Provo, UT: Ancestry.com Operations, Inc., 2015.

Michigan Department of Community Health, Division of Vital Records and Health Statistics. 1918. "1918 Eaton - 1918 Kent." *Michigan, Marriage Records*, 1867–1952. Microfilm: 139. Retrieved via Provo, UT: Ancestry.com Operations, Inc., 2015. Accessed March 16, 2018.

Monessen Daily Independent. 1917. "Concert Pleases." *Monessen [PA] Daily Independent* April 6, 1917, 1.

National Archives and Records Administration. 1924. "Certificates: 490350-490849, 12 Nov 1924–14 Nov 1924." *U.S. Passport Applications*, 1795–1925. Microfilm: 2666. Retrieved from National Archives at Washington, D.C. via Lehi, UT: Ancestry.com Operations, Inc., 2007.

Niemelä, J. 1997a. "Cultural Reflections in Finnish American Songs." *Journal of Finnish Studies*, 1.3: 100–492.

_____. 1997b. "Pontevasti kaikuivat laulut - Amerikansuomalaisten työläisten laulut 1900-1930- luvuilla Yhdysvalloissa." *Tyovaentutkimus*. http://www.tyovaenperinne.fi/tyovaentutkimus/1997/tt1997.html Accessed March 13, 2018.

_____. 1998–1999. "Who Do We Think We Are—The Finnishness in Finnish-American Songs." *Yearbook of Population Research in Finland*, 35: 114–132.

_____. 2003. "Finnish American Songs." Turku: Siirtolaisuusinstituutti/Immigration Institute, online publication, http://www.migrationinstitute.fi/fi/article/muut-aihepiirit/finnish-american-songs.

_____. 2007. "Hiski Salomaa (1891–1957)," in *The American Midwest: An Interpretive Encyclopedia*, ed. R. Sisson, C. Zacher, and A. Cayton. Bloomington: Indiana University Press, 396.

Niemisto, P. 2013. *Cornets & Pickaxes: Finnish Brass on the Iron Range*. Northfield, Minnesota: Ameriikan Poijat.

Olin, K. G. 1998. "Finns in the Gold Rush." *Swedish Finn Historical Society Quarterly* 7 (1&2): 1–5.

Olin, K. G. 2004. *Egen lyckas smed*. Jakobstad: Olimex.

Olin, K. G. 2013. *Alaska. Del 2. Guldrushen*. Jakobstad: Olimex.

Peltoniemi, Eric and Vesa Kaartinen. 2017. "Eric Peltoniemi Plays '*Punainen*,'" https://www.youtube.com/watch?v=SFlzXPuLsi8, accessed March 10, 2018.

Peltoniemi, Kip. 2001. Minnesota Tango: Music from the Finnish Triangle. Helsinki: Texicalli Records Oy, TEXCD 038.

Pitkänen, Silja and Ville-Juhani Sutinen. 2011. *Värssyjä sieltä ja täältä. Hiski Salomaan elämä ja laulut*. Helsinki: Kustannusosakeyhtiö Teos.

Päivälehti. 1899. "Suomalaisia hukkunut kaivosonnettomuudessa Amerikassa." 25–29.1.1899. Accessed digitally http://www.migrationinstitute.fi/files/pdf/uutisia_suomalaisista_siirtolaisista/kuolinilmoituksia.pdf.

Rausmaa, Pirkko-Liisa. 1981. "Kansantanssit," in *Kansanmusiikki*, ed. A. Asplund and M. Hako. Helsinki, Suomalaisen Kirjallisuuden Seura, 164–171.

Ross, Les, Sr. 2002. Tape recorded interview by James P. Leary. Negaunee, Michigan, July 22. Michigan Traditional Arts Program, Michigan State University.

Ross, Les, Sr., with Randy Seppala and Oren Tikkanen. 2014. *Lumber Jäkki: Old Finnish-American Songs & Harmonica.* CD. Laurium and Marquette, Michigan: no record label.

Saramo, Samira S. 2014. *Life Moving Forward: Soviet Karelia in the Letters & Memoirs of Finnish North Americans* (doctoral dissertation). YorkSpace Institutional Repository. Toronto: York University.

Sevander, Mayme. 1993. *Red Exodus: Finnish-American Emigration to Russia.* Duluth, MN: OSCAT.

Spottswood, R. 1990. *Ethnic Music on Records: A Discography of Ethnic Recordings Produced in the United States, 1893 to 1942, Volume 5: Mid-East, Far East, Scandinavian, English Language, American Indian, International.* Urbana: University of Illinois Press.

Sulkunen, Irma. 1989. "The Women's Movement," in *Finland. People, Nation, State,* ed. M. Engman and D. Kirby. London: Hurst & Company, 178–192.

Talve, Ilmar. 1998. *Finnish Folk Culture.* Helsinki: Finnish Literature Society.

Tamminen, Toivo. 1996. "Juho Koskelo: Singer and Instrumentalist," *Raivaaja,* September 25, 6, 12.

_____. "Antti Kosola: Pianist, Accordionist, Orchestra Leader," *Raivaaja,* July 23, 10, 16–17.

_____. 1998. "Aili and Lyyli Vainakainen," *Raivaaja,* April 8, 4.

_____. 1999a. "Laine-Toppila Orchestra," *Raivaaja,* April 28, 8, 10.

_____. 1999b. "The Maki Trio" *Raivaaja,* July 7, 6, 11.

U.S. Census Bureau. 1930. "Massachusetts, Worcester, Fitchburg." Fifteenth Census of the United States: 1930 Population. Washington D.C.: U.S. Census Bureau.

Virtanen, Hilary Joy. 2010. "What Official History Forgets Lives on in Song: On a Finnish American Parody of 'It's a Long Way to Tipperary,'" *Journal of Finnish Studies* 14:1, 46–52.

Virtanen, Leea. and Thomas A. DuBois 2000. *Finnish Folklore.* Helsinki: Finnish Literature Society.

Virtaranta, Pertti. 1993. *Amerikansuomi.* Helsinki: Suomalaisen Kirjallisuuden Seura.

Westerholm, Simo. 1992. "A Living Tradition: The Story of Finnish American Music," *Finnish Music Quarterly,* volume 4, 30–36.

Österlund-Pötzsch, Susanna. 2003. *American Plus—Etnisk identitet hos finlandssvenska ättlingar i Nordamerika.* Helsinki: Svenska Litteratursällskapel i Finland.

Contents